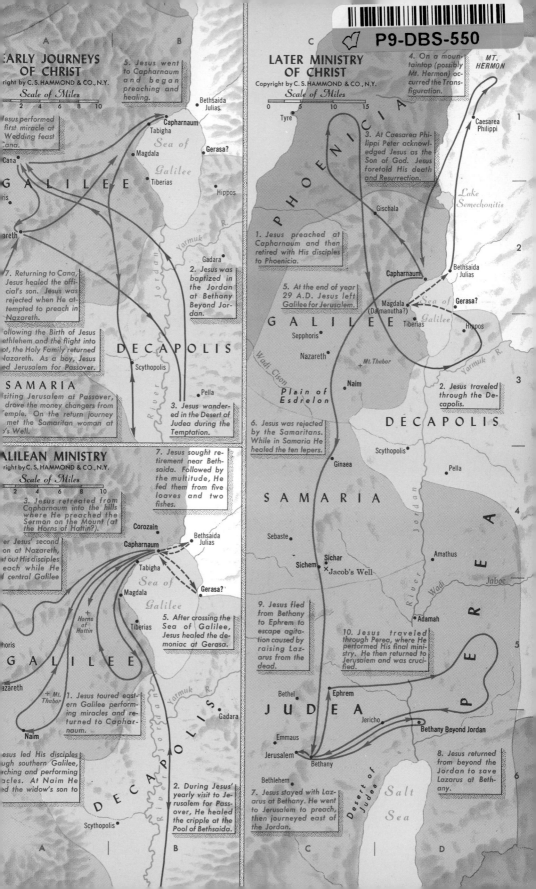

GOD'S KINGDOM
IN THE
NEW TESTAMENT

GOD'S KINGDOM
IN THE
NEW TESTAMENT

by

REV. MARTIN K. HOPKINS, O.P.

HENRY REGNERY COMPANY

Chicago   1964

Nihil Obstat:

Very Rev. J. S. Considine, O.P., S.T.M.
Rev. S. J. Oatis, O.P.

Imprimi Potest:

Very Rev. Gilbert Graham, O.P., Provincial

Imprimatur:

†Most Rev. Edward A. Fitzgerald, D.D.
Bishop of Winona
July 28, 1964

TO BROTHER ALPHONSUS, F.S.C.
DIRECTOR OF SAINT MARY'S COLLEGE PRESS
MY FIRST PUBLISHER

Foreword

It is with some hesitation that I undertake to introduce Father Hopkins' work to you, the reader. I am acutely aware that I am not a college teacher of Sacred Doctrine, and I recognize that in introducing a work such as this I am out of my medium. Yet in these past years, even from the somewhat remote vantage point of the seminary, I have become more and more impressed with the importance of introducing Sacred Scripture into college theology. And so, perhaps by way of introducing this book, I may be permitted to share with you some deep convictions on the subject.

At this moment we are facing a crisis in the teaching of Sacred Doctrine, a supreme crisis centered around the problem of *content*. The problem of method has been with us for some time and a solution is being reached. A dissatisfaction with the catechism question-and-answer routine and with the rote memorization of religion has evoked a kerygmatic approach that affects the gamut of Catholic education from grammar school to college. But this change, important as it is, does not touch the heart of the matter; for in the long run the problem of the way we communicate is subsidiary to the problem of what we communicate.

Since the time of the Catechism of the Council of Trent the substance of Catholic religious education has been a distillation of systematic theology, dogmatic and moral. The accompanying spiritual formation has been in terms of the piety of the post-medieval period, rather well illustrated in its span by *The Imitation of Christ*, and by the writings of St. Francis de Sales and the Little Flower. For those who would go deeper there were the mystical reflections of St. Teresa of Avila and of St. John of the Cross. This religious education rendered the Church of the past tremendous service and nothing should be said against it.

But now, under the impact of two great movements—ecumenism and liturgical reform—there has arisen within the Church the question of reorientating religious training. Catholicism shares a great heritage with other Christian bodies, but in the past religious education has emphasized more of what separates than of what unites. And, of course, one of the strongest unitive factors among Christians is the love of the Scriptures, the greatest of all theological sources, the inspired word of God Himself. During the whole patristic period, to know the Scriptures was to know Christ; but in the modern age it has been perfectly possible for a student to have the best Catholic religious training all the way through college itself without ever reading a single page of the Bible. However, since the dynamic impetus of the pontificate of John XXIII aroused the Catholic conscience about the obligations of Christian unity, the Bible has planted itself squarely across the path of Catholic ecumenism. It has become obvious that no dialogue is possible without speaking in biblical language, the Christian *lingua franca*.

At this same time of ecumenical awakening, the possibilities of liturgy for interior revival in the Church were coming to the fore. For centuries the liturgical services of the Church, although attended and loved, have not had their full role as an intelligible vehicle of Christian formation, their pedagogical role. Often private devotions and readings were used to make profitable the time spent at services, rather than allowing the liturgical text itself to instruct. But a grass-roots liturgical movement and the decision of Vatican II to permit the vernacular in the liturgy has totally changed the picture. We are involved in the greatest attempt in the history of the Church to make the Mass and Sacraments not only effective *ex opere operato,* but also subjectively meaningful and instructive. Once again the Bible plants itself across the path of liturgical progress. The Scriptures are the backbone of the liturgy, and liturgical expression is largely biblical. As the people are swept by participation into the heart of a liturgy in their own language, the need to understand the biblical passages they sing, recite, and hear becomes more imperative than ever before.

Thus both the external and internal aspects of Catholic revival lead us to the Scriptures which have not had their proper place in formal Catholic education. It is true that there has been constant encouragement from the Holy See by way of indulgences for reading the Scriptures. Moreover, there has been a small and often misunderstood core of Catholic intellectuals and scholars who have been enthusiastic propagandists for a scriptural movement. But the fact remains that the great religious challenges mentioned above are faced by a Catholic populace ninety-five percent of which has never read through the Bible. Only intensive biblical instruction can overcome this difficulty, and needless to say this instruction must be along the lines indicated by *modern* Catholic biblical studies. The classroom is, of course, no place for proposing untested or adventurous hypotheses; but the modern Catholic biblical movement is both scientific and prudent, and the conclusions on which there is agreement among modern Catholic scholars are well enough established to be presented to all in a way proportionate to their respective understanding.

Foreword

How is this biblical instruction to become part of Catholic religious education? Only the highest authorities in the Church can answer this question. We can only point out that a decision in depth is called for. The problem is not one of adding some scriptural orientation to existing courses whether they be on the grammar, high school, or college level; rather it is a question of making the Scriptures the basic religious textbook, the basic content of the courses, and the basic language of Catholic religious expression. The question that is raised is whether or not the Catholic Church will once again, as in patristic days, make the Bible the basic medium of religious instruction.

Since the amount of time available for religious instruction is limited, the decision on the question we have formulated may be an agonizing one, for it may involve curtailing many religious subjects that are dear to us. Much of what we now consider important religious knowledge may have to be sacrificed in favor of biblical knowledge. It is obviously desirable that in the course of their formal religious education our youngsters know about both Fatima and the Old Testament Patriarchs; but if the practical question of available time makes a choice necessary, which is to have primacy? It is desirable that our Catholic students know the precise scholastic theology of each of the sacraments; but if it has to be a choice between that and a detailed knowledge of the scriptural origins of the sacraments, which is to come *first?* On the advanced or college level what will one present *first:* a detailed training in the whole scholastic theory of the functioning of the interior life with the gifts and fruits of the Holy Spirit and the cardinal and moral virtues, or a thorough familiarity with Johannine and Pauline spirituality? The basic realities behind each are obviously the same; the basic Christian dogmas as professed in the Catholic Church are the same; but *which primary emphasis best meets the liturgical and ecumenical demands on today's Catholic?* In either a logical or a historical presentation of Christian thought, should not familiarity with the Scriptures come first as the basis of all that follows?

As we have stressed, only the authorities of the Church can totally reorientate the teaching of Catholic doctrine, and it may be some time before the radical imperative of making a decision is felt. In the meanwhile the needs of our times are already working on the principle of demand and supply. The demand to know the Bible has begun to influence the writing of grammar and high school religion textbooks. But what about the colleges? It is in our college students that the greatest potentialities of Catholic intellectual leadership will come to actualization. By way of progress, formal biblical courses are being introduced into the curricula of many Catholic colleges. The older "Life of Christ" course with its predominant apologetic, biographical interest is rapidly yielding to a course on the Gospels. It is being recognized that dogmatic and moral sections of college theology must be firmly grounded in biblical theology.

Such laudable changes have run afoul of a lack of college biblical textbooks. A first stopgap measure was offered in a flurry of biblical pamphlets. But more and more the answer has been sought in the complete scriptural textbook with the pamphlets as supplementary readings. Almost every Catholic publisher of textbooks in the country is rushing to meet the need. As far as I know, Father Hopkins' book is one of the first college textbooks (if not the very first) in the New Testament field. He has worked hard and carefully on this book after some years of experience in teaching the New Testament on the college level. The book is modern in its outlook and has a great deal of information packed within its covers. Its obvious liturgical interest is a valuable feature. Although no one textbook will meet the needs of all colleges, this should meet the needs of many. I must leave a judgment on pedagogical technique to those who teach in colleges. From my own position in the seminary all that I can say is that it would be a great boon to priestly education if students who enter the seminary after college had the biblical knowledge found in this book.

RAYMOND E. BROWN, S.S.
St. Mary's Seminary
Baltimore, Maryland

April 24, 1964

Preface

These notes are designed to be a continuation of their companion volume, *God's Kingdom in the Old Testament*. The introductory material and religious development found in the former work will be helpful but by no means indispensable to this study. This arrangement serves the twofold purpose of cutting down on the usual preliminaries, and allowing more space for actual concentration on the text of the New Testament. Thus, there are only two chapters of general introduction.

Like its Old Testament counterpart, this volume is meant to be a reading guide and college textbook, and is designed for a two-hour, one-semester course. Each of the twenty-seven chapters comprises one class assignment—with a few possible exceptions. It might be well to plan an extra "catching-up" class with Chapters 6, 10 and 16 as these chapters provide convenient points for tests. Since the main brunt of a college education falls on the amount of reading spontaneously undertaken by the student, extensive suggestions for additional work are offered at the end of each chapter.

The New Testament bears witness to the blossoming of the Kingdom of God on earth. Like the Old Testament, it is the product of the community in whose midst it was written. First came the living *kerygma* or proclamation of the Word; later the oral tradition found its way onto parchment. Each page of the New Testament eloquently testifies to the daily life and worship of the Apostolic Christian community. By way of completing this study, several non-inspired apostolic and patristic works are included in the assignments to illustrate how the *didache* (deeper implications of the "Good News") was assimilated and developed by the later Christian community.

Distinct recognition is paid to the importance of the literary history of the New Testament through the order of treatment of its various books, since this historical factor, together with the knowledge of Semitic literary genres carried over from the Old Testament, has proven to be indispensable. So it is neither by chance nor caprice that St. Mark's Gospel—the primitive proclamation—is studied first, followed by St. Luke's twofold work, Gospel-Acts. A detailed study of the merging Church is then pursued through the eyes of St. Matthew, supplemented by the more mystical approach of St. Paul and

St. John. Finally, the eschatological vision of the latter is captured in his Apocalypse.

Note that the study of the Psalms, generally one to a chapter, is continued in this work. Each psalm is chosen for its appropriateness to the subject matter of the chapter. In this way readers will be able to enlarge their appreciation of these inspiring religious prayers.

This edition contains revisions made in accordance with the teaching experience of the author and of others who have used the text before its publication in this present form. With few exceptions the spelling of proper nouns in the volume is that found in the Confraternity of Christian Doctrine Version of the Bible. The author wishes to thank the editors of this version for the use of their translation.

It is hoped these pages will increase not only the readers' knowledge of the Mystical Body, but also their love and loyalty towards its Head, Christ, as well as impart a deepened sense of Christian solidarity within this Body.

The author wishes to extend his thanks to the following publishers:

The Bruce Publishing Company for permission to quote from *Christian Life and Worship* by Gerald Ellard, S.J. (copyright 1956 by The Bruce Publishing Co.);

The Catholic Biblical Association of America for permission to quote from *The Catholic Biblical Quarterly*, Vol. 20 (copyright 1958 by the Catholic Biblical Association of America);

The Catholic University of America Press for permission to quote from *The Apostolic Fathers*, Vol. I, Fathers of the Church (copyright 1947 by Ludwig Schopp);

Doubleday and Company, Inc. for permission to quote from *The Book of the Acts of God* by G. Ernest Wright and Reginald H. Fuller (copyright 1957 by G. Ernest Wright);

Fides Publishers, Inc. for permission to quote from *New Horizons* by Barnabas M. Ahern, C.P. (copyright 1963 by Fides Publishers, Inc.);

Herder and Herder, Inc. for permission to quote from *New Testament Introduction* by A. Wikenhauser (copyright 1958 by Herder, Inc.), *God's Rule and Kingdom* by R. Schnackenburg (copyright 1963 by Herder and Herder, Inc.) and *My Father's Business* by G. Michonneau (copyright 1959 by Herder and Herder, Inc.);

The Liturgical Press for permission to quote from *The New Testament Reading Guide Series No. 1, Introduction to the New Testament* by R. A. MacKenzie, S.J., *No. 4, The Gospel of St. Matthew* by David Stanley, S.J., *No. 11, The Epistle to the Hebrews* by J. F. McConnell, M.M., and *No. 13, The Gospel of St. John, The Johannine Epistles* by Raymond E. Brown, S.S. (all copyright 1960–1963 by The Liturgical Press), to whom thanks is also due for permission to quote from *The Bible Today*, Vol. I (1962);

The Newman Press for permission to quote from *The Kingdom of Promise* by R. A. Dyson, S.J. and A. Jones (copyright 1957 by The Newman Press), *The Primacy of Peter* by Charles Journet (copyright 1954 by The Newman Press), and *The Mystery of Christian Worship* by Odo Casel, O.S.B. (copyright 1962 by The Newman Press);

Prentice-Hall, Inc. for permission to quote from *Understanding the New Testament* by H. C. Key and F. W. Young (copyright 1957 by Prentice-Hall, Inc.), and *Jesus: The Man, The Mission, and The Message* by C. Milo Connick (copyright 1963 by Prentice-Hall, Inc.);

The Henry Regnery Company for permission to quote from *Early Christian Worship* by Oscar Cullmann (Copyright 1953 by the Henry Regnery Company) and *The Paschal Mystery* by Louis Bouyer (copyright 1950 by the Henry Regnery Company);

Sheed and Ward, Inc. for permission to quote from *A History of the Church*, Vol. I, by Philip Hughes (copyright 1949 by Sheed and Ward, Ltd.) and *The Resurrection* by F. X. Durrwell (copyright 1960 by Sheed and Ward, Ltd.)

Grateful acknowledgment is also due to Rev. Raymond E. Brown, S.S., for his numerous and scholarly insights, as well as for writing the Foreword; and to Very Rev. J. S. Considine, O.P., S.T.M., for reading the manuscript and for his helpful suggestions.

Table of Contents

* Consult bibliography and assignments at the beginning of each chapter for full titles of works listed in this column. Those readings in parentheses are optional. Additional titles are given at the end of each chapter.

Table of Maps and Charts

Selected Bibliography

One of the most valuable features of this course will be the reading which the student undertakes to supplement the text and classroom lectures. The following is a list of the more basic sources. Those titles designated by an asterisk are particularly valuable for this course.

I. BY CATHOLIC AUTHORS

Texts of the Bible

The Confraternity of Christian Doctrine Version of the Bible is adequate, though not ideal. A new translation from the original Greek will be available in four or five years. The "New Testament Reading Guide Series" (Collegeville, Minn.: The Liturgical Press, 1960) contains the Confraternity Version text together with a valuable commentary. Especially recommended for this course are the following paperback volumes from the series.

AHERN, BARNABAS M., C. P. *The Epistles to the Galatians and to the Romans*, No. 7

BROWN, RAYMOND E., S.S. *The Gospel of St. John, the Johannine Epistles*, No. 13.

STANLEY, DAVID M., S.J. *The Gospel of St. Matthew*, No. 4 (revised in 1963).

SULLIVAN, KATHRYN, R.S.C.J. *St. Paul's Epistle to the Philippians, Ephesians, Colossians, Philemon*, No. 9.

The introductions and footnotes of *La Sainte Bible* (L'École Biblique de Jerusalem, 1961) are recommended to those who read French. An English translation is in preparation.

A handy instrument in the study of the four Gospels is S. J. Hartdegen, O.F.M., *A Chronological Harmony of the Gospels* (Paterson, N. J.: St. Anthony Guild Press, 1948), 222 pp.

Commentaries

AHERN, BARNABAS, C. P. *New Horizons*. Notre Dame, Ind.: Fides Publishers, Inc., 1963, 218 pp. Anthology of outstanding biblical papers by a modern scholar.

BIRD, T. E. *A Study of the Gospels*. Westminster, Md.: Newman Press, 1950, 152 pp. A harmonized exposition of the four Gospels. (Paperback)

*Bouyer, Louis. *The Meaning of Sacred Scripture*. Notre Dame, Ind.: University of Notre Dame Press, 1958, 258 pp. Penetrating insights into Old and New Testament themes, stressing the unity of the Bible.

Bullough, Sebastian, O. P. *The Church in the New Testament*. Westminster, Md.: Newman Press, 1944, 257 pp. Excellent treatise on the Acts of the Apostles. (Paperback)

——————. *St. Paul and Apostolic Writings*. Westminster, Md.: Newman Press, 1950, 338 pp.

Cerfaux, L. *The Four Gospels*. Westminster, Md.: Newman Press, 1960. Brief, scholarly introduction.

*Congar, Yves, O. P. *The Wide World My Parish*. Baltimore, Md.: Helicon Press, 1961, 188 pp. Contains an erudite analysis of the concept of salvation.

Danielou, Jean, S. J. *The Bible and the Liturgy*. Notre Dame, Ind.: University of Notre Dame Press, 1956, 372 pp. Very good work on symbolism in the Bible.

Dannemiller, L. *Reading the Word of God*. Westminster, Md.: Newman Press, 1960. Devotional aid.

Daniel-Rops, Henry. *Jesus and His Times*. New York: E. P. Dutton and Co., 1956, 479 pp.

*Davis, Charles. *Theology for Today*. New York: Sheed and Ward, 1963, 310 pp.

Dougherty, J. J. *Searching the Scriptures*. New York: Hanover House, 1959, 232 pp. A popular introduction to the books of both Old and New Testaments.

Durrwell, F. X. *The Resurrection: A Biblical Study*. New York: Sheed and Ward, 1960, 371 pp.

——————. *In the Redeeming Christ*. New York: Sheed and Ward, 1963.

*Dyson, R. A., S. J., and Jones, A. *The Kingdom of Promise*. Westminster, Md.: Newman Press, 1957, 222 pp. Concept of the Kingdom of God expertly carried from the Old Testament into the New Testament. (Paperback)

Feuillet, Andre. *L'Apocalypse: État de la question*. Paris: Desclee de Brouwer, 1963, 122 pp. Contains a valuable summary of the latest research on the Apocalypse.

Grollenberg, L. H., O. P. *Atlas of the Bible*. New York: Thomas Nelson and Sons, 1956, 166 pp. One of the best works of its kind; 35 maps.

——————. *Shorter Atlas of the Bible*. New York: Thomas Nelson and Sons, 1959, 196 pp. More concentrated than the larger work; 10 maps.

*Hartman, Louis F., C. SS. R., et al. *Encyclopedic Dictionary of the Bible*. New York: McGraw-Hill Book Company, Inc., 1963, 1334 pp. Monumental and authoritative.

*Hasseveldt, Roger. *The Church, A Divine Mystery*, 2nd ed. Notre Dame, Ind.: Fides Publisher's, Inc., 1960, 298 pp. A very helpful supplement to the Bible in understanding the Church.

Heaney, John J., S. J. (ed.). *Faith, Reason and the Gospels*. Westminster, Md.: Newman Press, 1962, 327 pp. Fifteen fine articles on problems about the Gospels; especially good are Chapters 13 and 14. (Paperback)

HERVIEUX, J. *New Testament Apocrypha.* (*Twentieth Century Encyclopedia of Catholicism,* vol. 72.) New York: Hawthorn Books, Inc., 1960, 188 pp.

HUNT, IGNATIUS, O.S.B. *Understanding of the Bible.* New York: Sheed and Ward, 1962, 207 pp. Brief introduction to the books of the Old and New Testaments reflecting the latest scholarship.

LAGRANGE, M. J., O. P. *The Gospel of Jesus Christ,* 2 vols. Westminster, Md.: Newman Press, 1938.

*MONRO, MARGARET T. *Enjoying the New Testament.* New York: Doubleday & Co., Inc., 1962, 199 pp. A popular exposition tracing the literary development of the books. (Paperback)

*ORCHARD, SUTCLIFFE, *et al.* *A Catholic Commentary on Holy Scripture.* New York: Thomas Nelson and Sons, 1953, 1312 pp. Commentary on each verse of the Bible; somewhat outdated. Especially recommended is the article by M. Benevot, S. J., and Ralph Russell, "Christianity in Apostolic Times: Doctrine and Practice," cols. 629–660.

RAHNER, HUGO, *et al.* *The Church: Readings in Theology.* New York: P. J. Kenedy and Sons, 1963, 242 pp.

RICCIOTTI, G. *The Life of Christ.* Translated by I. Zizzamia. Milwaukee, Wis.: Bruce Publishing Co., 1947, 703 pp. One of the best, with much valuable background material.

ROBERT, A., and TRICOT, A. *Guide to the Bible,* 2 vols. New York: Desclee Co., Inc., 1955. Thoroughly scholarly and complete introduction to the Bible.

SCHILLEBEECKX, EDWARD. *The Layman in the Church and Other Essays.* Staten Island, N. Y.: Alba House, 1963, 91 pp. An authoritative treatment of the layman's role.

*SCHNACKENBURG, RUDOLPH. *God's Rule and Kingdom.* New York: Herder and Herder, 1963, 365 pp. An up-to-date, provocative treatment of a burning question.

————————. *New Testament Theology Today.* New York: Herder and Herder, 1963, 133 pp. Summary of latest Catholic and Protestant studies.

SHEEN, FULTON J., BISHOP. *Life of Christ.* New York: McGraw-Hill Book Company, 1958, 473 pp. Helpful applications to modern life.

STANLEY, DAVID, S. J. *Christ's Resurrection in Pauline Soteriology.* (Analecta Biblica, No. 13.) Rome: Pontifical Biblical Institute, 1961, 313 pp. Complements Durrwell's book.

————————. "From Kingdom to Church," *Theological Studies,* vol. 16 (1955), 1–29. Excellent insight into the structural development of early Christianity.

STEINMUELLER, J. E., and SULLIVAN, KATHRYN, R. S. C. J. *Catholic Biblical Encyclopedia, New Testament.* Some of the articles are outdated.

VANN, GERALD, O. P. *The Paradise Tree.* New York: Sheed and Ward, 1959, 320 pp. Superb treatment of biblical symbolism.

*WIKENHAUSER, A. W. *New Testament Introduction.* Translated from the German by Joseph Cunningham. New York: Herder and Herder, 1958, 580 pp. Highly recommended.

Selected Bibliography

Liturgical and Patristic Materials

*BOUYER, LOUIS. *Liturgical Piety.* Notre Dame, Ind.: University of Notre Dame Press, 1954, 284 pp.

———————. *The Paschal Mystery.* Chicago, Ill.: Henry Regnery Co., 1950, 347 pp. A commentary on the last three days of Holy Week; many patristic references.

*CYRIL OF JERUSALEM, SAINT. *Mystagogical Catecheses.* (A Select Library of Nicene Post–Nicene Fathers of the Christian Church, Vol. VII.) Grand Rapids, Mich.: William B. Eerdmans Publishing Co., pp. 144–157.

*DAVIS, CHARLES. *Liturgy and Doctrine.* New York: Sheed and Ward, 1960, 123 pp. Masterful summary.

DIEKMANN, GODFREY, O. S. B. *Come Let Us Worship.* Collegeville, Minn.: Liturgical Press, 1961. An anthology of the author's addresses at the North American Liturgical Conferences.

ELLARD, GERALD. *Christian Life and Worship.* Milwaukee, Wis.: Bruce Pub. Co., 1956, 426 pp.

*FREMANTLE, ANNE (ed.). *A Treasury of Early Christianity.* New York: New American Library, 1960, 511 pp. Selections from *Fathers of the Church.* (Students should obtain a copy of this book for the course.)

JOHN CHRYSOSTOM, SAINT. "Catechesis III," *Worship* (April, 1960) 241–247.

*JUNGMANN, JOSEF, S. J. *The Early Liturgy.* Notre Dame, Ind.: University of Notre Dame Press, 1959, 314 pp.

———————. *Public Worship.* Collegeville, Minn.: Liturgical Press, 1957, 249 pp. Chapter 8 is a good treatise on the Divine Office.

———————. *The Sacrifice of the Church.* Collegeville, Minn.: Liturgical Press, 1955, 71 pp. Four essays.

PARSCH, P. *Church's Year of Grace,* 5 vols. Collegeville, Minn.: Liturgical Press, 1957–1959.

SCHOPP, LUDWIG. *The Apostolic Fathers.* (*Fathers of the Church,* Vol. I.) New York: Cima Publishing Co., 1947, 401 pp. This volume of the series contains "The Letters of St. Clement and St. Ignatius of Antioch," the "Martyrdom of St. Polycarp," "The Didache," and "The Shepherd of Hermas."

Twenty Four Psalms and a Canticle. Gregorian Institute of America, 1955, 59 pp. English translation of the Psalms from the Jerusalem Bible according to Gelineau notations.

II. BY NON-CATHOLIC AUTHORS

Texts of the Bible

(These texts may be used by students of Scripture according to Canon 1400.)

The Bible: An American Translation is an accurate translation by Smith-Goodspeed published by the University of Chicago Press, 1931.

New English Bible is the latest English version of the New Testament published by the Oxford and Cambridge University Presses, 1961.

Revised Standard Version by the National Council of Churches is the modern American revision of the King James Version, 1952.

Commentaries

BARRETT, C. K. *The New Testament Background: Selected Documents.* New York: Harper and Row (TB 86), 1961, 232 pp.

BULTMANN, RUDOLPH. *The History of the Synoptic Tradition.* London: Basil Blackwell, 1962. The student will perhaps find an easier explanation of this author's concept of the Gospels in Rudolph Bultmann and Karl Kundsin, *Form Criticism* (New York: Harper and Row [TB 96] 1962), 161 pp.

BUTTRICK, G. A. (ed.). *The Interpreter's Dictionary of the Bible,* 4 vols. Nashville, Tenn.: Abingdon Press, 1962. An authoritative work.

CONNICK, C. MILO. *Jesus, the Man, the Mission and the Message.* Englewood Cliffs, N. J.: Prentice-Hall, 1963, 462 pp. Reflects latest research of form critics.

CULLMAN, OSCAR. *Peter, Disciple-Apostle-Martyr.* Philadelphia, Pa.: Westminster Press, 1952, 252 pp. This book should be studied in conjunction with Charles Journet's *The Primacy of Peter* (Westminster, Md.: Newman Press, 1954), 144 pp. Cullmann is also noted for his *Christology of the New Testament* (Philadelphia, Pa.: Westminster Press, 1959).

DODD, C. H. *The Bible Today.* New York: Cambridge University Press, 1961, 168 pp. (Paperback)

—————. *The Interpretation of the Fourth Gospel.* New York: Cambridge University Press, 1953.

—————. *New Testament Studies.* Manchester: Manchester University Press, 1953, 182 pp.

—————. *The Parables of the Kingdom,* rev. ed. New York: Charles Scribners' Sons, 1961, 214 pp.

HASTINGS, J. H. (ed.). *Dictionary of the Bible,* rev. ed. New York: Charles Scribners' Sons, 1963.

HUNTER, A. M. *The Work and Words of Jesus.* Philadelphia, Pa.: Westminster Press, 1950.

JEREMIAS, JOACHIM. *The Parables of Jesus.* New York: Charles Scribners, 1963.

*KEY, H. C., and YOUNG, F. W. *Understanding the New Testament.* Englewood Cliffs, N. J.: Prentice-Hall, 1957, 492 pp. A liberal Protestant interpretation.

MANSON, T. W. *The Servant-Messiah.* New York: Cambridge University Press, 1961, 104 pp. Illustrates Christ's fundamental role as the Suffering Servant of Isaia. (Paperback)

PRICE, J. L. *Interpreting the New Testament.* New York: Holt, Rinehart and Winston, 1961, 572 pp. An excellent text.

ROWLEY, H. H. *The Unity of the Bible.* Cleveland, Ohio: Meridian Books, (LA 16), 1957, 232 pp. Brings out the continuity of Old and New Testaments. His doctrine on the limitation of Baptism to adults is unacceptable to Catholics, however (cf. Chap. 6).

TAYLOR, VINCENT. *Formation of the Gospel Tradition.* New York: The Macmillan Co., 1957. A well-balanced presentation.

————. *The Gospel According to St. Mark.* London: The Macmillan Co., 1955.

WRIGHT, G. E., and FULLER, R. H. *The Book of the Acts of God.* Garden City: Doubleday & Co. (Anchor Book A222), 1960, 420 pp. A fine presentation of salvation history, though not all of the conclusions are acceptable to Catholics.

GOD'S KINGDOM
IN THE
NEW TESTAMENT

Chapter I

Dawn of the Kingdom: The Continuity of Scripture

READINGS: *"The Conception of Our Gospels as Salvation History,"
Theological Studies, 20, (Dec. 1959), 561–588. (Also in Heaney,
Faith, Reason and the Gospels, Chap. 14.)*

We have dared to call the Bible the "pre-incarnate Word of God."
This designation reveals the dynamic proportions of the biblical story.
The Word in question is no longer viewed as merely a written message but rather as an eternal moment in history, climaxing in the appearance of the Author of that message. Sacred Scripture is anything
but a dead letter; it is a panoramic glimpse of the timelessness of God
captured on the frail pages of a scroll. Human events provide the
background and much of the medium of this divine Self-revelation;
but long after the created actors have died, the Principal Author continues the dialogue. No better introduction to the New Testament
could be offered than a brief resumé of the communication between
God and man.

Old Testament Salvation History: The Plot Begins

This divine communication began the day on which man was created in the Garden of Eden. Until they disobeyed God, Adam and
Eve lived in a state of divine friendship. God could be found "walking
in the garden in the cool of the day."[1] We are told that both Henoch
and Noe "walked with God"[2] in a nostalgic denotation of the sort of
divine intimacy which would have been normal to mankind had our
first parents not sinned. But with the Fall divine friendship was for-
feited, the line of communication between God and man was broken,
and divine-human relations strained. It was God Himself Who took
the initiative in restoring communications almost immediately when
He promised Adam and Eve redemption. But the damage was done;
man's intellect was darkened, his will weakened, and he was prone to
live more according to his passions than according to his reason.

Neither exegetes nor scientists can tell us for certain whether or
not the era of the so-called "Cave Man" ensued immediately. What-

---

[1] Gen. 3:8.
[2] *Ibid.*, 5:22 and 6:10.

ever man's physical condition became outside of the Garden, his moral life deteriorated rapidly without God, as the fourth chapter of the Book of Genesis clearly shows. The return of mankind to the divine intimacy of Paradise—laboriously begun through the Patriarchs, formalized in the Mosaic Law and finally re-established in the incarnation and death of Jesus Christ—does not make for dull reading to those who have been initiated to the Scriptures. We may go even further and say that the grandeur of God's plan in accomplishing this rapprochement can scarcely be appreciated apart from the Bible. But we are getting ahead of our story: what we now call Sacred Scripture existed at this time only in the form of Tradition.

The text of the first promise of human "redemption" (later to be recorded in the third chapter of the Book of Genesis) indicates the general lines which man's rehabilitation would have to take. The powers of evil had won a decisive victory in the Fall, thereby obtaining an enslaving influence over the human race. These powers (later to be identified with the devil) would have to be crushed by a counter-victory to be won by the "seed of the woman" in the name of the human race. In the meantime man would have to toil and to sweat.

The progressive degradation of humanity following the Fall provided God with an occasion to intervene in human affairs. The purging waters of the Deluge constituted a "new creation" in the physical order, inaugurating a "new human race," as it were, in the Patriarch Noe. With him God made his first covenant, symbolized by the rainbow. His second covenant with Abraham represented a furthering of the moral regeneration of humanity which would find its perfection in those descendants in whom "all nations of the earth" were to "be blessed."[3] Faith in the redemption-to-come became the official medium of justification for a chosen segment of the human race. Through God's provision for physical hygiene contained in the ritual of circumcision and the dietary laws, they were expected to develop a delicacy of conscience which would lead them to greater intimacy with their Creator.

The Israelites (as the Jacobites came to be called after the Exodus events) were further separated from non-Israelites or Gentiles and sealed as God's people with the ratification of the Mosaic Law. This third covenant spelled out the demands which God made of them in order that they might inherit the promises given to Abraham, including the repossession of Palestine. Its precepts regulated every aspect of their life: religious, civil, and moral. God Himself carved out the heart of the covenant, the Ten Commandments, on tablets of stone. The other precepts and related historical data drawn from Israelite

---

[3] Gen. 12:3. This begins the "Hebrew" period of Old Testament history.

tradition and completed by divine revelation were gradually written down by Moses and his successors. *Here we have a milestone in the history of divine communication: The beginning of Sacred Scripture.* If the date of the Exodus (c. 1250 B.C.) based on the latest archeological research is correct, then we have here the approximate date of the birth of Sacred Scripture. It must be carefully noted, however, that scholars today generally agree that only a fraction of the Pentateuch as it now stands was committed to writing during the lifetime of Moses. Centuries would elapse before the rest of the oral tradition would find its way onto parchment under divine inspiration.

With the departure of the Israelites from Egypt and their subsequent re-entry into Palestine under Josue, a people became a nation. Their national character was assured through the conquest of the land which the Lord promised to Abraham and to his descendants. During these golden years of the theocracy God communicated with His people through sporadically chosen individuals known as "Judges." Then, when the people insisted on having a king in imitation of their pagan neighbors, God yielded to the transferral of political authority into the hands of the "Lord's Anointed," as the king was called. The four Books of Kings deal with this era. However, the mind of Yahweh was not revealed exclusively through the king; God continued to raise up other men—*prophets* like Elias, Amos and Jeremia—to exhort and to teach His chronically rebellious subjects. In fact, it was principally from the prophets that the Old Testament was completed. We read in the Book of Isaia Yahweh's declaration that "my word . . . shall not return to me void, but shall do my will, achieving the end for which I sent it,"[4] and the Wisdom literature corroborates the dynamic power of the divine word.[5]

The Kingdom of God was, indeed, to be established on this earth and its true King was to belong to the Davidic dynasty. But it was not to be merely an earthly kingdom limited to a single racial stock. If divine sonship was to be restored to the human race, *the Kingdom of God would have to be a spiritual entity transcending national bonds and geographical dimensions.*[6] It is in this light that we must view the calamities which overtook the Davidic Kingdom following the death of Solomon about the year 932 B.C. Outraged by the excesses of this worldly-wise man, the Northern Tribes seceded and set up their own government at Samaria. This move represented a religious as well as a political schism, since the only legitimate place for offering sacrifice

---

[4] Is. 55:11.

[5] *E.g.,* Sir. 24, Prov. 8, Wis. 7, etc. St. John will complete the revelation by supplying the identity of the Word of God as a Person, God's own Son.

[6] Cf. The Gospel of St. Matthew.

was at Jerusalem, located in the Southern Kingdom, Juda. God permitted the schismatic Kingdom of Israel to fall to the Assyrians in the year 721 B.C. Deported to Nineve never to return, these unfortunate Jews became known as the "Lost Tribes." The Kingdom of Juda managed to carry on the Davidic dynasty another century and a half until their infidelities forced God to punish them at the hands of the Babylonians in 587 B.C.

With the fall of Jerusalem, and especially the destruction of their precious Temple symbolizing the presence of Yahweh among them, the Jews should have been able to read the handwriting on the wall. The prophets had been most explicit; the People of God would have to undergo a change of heart, but this would not be the product of any human endeavor. The new and eternal covenant to be established would not consist essentially in a worldly monarchy but rather in an intimate, personal relationship with Yahweh and would be characterized by social justice.[7] In the winning of the victory over the devil, the material would have to yield to the spiritual: the Kingdom of Israel must be supplanted by a worshipping community which would bear witness to the messianic fulfillment and prepare for the final consummation of all things.[8]

Final Clues: The Plot Thickens

The Old Testament proposes a mystery; it is a problem book. It does not furnish all of the clues, and the solution comes only in the New Testament. Using the New Testament as a guide, it is quite easy for us to pick out the key passages; but for even such sincere Jews as Zachary, Elizabeth, the Apostles, etc., the texts were far from clear and often bewildering. The basic promise made to David and renewed with Solomon (cf. II Kgs. 7:11–13; III Kgs. 9:4–5) was later reapplied to that idealized Davidic descendant who would be the "anointed" (Messia) of the Lord and the Savior of His people. In another passage, the characteristic of priest is added to that of Messia:

> The Lord said to my Lord: 'Sit at my right hand till I make your enemies your footstool.' The scepter of your power the Lord will stretch forth from Sion: 'Rule in the midst of your enemies. Yours is princely power in the day of your birth, in holy splendor; before the daystar, like the dew, I have begotten you.'
> The Lord has sworn, and he will not repent: 'You are a priest forever, according to the order of Melchisedec.'[9]

---

[7] Cf. Jer. 31:31 and Am. 5:11–15. "Jew" is a post-Exilic designation.

[8] These themes will be developed in the Acts of the Apostles and the Apocalypse.

[9] Ps. 109:1–4. Jewish tradition, however, takes Melchisedec as a common noun, translating it as "a righteous king." Deut. 18:15 adds the characteristic of prophet; cf. John 1:21.

With the exception of the Essenes, the Jews tended to overlook the priestly qualities of the promised Messia; the Levitical priesthood was the only one they knew, and the Messia had to be of the Tribe of Juda. Moreover, the author of the Book of Daniel describes a vision of God's "holy ones" triumphantly inheriting an everlasting kingdom. The sacred author personifies this holy people—understood to be Israel—under the title "son of man." By the time of Christ, apocalyptic literature had developed the concept to the proportions of a pre-existent, heavenly conqueror who would crush all evil in the world and bring about God's rule over the earth. The Danielic passage reads:

> I saw one like a son of man coming on the clouds of heaven; when he reached the Ancient One and was presented before him, he received dominion, glory, and kingship; nations and peoples of every language serve him.
> His dominion is an everlasting dominion that shall not be taken away, his kingship shall not be destroyed. (Dan. 7:13–14)
> "But the holy ones of the Most High shall receive the kingdom, to possess it forever and ever."[10]

In stark contrast to the appealing character of this "son of man" was another Old Testament figure described in the Servant Songs of Isaia, especially the Fourth Song (below). A similar figure had already been depicted in Psalm 21. In the Isaian passage, as in the Danielic passage above, Israel is personified: this time as the "Servant of Yahweh," a despised, rejected, and dying sufferer who offers his life for the sins of his people.

> He was spurned and avoided by men, a man of suffering. . . . But he was pierced for our offenses, crushed for our sins; upon him was the chastisement that makes us whole, by his stripes we were healed . . . like a lamb led to the slaughter or a sheep before the shearers, he was silent and opened not his mouth.
> Oppressed and condemned, he was taken away. . . . When he was cut off from the land of the living, and smitten for the sin of his people, a grave was assigned him among the wicked and a burial place with evildoers, though he had done no wrong nor spoken any falsehood.[11]

In retrospect we Christians can appreciate the unique accomplishment of Christ in reconciling these apparently disparate characteristics in His own Person. But we must be careful not to demand such a reconciliation from the Jews as the Old Testament was completed

---

[10] Dan. 7:18. See also the portion of I Enoch cited in C. K. Barrett, *The New Testament Background: Selected Documents* (New York: Harper and Row, [TB 86,] 1961), p. 232.

[11] Isa. 53:3, 5, 7–9. Here again the subject is a group—the new Israel—but the title "servant" could also be verified of a single person in line with Semitic literary practice.

shortly after 100 B.C. Their human and understandably nationalistic notion of redemption conspired with the political misfortunes of Palestine following the Greek conquest of 330 B.C. to create a limited messianic expectation. We can readily understand how Israel, suffering under the domination of one pagan ruler after another, permitted the glorious qualities of the kingly "son of man" described by Daniel to occupy the center of her messianic outlook without perceiving any necessity of incorporating the role of the "servant of Yahweh" into the picture. One of the liabilities of the part played by the Jews as God's Chosen People, separated from Gentile contamination by a series of striking divine interventions in history, lay in Israel's difficulty in recognizing the unsavory servant-role to be played by the remnant. That the sufferings of Israel—or of any other nation on the face of the earth—were scarcely adequate to satisfy the price of human redemption goes without saying. But what her corporate sufferings were designed to effect was the ability to be transformed into the New Israel by allowing herself to be identified with and recapitulated in the mysterious individual at the center of the hourglass of salvation history. To such a one the inspired clues pointed; but it would take the eyes of faith rather than those of reason to discover the true pattern. The Servant Songs offered little consolation to a harassed minority group; yet, they could be ignored only at deadly peril. That the Servant was ignored is a matter of history: "He came unto his own, and his own received him not. (John 1:11)[12] Because she fell into the very human,

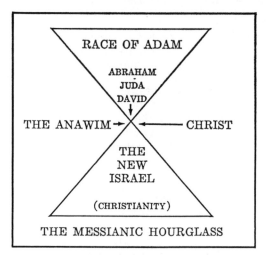

THE MESSIANIC HOURGLASS

---

[12] It is St. Mark's Gospel which will most clearly identify the Messia with the Servant. The Anawin were humble, devout Jews prepared to do God's will. Cf. Chap. IV.

natural fault of viewing her messianic heritage through the eyes of nationalism rather than of supernatural faith, the tiny state of Israel was erased from the surface of the earth.[13]

The Mystery Solved: The New Testament

Begun scarcely more than a century after the completion of the Old Testament, the books of the New Testament continue the thread of salvation history, depicting clearly the divine solution: God sent His Own Son, the eternal, pre-existent Word, to unite the two apparently incompatible messianic characteristics in His sacred Person and thus to bring mankind the awaited redemption. As the Incarnate Word, Jesus Christ spelled out the last chapter of His Father's official communication with the human race and transformed the Davidic Kingdom into a supernatural organism, His own Mystical Body. It was not enough that He be a descendant simply of Abraham and come as the New Israel and the New Moses. His universal redemptive mission demanded that He also fulfill the role of the New Adam. The first "earthy man" who betrayed his role must be redeemed by the second "heavenly man." It was Christ's unique contribution to recapitulate both of these elements in His divine personality: here is the heart of the Christian mystery.[14]

We find at the end of the New Testament a fitting climax to the history of salvation as we are taken back to Paradise where the drama had had its beginning:

> And he showed me a river of the water of life, clear as crystal, coming forth from the throne of God and of the Lamb. In the midst of the city street, on both sides of the river, was the tree of life, bearing twelve fruits, yielding its fruit according to each month, and the leaves for the healing of the nations. (Apoc. 22:1-2.)

In the midst of the defection of the majority of His Chosen People, God saved for Himself a faithful remnant to serve as the nucleus of the New Israel. The first chapter of St. Luke's Gospel introduces us to the charter members: Elizabeth, Zachary, and John; Mary and Joseph. Free from the prejudices of the false messianic view (as the Benedictus and especially the Magnificat illustrate), these devout souls received the Lord with open hearts and were in turn given "the power of becoming sons of God . . . born not of blood, nor of the will of the flesh, nor of the will of man, but of God" (John 1:12-13). Here is the fulfillment of the highest aspirations of the Old Testament—the last

---

[13] The burden of universalism will be vindicated par excellence in St. Luke.

[14] This is likewise the heart of St. Paul's doctrine. Cf. 1 Cor. 15:44-49.

7

stage and final terms of human salvation. We find in the New Testament the full restoration of the line of communication between God and men.

The point which emerges from this resumé of the People of God is the inescapable urgency of studying each book of the Bible *in its proper context of salvation history*—that is, in conjunction with cognate inspired books. This has been our plan in going through the Old Testament, and we shall continue the procedure in the New Testament. How absurd, then, to *begin* the study of Sacred Scripture with the books of the New Testament! This is to get an answer before any question has been asked; to be furnished with a solution to a non-existent problem. God has chosen to unfold His mysterious plan of human salvation on the stage of history—a very particular history—that of the Jews. To grasp His plan, we would do well to follow His divinely inspired pedagogy by recognizing in the New Testament the continuation of the Old. Nor may we conclude that once the pieces of the puzzle have been put together by a perusal of the whole Bible, the Old Testament can then be scuttled. If it is true that "the New Testament lies hidden in the Old," it is likewise true that the former sheds a new luster on the latter, bringing forth previously unsuspected insights into the divine economy of salvation. This economy is capable of nourishing the highest Christian mysticism—but only when it is seen and pondered in its entirety.

Literary Continuity of the Two Testaments

One often begins the reading of the New Testament under the supposition that its literary style departs abruptly from that of the Old Testament. The following considerations, together with the realization that most of the New Testament authors were Semites writing little more than a century after the completion of the Old Testament, should help to dispel this erroneous attitude:

1. In the composition of both Old and New Testaments, the inspired writing reflected and was largely based upon the *oral traditions of the community*. Even though some of the writings were composed for Gentiles, they would nevertheless reflect strongly their Semitic atmosphere. And we know that the Gentile Luke was profoundly influenced by the catechesis of St. Paul who was a Jew to the core.
2. For the Evangelists as well as for the Old Testament authors, history remains an *art* rather than a science; hence, we find virtually the same literary liberties in the New Testament. The order followed in the Gospels is *logical* rather than chronological, for the most part. The reason is the same: the sacred authors are giving us a *theology of history*, not a history of theology. Few dates are given.

8

3. Authorship is still to be reckoned according to the Oriental standard of authority rather than actual composition. The "author" is the man who stands behind the tradition and gives it substance, whether or not he ever wrote a word. As in the case of the Old Testament, the editing of a manuscript by a later hand and the use of a pseudonym do not constitute a falsification of the record. We know also that a number of sacred authors used secretaries (e.g., Jeremia and St. Paul). Today, exegetes are laying less and less stress on equating authenticity with proof of specific authorship.
4. Just as we admit today the existence of the four documents (J, E, P, D) in the composition of the Old Testament, so do Catholic scholars now admit the existence of a primitive, lost Gospel plus one or more Logia documents (cf. Chap. II).
5. The New Testament bears a distinctly *liturgical* stamp, as does the Old Testament.
6. The New Testament likewise betrays a very distinct development of dogma (e.g., regarding the Parousia), but with this difference: it contains the *antitypes* of Old Testament types now fulfilled, and hence the *final terms of salvation.*
7. On the supernatural plane, the quality of *inspiration* guarantees the substantial continuity of the two Testaments as well as inerrancy.

The Canon of the New Testament

Just as in the early Church there were doubts about seven books of the Old Testament canon, so also did it happen that seven New Testament books came in for special scrutiny. Some doubts were over authorship; e.g., whether or not St. Paul composed the Epistle to the Hebrews. Other doubts involved doctrine; e.g., Martin Luther attacked the Epistle of St. James because of its insistence on good works with faith. At the time of the Reformation, some or all of these seven books were excluded from the Protestant Bibles, but eventually found their way back in. Today both Catholic and Protestants recognize twenty-seven books as comprising the New Testament; Jews, of course, reject the whole of them. The Apocalypse is known in non-Catholic circles as Revelation. Catholic canonicity was on the way to being established c. 400 A.D.

For Catholics, the only adequate criterion of canonicity is the authority of God Himself as manifested through the Church. Auxiliary criteria are: 1) orthodoxy of doctrine; 2) "Apostolic" origin (i.e., written by an eyewitness of the events or an associate of an eyewitness); 3) use in the liturgy; 4) the testimony of scholars. In declaring that the Latin Vulgate is substantially in accordance with the original manuscripts of the Bible, the Council of Trent gives us adequate assurance that our American translations from the Vulgate are doctrinally satisfactory (though not taken from the original Greek). In the list of New Testament books below, those preceded by an asterisk are deuterocanonical.[15]

I. "HISTORICAL" BOOKS	II. "DOCTRINAL" BOOKS		
Gospel of St. Matthew			"CATHOLIC"
Gospel of St. Mark		EPISTLES OF ST. PAUL	EPISTLES
Gospel of St. Luke			
Gospel of St. John	Romans	I Thessalonians	*St. James
Acts of the Apostles	I Corinthians	II Thessalonians	I Peter
	II Corinthians	I Timothy	*II Peter
	Galatians	II Timothy	I John
III. "PROPHETICAL" BOOK	Ephesians	Titus	*II John
	Philippians	Philemon	*III John
*Apocalypse (Revelation)	Colossians	*Hebrews[16]	*St. Jude

The Political Situation in Palestine[17]

Palestine came under Roman domination in 63 B.C. when Pompey decided a fraternal Hasmonean dispute in favor of Hyrcanus II, who was supplanted by Antigonus in 40 B.C. Through intrigue and the influence of Octavian, Herod (the Great) succeeded Antigonus in 37 B.C. as King of Jerusalem. An astute statesman, this crafty Idumean extended his domain to include all of Palestine and more which he gained from Augustus, as Octavian was now called, after the latter's crucial victory over Antony at Actium (31 B.C.). The cruel but clever neurotic king was thoroughly despised by his Jewish subjects because of his Edomite blood, even though he rebuilt the Temple (the third and the last). Yet this monster, whose purges included members of his own family, managed to retain his throne until his miserable death in 4 B.C., about two years after the birth of Christ. Herod had arranged for his three surviving sons to succeed him: *1)* Archelaus became ethnarch of Judea, Samaria, and Idumea; *2)* Herod Antipas (who married Herodias illegally) became tetrarch of Galilee and Perea; *3)* Philip reigned as tetrarch of Trachonitis, Ituraea, etc., in the northeast of Palestine. Because of egregious misrule, Archelaus was deposed in 6 A.D. in favor of Roman procurators. Pontius Pilate held this office from 26–36 A.D. (note chart on p. 62).

---

[15] Although some of these seven books were rejected by certain Protestant sects at the time of the Reformation, they are generally accepted today by most Christian bodies. It took the Council of Trent to settle canonicity finally for Catholics.
[16] Today scholars no longer ascribe Hebrews to St. Paul.
[17] Cf. Martin Hopkins, O.P., *God's Kingdom in the Old Testament,* (Chicago, Ill.: Henry Regnery Co., 1964) p. 228.

Suggested Readings

Bird, *A Study of the Gospels,* pp. 19–34.
Davis, *Theology for Today,* Chap. 7, 14.
Dirksen, *A Life of Christ,* pp. 309–355.
Dyson and Jones, *The Kingdom of Promise,* pp. 121–134.
Fernan, *Christ as Prophet and King,* pp. 85–134. Extensive background material.
Hasseveldt, *The Church: A Divine Mystery,* pp. 102–131.
MacKenzie, *Introduction to the New Testament* (New Testament Reading Guide
   Series, No. 1), pp. 5–14.

For Further Study

1. Is history merely a record of occurrences? Is it an art or a science? Does it admit of a selection and interpretation of events? Are the Gospels history?
2. What is meant by the term "salvation history"? God's "Self-revelation"?
3. In what sense is it true that "there is only one gospel . . . which is older than the Gospels"?
4. To what literary genre do Luke 3:23 and Matthew 1:1–17 belong? How are they reconciled? (See Chap. V.)

The Quest for the Historical Jesus: Form Criticism and the Shaping of the New Testament

READINGS: *Acts of the Apostles 1–5; Psalm 2. Vincent O'Keefe, S. J., "Towards Understanding the Gospels,"* Catholic Biblical Quarterly, 21 (April, 1959) pp. 171–189. (Also in Heaney, Faith, Reason and the Gospels, Chap. 13.)

In 1906 the now famous medical missionary, Dr. Albert Schweitzer, published a book which was soon afterward translated into English with the title, *The Quest for the Historical Jesus.* His conclusion was that we shall never be able to get at the *real* Jesus because of the "distortions" which have crept into the Gospels—even that of St. Mark, which was presumed to be the most primitive. But he feels that the life of Jesus does make sense if we accept Him as an eschatologist, i.e., as one who identified the coming of the Messia with the immediate inauguration of the heavenly phase of the Kingdom of God. Hence, His ethical pronouncements were meant merely as a "provisional" morality until the end-time became a reality. Witness, for example, the idyllic communism of the early community of Christians eagerly awaiting the return of Jesus. According to the eschatologists, this can be explained only by the fact that His plans had been temporarily side-tracked by a gradual realization on His part that the inauguration of the Kingdom demanded His own expiatory death rather than a fresh purification of the Jewish nation as a whole.

While Catholic scholarship refuses to admit the distortion of the Gospels alleged by many modern exegetes, they are nevertheless enlarging their view on the degree of editorship which went into the final formulation of the New Testament. It has always been realized that the New Testament, just as the Old Testament, first existed as tradition within the community. The crucial question is the *exent* to which the faith and aspirations of the people involved had modified that tradition in the period before it found its way into written documents, especially the Gospels. Many critics, such as Dr. Schweitzer, have so stressed the impact of faith (mixed with wishful thinking) on the "facts" of Jesus' life that they have ended up in skepticism.

They attempt to bolster their conclusions by the assertion that first-century Christians had no interest in the biography of Christ but concentrated exclusively on His cult; thus, we find in the Gospels and Epistles very few dates and other details about the life of Christ in addition to the alleged distortions.

It is a universal Catholic belief that the autographs of the New Testament were inspired documents and that the approved versions in use today are substantially in accord with those original texts. Since inspiration makes God the principal Author, there cannot be any distortions. As noted in the last chapter, the editing of a manuscript does not necessarily falsify it. In fact, many manuscripts would tend to mislead the reader unless someone who understood the facts narrated were to validate the account by supplying background details, presuppositions, explanatory notes, etc., through a process of editing. This process might well involve selection of materials, modification or even alteration of details to do justice to both the original author and the reader. That the New Testament (as well as the Old) did go through such a process of editing is an incontestable fact. To attempt to reconstruct the original documents and (even more so) the tradition which lay behind them is a delicate and not always completely successful task. However, certain general lines of procedure on the part of the apostolic teachers and writers of the "Good News" can be laid down with a fair degree of certitude.

The "Evangelium" or Preaching of the "Good News"
(Acts 1–5)

Before the events narrated in the New Testament were written down they had already been preached for at least two decades by 1) Christ, Who announced the "Good News" (this is the meaning of the word *Gospel*) of the arrival of the Kingdom of God; and 2) the Apostles, who reproduced His preaching in the context of His salvific death and Resurrection. Only in the second century does Gospel come to mean a document. The most primitive record of the preaching of the early Church is found in the Acts of the Apostles 2–5; 10:37–42 and 13:23–31. The first chapter of Acts is devoted to an account of the Ascension and the choice of Matthias to succeed Judas. Chapter 2 recounts the story of Pentecost and its effect on the apostolic community.

Under the stimulus of the Holy Spirit, St. Peter preached his first sermon, citing Joel's messianic vision and identifying the Apostles' charismatic tongues as its fulfillment.[1] Then Peter has recourse to

---

[1] This prophecy was treated in *God's Kingdom in the Old Testament*, p. 216. In the typical Old Testament telescoping of events, the Day of the Lord and Last Judgment are contiguous.

Psalms 15 and 109 to clinch his main thesis: the Messia, admittedly of the Davidic line, would have two distinguishing characteristics: incorruptibility (Ps. 15) and ultimate exaltation (Ps. 109). David himself possessed neither: not incorruptibility, for "his tomb is with us to this very day" (Acts 2:29); nor was he exalted, because in Psalm 109 David expressly affirms this prerogative not of himself but of his seed, the Messia. Christ fulfilled the exigency of incorruptibility by His Resurrection, and the Ascension completes His exaltation.[2] The primitive character of this sermon is indicated by the fact that as yet little stress is laid on the saving value of Jesus' death, and by the feverish expectancy of the Parousia evidenced by the idyllic voluntary dispossession described in 2:44.

In Acts 3, Peter's sermon to the people occasioned by the cure of the lame man leans heavily upon the Servant-Messia theme developed in Second Isaia: suffering was to be the indispensable door to salvation (v. 18; in 4:27 Jesus is actually designated as God's "holy servant"). This same type of primitive catechesis is found in St. Paul's writings, which were perhaps the first New Testament documents to be recorded. An example is contained in Philippians 2:5–11, now generally conceded to be an early Christian hymn incorporated by the apostle into his epistle: "Have this mind in you which was also in Christ Jesus,

> Who, while he kept his character as God,
> Did not consider his divine equality
> Something to be proudly paraded.
>
> No, he despoiled himself,
> By taking on the Servant's character,
> Becoming similar to mortal men.
>
> And looking outwardly like any other man,
> He carried self-abasement, through obedience,
> Right up to death, yes, death by the Cross.
>
> Therefore did God in turn immeasurably exalt him,
> And graciously bestow on him the Name,
> Outweighing every other name;
>
> That everyone, at Jesus' Name,
> Should bow adoring: those in heaven,
> On earth, in the infernal regions,
>
> And every tongue take up the cry
> 'Jesus is Lord,'
> Thus glorifying God his Father.[3]

---

[2] Cf. also Acts 13:35–37, and John 12:34.

[3] Fr. David Stanley's translation in "Carmenque Christo Quasi Deo Dicere . . .", *Catholic Biblical Quarterly*, 20 (1958), p. 180, in which Christ is honored with the title "Lord."

Liturgical Orientation of the Early Preaching

St. Paul's unabashed borrowing of what evidently seems to be an early Christian hymn enshrining a profession of faith is by no means an isolated incident in New Testament writings. Other instances are found in Ephesians 5:14; I Timothy 3:16; Colossians 1:13–20; I Peter 1:3–5; John 1:1–18; Apocalypse 5:9–10, 12, 13 and 15:34. Thus, rather than providing a source of liturgical texts, these writings reflect already existing formulas and are profoundly influenced by them. It seems, for example, that St. Peter's first epistle contains almost a complete baptismal liturgy. In addition there are fragments of early creeds (Rom. 10:9, I Cor. 12:3); doxologies (II Cor. 1:3–4); acclamations ("Maranatha" in I Cor. 16:22); and Eucharistic liturgies (Mark 14:22–25; I Cor. 11:23–25). This theme will be developed at greater length in subsequent chapters.

From Kerygma (Proclamation) to Didache (Teaching)

Already we can note a progression in the Church's understanding of the character of the Messia in Philippians 2:5–11: the expiatory value of His death and a clear statement of His divinity. Undoubtedly some individuals had copied down certain phrases and recollections of the Master, as also some of His miracles. Other persons began selecting and combining groups of related pericopae. By the time the four Evangelists (in the literary sense) began their scribal activity at the request of the faithful, there must have been a copious supply of written materials to fall back on. These materials would be basically either *Logia* (sayings) of Christ or *narratives* (action accounts, e.g., miracles). The task of the sacred author would be largely that of editing. He would have to select carefully his pericopae, then insert them into the loose outline of Christ's life which he possessed, and finally add connecting words and phrases. St. Mark's Gospel and Acts (especially 10:37–42) gives us a fair replica of this outline or framework: *1)* preaching of John the Baptist; *2)* baptism of Christ; *3)* the ministry in Galilee, with healings and exorcisms; *4)* the growing opposition of the Pharisees leading to Christ's semi-retirement with His apostles; *5)* the final journey to Jerusalem; *6)* the Passion, death, and Resurrection.

In order to effect the amalgamation of a number of disparate elements in their accounts, the sacred authors would have to impose an artificial character on their work. Many apparently *temporal* connectives, for example, would have to be *literary:* "At that time" might actually be several weeks or months later. Two or even three visits could be included in the phrase, "And he came to Nazareth." Besides reflecting different stages of the oral tradition, each Evangelist would have his own proper sources to draw from. Not one of these authors aimed at pure biography; nor were they satisfied with mere *kerygma* (proclamation of the bare essentials of salvation) but wrote to provide *didache* (advanced teaching, "theology") for a specific audience. The Gospels do, indeed, contain history; but they are better described as testimonials to faith with an apologetic end in view. As Fr. Barnabas Ahern states the case:

> We know now that events are recorded in the Gospels not merely because Jesus performed them, but, above all, because the early Christian community cherished them as directives for Church life and guide-lines for personal conduct. Every unit of the Gospel shows the mark of community use. Miracles are related not as documentary accounts of the deeds of Christ but as terse action photos of the messianic mercy which He is always ready to renew. The Last Supper is recounted in the synoptics not as a photographic reproduction of all that took place but as a sacramental rite which is constantly being renewed in the "breaking of bread." Some of our Lord's most telling pronouncements are preserved in the Gospel not because they were intended for the use of future biographers but because they were used every day in the life of the community to meet the challenge of its foes and to form Christlike attitudes in men and women who, though followers of Christ, had never seen Him. Like the history of Israel, the history of Jesus is a saving history. For thirty years before the composition of the first Gospel, the events of His life were told and re-told with sublime faith in their present efficacy. The works of His human life mark the culmination of God's saving action in the world of men. Like all sacred history, therefore, they are dynamically relevant in every age: 'Jesus Christ is the same, yesterday and today, yes, and forever.' (Heb. 13:8)[4]

Thus, we can distinguish a variety of themes among the New Testament authors.

WORK	MAIN THEME	SPECIAL MEDIUM
St. Mark	"Son of man" and "Servant" identified in Christ.	Miracles, secrecy.
St. Luke's Gospel	Christ is universal Savior.	New Exodus by a New Adam.
Acts of the Apostles	A Jewish worshipping community becomes the Christian Church under the guidance of the Holy Spirit.	Biography, travelogue, primitive kerygma.

[4] Fr. Barnabas Ahern, *New Horizons* (Notre Dame, Ind.: Fides Publishers, 1963), pp. 22–23.

WORK	MAIN THEME	SPECIAL MEDIUM
St. Matthew	Christ is the New Moses; God's reign has found a beach-head in the Christian community.	The "Five Discourses"; fulfillment of Old Testament prophecies.
St. Paul	Fulfillment of the mystery: God's plan to recapitulate men in Christ, Whose Body is the Church.	The "Heavenly Man's" victory over Satan, thereby releasing the "earthy man," Adam, from bondage.
St. John's Gospel	The life-giving mission of the Son of God descended from above.	Signs and symbols; new rites to replace the old.
Catholic and Pastoral Letters	Conflict with heresy; further instruction on the Christian life.	Applied ethics for Christians in the world.
Apocalypse	Conflict with the Roman Empire; Church versus State.	Theology of history; the liturgy of heaven.

Summary of Non-Catholic New Testament Criticism

Before turning to form criticism, it would be well to survey briefly the path of higher criticism of the nineteenth century (cf. *God's Kingdom in the Old Testament*, Chap. I). After its first wave of enthusiasm, that bold attempt to debunk the Bible through a "philosophical" approach yielded to the documentary period and the four distinguishable Mosaic Traditions. Although this second phase had much of permanent value, it was succeeded by the comparative religious approach which ended up (as the philosophical era had) in reducing Scripture to myths and pagan mysteries. From this conglomeration emerged liberal Protestantism—a sort of vague, agnostic clinging to the Christ of faith. The impetus behind this whole process was furnished by a German scholar named H. S. Reimarus, whose ideas we shall trace briefly.

Pioneering during the philosophical era, Reimarus' study led him to the conclusion that Jesus was fundamentally a political agitator who gathered a following in the hope of shaking off the shackles of Roman rule. Unfortunately, He was arrested, tried, and condemned to death. In order to save the cause, His disciples shrewdly made a martyr out of Him, assigning a sublime, expiatory motive to His death. They stole His body and then claimed He had arisen, and the myth of Christianity caught on. Reimarus never had the courage to publish his work, but after his death a friend and admirer published excerpts from it. It is remarkable to note that this and virtually every other rationalist conclusion have been abandoned after a short spurt of popularity as new theories are proposed. Basically the quest of subsequent scholars was that formulated by the "founder of Liberal Protestantism," A. Ritschl: how to distinguish the Christ of history" from the "Christ of faith." The "dilemma" is pictured below.

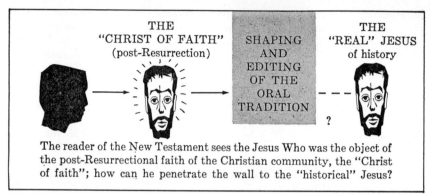

THE
"CHRIST OF FAITH"
(post-Resurrection)

SHAPING
AND
EDITING
OF THE
ORAL
TRADITION

THE
"REAL" JESUS
of history

?

The reader of the New Testament sees the Jesus Who was the object of the post-Resurrectional faith of the Christian community, the "Christ of faith"; how can he penetrate the wall to the "historical" Jesus?

THE PROBLEM OF THE "HISTORICAL" JESUS

Form Criticism: The New Higher Criticism—Evaluation

Actually a refinement of higher criticism, form criticism had been employed by Hermann Gunkel (d. 1932) in his work on Genesis and especially the psalms (cf. *God's Kingdom in the Old Testament*, Chap. XXI). It represents an effort to determine the original form of the oral tradition behind the New Testament by reconstructing the "life-situation" *(Sitz im Leben)* in which it was shaped by the Evangelist. The movement was accelerated after World War I by K. L. Schmidt, M. Dibelius (1919), and R. Bultmann (1921 ff.). To find the life-situation of a given work, e.g., the Gospel of St. Mark, it is necessary to separate out all of the pericopae (independent units) which have been amalgamated by the editor who added the framework and connective links. This separation can be accomplished, says the school, by classifying the pericopae into literary types. The following schema of these "forms" is representative:

1. APOTHEGMS (paradigms, anecdotes) are *stage-settings for sayings of Christ.* (E.g., the disciples' plucking of corn on the Sabbath gave Christ the occasion of declaring His lordship over the Sabbath, Mark 2:23–28). These are largely artificial.
2. MIRACLE STORY (*Novelle* according to Dibelius) is an *act of power* introduced to enhance the doctrine. These have little historical value, according to the critics.
3. PURE DISCOURSE *(parenesis)* embraces isolated phrases (Sermon on Mount and parables). This class of pericopae possesses the greatest face value.

4. LEGENDS (myths) are fictional additions to the text (stories of the infancy and the Resurrection). These have been introduced by the Evangelists to convey delicate theological lessons.

Having determined the classification of a pericope, the form critic is in a position to establish its life-situation: the nature of the audience, the preacher's purpose in making a given statement, etc. The final step is to decide what Jesus and His followers actually said and did. For example, we learn from this process that St. Peter's confession of Christ's divinity must have occurred after the Resurrection rather than during His public life (cf. Chap. XIV, two-page chart for additional examples). Although frequently carried to excess, form criticism has provided biblical exegetes with a valuable tool.[5] The following detailed analysis will help to illustrate its potentialities and its limitations.

CLAIM OF FORM CRITICS	EVALUATION
1. The Gospels are basically compilations (pericopae) artificially linked together, since the early Christians and Evangelists had no interest in Christ's biography.	1. The first part is true: the Gospels do represent compilations of material. However, not all connective narratives stem from the Evangelists; at least a skeletal framework was included in the primitive oral tradition (e.g., Acts 10:37–42).
2. Christianity served as a creative power, manufacturing events in the life of Christ—especially miracles. (Note that no account is taken of the fact that many of these episodes can be traced back to eyewitnesses.)	2. The Christianity community—like any other community—tended to shape and conserve, rather than to create, traditions about Jesus. It is normally individuals who create events, since the community lacks this dynamism.
3. The classification of pericopae shows that some miracles resemble Hellenistic accounts, and hence were probably "borrowed" to serve as teaching devices.	3. This assumption is unfounded, especially since heathen "miracles" simply exalted the wonder-worker, whereas Christ used them as works of mercy, not primarily as apologetics.
4. The classification of pericopae is the key to their historicity (i.e., their correspondence to the actual words and deeds of Jesus).	4. This is denied; form criticism must be supplemented by literary criticism embracing the contents of the passage as well as its form.
5. Form criticism shows that the date of the written source of a pericope does not determine its degree of reliability, but rather the tradition behind it determines that.	5. This is true, and is one of the valuable insights furnished by the method of form criticism.

[5] A decree of the Pontifical Biblical Commission dated April 21, 1964 gives official sanction to the use of form criticism by Catholic scholars, but warns against abuses.

Largely through the aid of form criticism, biblical scholars have been able to recognize many diverse factors in the Gospels and other New Testament books:

1. *The language factor.* Jesus probably made most of His pronouncements in Aramaic; our Greek text does not always carry the accuracy or the richness of the original term (e.g., the Greek word *porneia* in Matt. 5:32, 19:9, and Acts 15:29).
2. *The social factor.* The common life of the primitive community entailed class and racial integration with its accompanying factions, e.g., I Corinthians.
3. *The liturgical factor.* Already discussed in this chapter.
4. *The catechetical factor.* Considerations of how best to present Christianity to new converts, e.g., I Peter is probably using a baptismal liturgy.
5. *The didactic factor.* Setting up rules for the community based on Jesus' own preaching, e.g., the Sermon on the Mount.
6. *The ecclesiastical factor.* Structural developments in the community had to be taken into account as it emerged from Temple and Synagogue to become a distinct organization (cf. Matt. 18 and the Pastoral Epistles).
7. *The historical factor.* Great pains were taken by the sacred authors to identify their written accounts with genuine happenings in the life of Jesus (cf. I Cor. 13:23ff. and 15:1–11). Many readers would have been eyewitnesses of the events.
8. *The psychological factor.* A deepening penetration over the years by the apostles of the mysteries of faith enabled them to recall and grasp forgotten phrases of Christ embodying this new understanding, e.g., the doctrine of the Trinity.
9. *The apologetical factor.* Although this element is present in nearly all of the New Testament books, it stands out in some which seem to have been written expressly to encourage Christians in time of persecution or heresy: the Apocalypse; II Peter; Colossians.

The "Synoptic Problem"

The first three Gospels are known as the "Synoptics" (from the Greek word meaning "see together") because when their parallel passages are laid out side by side they manifest a notable agreement. This fact is made very evident by a harmony of the Gospels; such a work shows the Fourth Gospel to be in a different idiom from the first three. At the same time the presence of unmistakable differences is apparent among the Synoptics. It is this *simultaneous existence of similarities together with dissimilarities* which constitutes the so-called Synoptic problem and which demands some sort of solution.

The similarities can be explained by: *1)* the use of common sources. All of the four Gospels had, as we have seen, their remote sources in the preaching of Christ and the Apostles, from which the primitive oral teaching or catechesis was formed. The proximate sources of the synoptics comprise one or more collections of "Logia" or sayings of Christ (called "Q" in Protestant circles from the German word *Quelle* meaning "source") plus a lost Aramaic version of St. Matthew's Gospel. Protestant scholars generally deny the existence of the latter and maintain that Mark is the most "primitive" Gospel source. Catholic critics see Mark as the bridge between Matthew Aramaic and the Greek version of the same (which, hypothetically, is more of a paraphrase than a translation). *2)* Mutual dependence. Form criticism reveals that both Matthew Greek (the Gospel which we possess today) and Luke depend upon Mark but not upon each other. About one-third of St. Luke's Gospel has been taken bodily from St. Mark, as will be illustrated in Chapter 4. If we date St. Mark 65–70 A.D., then Luke was probably composed about 70 A.D. (before the fall of Jerusalem —?) and Matthew some time after the fall (70–80 A.D.?).

Discrepancies among the synoptics are traceable to: *1)* the peculiar background and style of each. Just as Isaia and Amos contrast vividly as to style, so do Luke and Mark. *2)* Proper source(s) of each Evangelist. St. Mark's Gospel stems from St. Peter's catechesis in Rome; St. Luke was disciple and secretary to St. Paul. St. Matthew and St. Luke each had his proper infancy source. *3)* Difference of purpose and audience. All three Synoptics offer us theological rather than biographical works. In addition, each Evangelist had his proper audience to keep in mind in presenting his story. The following chart will help to clarify the formation of the Synoptic Gospels.

FORMATION OF THE SYNOPTIC GOSPELS

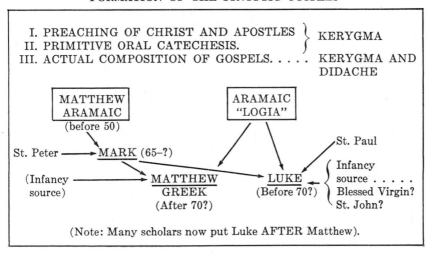

21

Psalm 2: The Triumph of the Messia
(Cf. Psalm 131: 11–12; II Kings 7: 11–13)

Here is one of the "Coronation Psalms" idealizing the newly-crowned monarch. As in the case of Psalm 15:10, certain passages of this pre-Exilic poem(notably Yahweh's messianic decree in vv. 7–9) extend beyond the type (Solomon?) and compenetrate the anti-type (Christ, in Whom alone they attain fulfillment). The Psalmist beholds in a vision the Gentile nations conspiring against God and His Anointed ("Messia") in verses 1–3. Amused at their puny audacity, Yahweh counters with the decree whereby He designates the Messia-King. The latter corroborates the decree by declaring himself the "Son of God" (vv. 4–9). The Psalmist concludes with a warning to the kings of the earth to submit to the messianic rule lest they be crushed (vv. 10–12).

Suggested Readings

Bible de Jerusalem, pp. 1283–1289.
Dodd, *New Testament Studies,* pp. 1–11.
Flanagan, *Acts of the Apostles* (New Testament Reading Guide Series, No. 5), pp. 3–25.
MacKenzie, *Introduction to the New Testament* (New Testament Reading Guide Series, No. 1), pp. 14–23.
Orchard, *A Catholic Commentary on Holy Scripture,* cols. 604–609.
Ricciotti, *The Life of Christ,* Chap. 13.
Rigaux, "Historicity of Jesus and Recent Exegesis," *Theology Digest,* IX (Winter, 1961), 26–32. (Same article appears as Chap. 12 in Heaney, *Faith, Reason and the Gospels.*)
Wikenhauser, *New Testament Introduction,* pp. 1–10, 150–155, 221–277.

For Further Study

1. What is the difference between *didache* and *kerygma*? Which came first?
2. Why is the "eschatological" explanation of the life of Jesus not only harmful, but positively vicious?
3. What use do both St. Peter and St. Paul make of Psalm 15?
4. What is the significance of the phrase, "Jesus is Lord?"
5. What is the value, if any, of form criticism?

Chapter III

St. Mark's Gospel:
The Primitive Proclamation

READINGS: *St. Mark 1–10; Psalm 81; Bouyer,* The Meaning of Sacred Scripture, *Chap. 16. (Note: Mark 1:34; 6:5, 13; 7:20; 10:45.)*

After centuries of neglect the Gospel of St. Mark has come into its own in the twentieth century. The early Church preferred St. Matthew. The earliest known commentaries on Mark appear only in the fifth and sixth centuries; in the patristic age it was explained but rarely. As the Second Evangelist was thought to have abridged Matthew's more complete account, it was sufficient to study the First Gospel.

Mark, however, found favor with the late nineteenth-century critics, who regarded his work as a simple, untheological 'Life of Jesus.' The early twentieth century discovered the presence in Mark of the 'messianic secret,' a theme supposedly invented by the evangelist to explain away the inconvenient fact that Jesus' real mission went unsuspected during His earthly life, even by His most intimate disciples. The theory was an exaggeration, of course, but it did point out that Mark was truly aware of the mystery surrounding the person of Jesus Christ. In recent years the study of the apostolic preaching has increased the popularity of Mark's Gospel and has shown it to be nearest to that teaching in form and content and in the picture it gives of Christ.[1]

It is in these terms that Father David Stanley, S.J., characterizes the "emergence" of St. Mark's Gospel, orientating it as the most "primitive" of the four. Though edited (as were the others), the second Gospel takes us back into closer proximity to the words and especially the deeds of Jesus. St. Mark gives us not the Jesus Who speaks but the Jesus Who acts. His Gospel has been called a "passion narrative prefaced by an outline of Jesus' ministry," obviously an oversimplification, but still containing much truth. The almost crude language and style of this shortest (661 verses compared with 1148 of St. Luke) Gospel matches its kerygmatic approach. Though possessing the vividness of an eye-witness account in many spots, e.g, 8:24 and 9:2, its vocabulary is drab and repetitious. Little imagination is employed in

---

[1] *The Bible Today,* I (1962), p. 59: "Mark and Modern Apologetics" p. 59. Cf. also Orchard, *A Catholic Commentary on Holy Scripture* (New York: Thomas Nelson and Sons, 1953) col. 724b.

connecting the pericopae: "and," "straightway," "entering" (a house), "on the way" are used over and over again. Originally written in Greek, Mark's Gospel betrays more Aramaisms than even St. Matthew's version of the "Good News." But it also contains a generous supply of Latinisms such as *denarius, quadrans, centurion, legion, praetorium,* etc. This last fact leads up to another line of thought.

Relation of St. Mark's Gospel to St. Peter

About 130 A.D. Papias, Bishop of Hierapolis in Phrygia wrote in defense of the second Gospel:

> This, too, the Old Man said: 'When Mark became [sc. by writing his Gospel] the interpreter of Peter, he wrote down, though by no means with full detail [though not without gaps in his narrative], as much as he accurately remembered of the words and works of the Lord: for he had neither heard the Lord nor followed Him, but he subsequently joined Peter, as I said. Now, Peter did not intend to give a complete exposition of the Lord's ministry, but delivered his instruction to suit the varying needs of the people. It follows, then, that Mark was guilty of no blunder if he wrote, simply to the best of his recollections, an incomplete account. For, of one matter he took forethought—not to omit anything he had heard or to falsify in recording anything.'[2]

This early testimony represents the constant tradition of the Church regarding Mark's association with St. Peter in Rome, supported by other witnesses and the Latinisms just referred to. If we assume that St. Mark is identical with the John Mark of the Acts of the Apostles (a thesis generally conceded today), then we can reconstruct this "biography" of him: He is first designated in Acts 12:12 as the son of a certain Mary whose house was used for prayer meetings. Next, he ("John") is described as deserting Paul and Barnabas at Pamphylia, for which act St. Paul refuses to take him on his second missionary journey (Acts 13:13 and 15:38). A quarrel ensues, with Mark and Barnabas (his cousin, Col. 4:10) pairing off and Paul taking Silas with him instead. But later on Paul and Mark were reconciled, as we learn from Philemon 24, and II Timothy 4:11, where Mark is described by St. Paul as "useful to me in the ministry." These epistles were written from Rome, as was also the reference in I Peter 5:13 to Mark as "my [Peter's] son." Finally, it is worthy of mention that the young man who fled naked from the soldiers in Gethsemani—described only in Mark 14:51–52—may be none other than the Evangelist himself. Tra-

---

[2] Quoted from *The Apostolic Fathers* (*The Fathers of the Church,* Vol. I [New York: Cima Publishing Co., 1947]), p. 377.

dition affirms he was martyred in Alexandria, Egypt. That St. Mark reproduces the oral catechesis of St. Peter, then, cannot be reasonably doubted.

St. Mark's Identification of the "Servant" and "Son of Man" in the Son of God

The Second Gospel contains no Sermon on the Mount; in fact, there are only two extended discourses in the whole book: the three parables in Chapter 4 and the eschatological discourse in Chapter 13. From Christ's baptism until His resurrection St. Mark's account portrays Him on the move, His days so crowded with activity that there is seldom time to rest. Nevertheless there is a unifying theme; in the words of G. E. Wright and R. H. Fuller, "the figure of the *servant* (from the Book of Isaia) gives a unity to all that Jesus said and did from the moment of his baptism to his death upon the cross. Remove that background, and his life breaks up into a series of unrelated fragments."[3] And it is St. Mark who gives us this thread in the most explicit fashion.

For W. Wrede and his followers, the pivotal theme consisted in the element of secrecy which is clearly a part of Mark's technique. As Fr. Stanley notes, however, this concept was developed by them to explain away this technique as a mere literary device introduced to hide the alleged fact that Christ never claimed to be the Messia and was not recognized as such during His earthly career. Contrary to Mr. Wrede's contention, the "messianic secret" is part of St. Mark's apocalyptic genre employed by the Evangelist to show that Jesus' true nature is a mystery which can be grasped only by faith. The miracles which St. Mark recounts (and on which he places more emphasis than the other Evangelists) are acts of divine power to help men to believe, but they do not dispense with the need of faith. Indeed, Christ's miracles must be hidden from those who are ill-disposed to believe.

St. Mark follows the simple outline of the kerygma noted on page 15, beginning with the preaching of John the Baptist and ending with the Resurrection.[4] In order to grasp the effect of the kerygma, it is best to read through the Gospel without too much distraction. The following topical ideas will suffice as a guide; specific exegesis will

---

[3] G. E. Wright and R. H. Fuller, *The Book of the Acts of God* (Garden City: Doubleday, 1960) p. 277. Cf. also T. W. Manson, *The Servant Messiah* (New York: Cambridge University Press, 1961), especially Chap. 4.

[4] Mark 16:9–20 seems to have been added by a later editor. It includes accounts of Christ's apparitions after the Resurrection as well as the account of His Ascension. It is, however, part of the inspired Gospel.

be supplied in conjunction with St. Matthew's Gospel. These topics, it will be noticed, cut across the chronological order; they are *thematic* divisions.

Topical Development of St. Mark's Account

1. *Proclamation.* It was generally believed that the advent of the messianic era would be heralded in a very special manner, e.g., by the return of Elias (*Mal.* 3:23). Isaia 52:7–10 contains a model; this passage presaged the return from the Babylonian Captivity. St. Mark's Gospel begins abruptly with the appearance of the New Elias, John the Baptist. Mark 1:3 is an accommodated mixture of Malachia 3:1 and Isaia 40:3; such free use of texts was commonplace among Jewish rabbis. The message: Men must prepare themselves for the Messia by baptism and penance.

2. *Theophany.* Some sort of epiphany would be called for to identify the Messia, such as Isaia 60 or 63:1, 11, 19. In the case of Jesus, this is accomplished by the voice and dove at His baptism (the messianic anointing or confirmation). The phrase, "Thou art my beloved Son" reflects Psalm 2:7; "in thee I am well pleased" refers the reader to the first Servant Song, Isaia 42:1.

3. *Conquest of Satan.* "And immediately the Spirit drove him forth into the desert . . . forty days and forty nights . . . being tempted the while by Satan . . . and (he) was with the wild beasts" (Mark 1:12–13). Many images are amalgamated here to suggest the real issue: the struggle with the devil, undoing the mischief of Adam and reclaiming the dominion of Paradise. Matthew and Luke will expand this theme.

4. *Miracles.* Imitating the prophets, Christ gathers a core of disciples in whom to seal up his message (cf. Isa. 8:16). The messianic signs (Isa. 35:5ff.) begin with the exorcism of a demoniac: Christ's first onslaught against the powers of evil. The demon proclaims Him and is ordered to hold his peace. Other wonders follow quickly: the cure of Peter's mother-in-law, the healing of a leper, then a paralytic. Mark 1:34 and its context suggest that the vast sea of human misery and diseases is but a corollary of Satan's tenure.[5] The cure of the paralytic in Chapter 2 goes beyond messiaship and, coupled with the forgiveness of the man's sins, sug-

---

[5] It is interesting to note that in Mark 1:21–39 we have what appears to be an original continuous narrative depicting a typical 24-hour period in Christ's busy apostolate. He worked during the day and spent most of the night in prayer: His was the *apostolic* or "mixed" way of life—action flowing from contemplation. For evidences of the "primitiveness" of Mark, compare Mark 5:30, 32 with Matt. 9:22; Mark 6:5–6 with Matt. 13:58.

gests Christ's divinity. It is in this context that He first designates
Himself as "Son of Man"—subtly insinuating that He is also the
"Son of God" (cf. Mark 1:1).

5. *Conflict with the Pharisees.* The Scribes and Pharisees have been
alerted by the claim to forgive sins made by Jesus. A series of episodes, artfully arranged by Mark, now ensues to set the stage for
Christ's ultimate fate. In attending the banquet accorded Him by
Levi (publican just called to be a disciple), Christ is accused of
dining with sinners: His reply is that He is the physician of sick
souls. When they accuse Him of neglecting the traditional fasts, He
identifies Himself as the bridegroom preparing the messianic banquet. In answer to the charge of working on the Sabbath (by plucking a few ears of grain), Jesus declares that He is Lord of the Sabbath. Finally, the cure of the man with the withered hand—also on
the Sabbath—results in the beginning of the plot to kill Him. He
brands their gossip campaign against Him as blasphemy against
the Spirit, and counters by selecting His twelve apostles. Not even
His own relatives are completely loyal: they think Him beside Himself ("mad"). Jesus gives the standard of His *true* kinsmen: doing
the will of God (3:35).

6. *Messianic secret.* After every miracle Jesus strictly enjoins silence
(though His beneficiaries consistently ignore this injunction), and
His popularity daily increases. Exceptions to the secrecy rule do
occur, as in the case of the demoniac of Gerasa (who even becomes a local apostle—5:19) and the Syrophoenician's daughter
(7:26–30): but both of these miracles occurred outside of Jewish
territory. Careful reasoning must convince us that this is not merely
a literary device of St. Mark to gloss over the allegation that Christ
made no pretensions to messiaship. Rather, it is the Evangelist's
factual portrayal of Jesus as the Servant of Isaia, "not crying out,
not shouting, not making his voice heard in the street" (Isa. 42:2;
cf. also 49:2, 53:1).

7. *Prophet and teacher.* Christ's teaching career is drastically curtailed
in St. Mark's account. The secrecy of Jesus' actions is carried over
into His teaching by means of a wisdom genre, the parable. The
purpose of this genre is not primarily to obscure the doctrine; Mark
4:11 must be understood in its Isaian context. The mysteriousness
of the parables betokens the fact that the coming of the Messia and
his kingdom are mystery events.

8. *Liturgical interlude.* The mission of the Twelve (6:7ff), sent out by
pairs in apostolic poverty, touches off a series of liturgical allusions.
(a) Sick people are "anointed with oil . . . and healed" (6:13).
The Council of Trent decreed that this anointing "insinuated" the

institution of the sacrament of Last Anointing, which is "promulgated" in James 5:14–15. *(b)* In both accounts of the multiplication of the loaves a liturgical formula is employed; in 6:41, Jesus is described as "looking up to heaven," whereupon He "blessed and broke the loaves, and gave them to His disciples . . ." (cf. 14:22–25). *(c)* At the conclusion of His denunciation of the Pharisees, the dietary laws, a very important section of the ceremonial precepts, are abrogated explicitly (7:20). *(d)* In the healing of the deaf-mute a baptismal formula is used by Christ, Who "put his fingers into the man's ears, and spitting, he touched his tongue. And looking up to heaven, he sighed, and said to him, 'Ephpheta,' that is, 'Be thou opened' " (7:33–34). *(e)* Spittal is also used in healing the blind man in 8:23 (note vividness of description in 8:24).

Turning-Point in Christ's Career: Peter's Confession and the Doctrine of the Cross

After His scathing rebuke of their formalism in worship in Chapter 7, Jesus' relationship with the Pharisees reaches the breaking-point, and He refuses them a sign in 8:12 (but see Luke 11:29–30 for the "sign" of Jona). Even His own townspeople have rejected Him (6:1–6). John the Baptist's death is a further warning of Herod's enmity (cf. 6:16), and Jesus goes into semi-retirement to concentrate on the training of His apostolic band. His climactic question at Caesarea Philippi regarding His true identity elicits an act of faith from Peter. St. Matthew's Gospel gives us Peter's post-Pentecostal understanding of both Jesus' messiaship and divinity (16:16), but St. Mark's account contains reference only to His messiaship—and that a very imperfect notion, as we learn three verses later.[6] With the triple prediction of the Passion, death, and Resurrection, we have arrived at the literary center of St. Mark's Gospel. Each time, that prediction falls on uncomprehending ears—as does the "doctrine of the cross": "For he who would save his life will lose it; but he who loses his life for my sake and for the gospel's sake will save it" (8:35). Not even the glimpse of Christ's glorified body granted to Peter, James, and John in the *Transfiguration,* identifying Him as the new Lawgiver (Moses) and Prophet (Elias), is sufficient to confirm their faith in a Servant-Messia Who must suffer and die. In answer to their query, He identifies the Baptist with Elias. Note their incomprehension in 9:9.

At this point St. Mark inserts into his already overcrowded outline a series of short discourses. The disciples' failure to cast the devil out of the little boy illustrates the need of asceticism (9:28). Their argu-

---

[6] This passage will be treated in greater detail, along with the Transfiguration, in Chap. XIV.

ment over the occupancy of the first places in the kingdom (9:33) and the request of James and John (10:37) give rise to a lesson on humility: "If any man wishes to be first, he shall be last of all, and *servant* of all" (9:34). In the Markan report of Jesus' teaching on divorce, we find this Evangelist less "primitive" than either Matthew or Luke: the prohibition has been adapted to a Roman audience (10:12), for a woman had no right to institute divorce proceedings under the Mosaic Law. The refusal of the rich young man to embrace voluntary poverty as a condition of the apostolate (10:22) launches Jesus into a discourse on the danger of wealth. In the third prediction of the passion there is a veiled allusion to the third Servant Song (Isa. 50:6). This reference is followed shortly by the key to Mark's Gospel: " . . . for **the Son of Man also has not come to be served but to serve, and to give his life as a ransom for many**" (10:45). Note, finally, that Bartimeus is not ordered to keep quiet when he proclaims Jesus "Son of David" before his cure (v. 48); the secret is out, and the last trip to Jerusalem has begun!

Psalm 81: Condemnation of the "Sons of God" (Cf. Psalm 57)

In this solemn court scene, the Psalmist conceives Yahweh as Judge of the earth, rebuking His human representatives for their unjust decisions (cf. Isa. 3:13–15 and Dan. 13). Verses 1–5 express the divine accusation: their crime of partiality toward the rich. In verse 1 these men are termed "gods"; in verse 6 the description is repeated along with the epithet "sons of the Most High" (= "sons of God;" cf. Ps. 57:1). Christ cited this passage in John 10:34 when the Jews were about to stone Him for calling God His father. The final verse is a prayer that God will vindicate His sovereign dominion by coming in person to judge the world.

Placing Psalm 81 in its proper literary genre poses a difficulty. The fact that it contains a complaint would seem to qualify it as a Psalm of Lament. However, the objective presentation of the injustices as a violation of the rights of Yahweh raises it to the more speculative level of a Wisdom Psalm. Its twin, Psalm 57, would likewise fit into this category. The point to note here is the generic use of the term "son of God" by the Jews. In employing this designation of Himself, Christ not only fulfilled it but utterly transformed it.

Suggested Readings

Hunt, *Understanding the Bible*, Chap. 23.
Manson, *The Servant Messiah*, Chap. 1–4.
Orchard, *A Catholic Commentary on Holy Scripture*, col. 724–735.
Sloyan, *The Gospel of St. Mark* (New Testament Reading Guide Series, No. 2), pp. 3–84.
Wikenhauser, *New Testament Introduction*, pp. 155–173.

For Further Study

1. In what sense is St. Mark's Gospel "primitive?"
2. Which parable is proper to St. Mark, and what does it teach?
3. How does Mark 6:5 manifest the "primitiveness" of this Gospel?
4. Explain, "Thus He declared all foods clean."
5. Was the resurrection of the body a clear, well-delineated concept in contemporary Judaism (cf. 9:9)?
6. In what sense was Peter's confession the turning point in Christ's career?

Chapter IV

St. Mark's Passion Account and I-II Thessalonians: Servant, Son of Man, The Parousia

READINGS: *St. Mark 11–16; I–II Thessalonians; Psalm 117.* (*Note: Mark 11:10; 12:10, 26, 35; 14:62; 15:39; I Thessalonians 4:15–17; II Thessalonians 2:3, 7; Psalm 117:22–26.*)

Bartimeus' reference to Jesus as "Son of David," no doubt intended as a messianic title designed to win the Master's favor, testifies to the revival of Jewish hopes in the return of a Davidic prince to the leadership of Israel. Dampened by the disappearance of Zorobabel, these repressed hopes seem to have reappeared during the pitiful performance of the Hasmonean dynasty when the titles of king and high priest were usurped by the ineffectual incumbents. The "Psalms of Solomon," a Pharisean manifesto composed about 50 B.C., gives us one of the best expressions of Jewish messianism of the period. This prince of the line of David is to possess the qualities of wisdom, justice, and sinlessness; the "Chosen of the Lord" will not be divine, "for the Lord Himself is his king." He will conquer the Gentiles, not by violence, but "by the word of his mouth," and they shall be forced to serve under the yoke of the "sons of their God" (the Jews). This concept agrees with the prophets (e.g., Isaia, Daniel) in depicting the Messia as a king and prophet who will establish a kingdom on this earth; but it falls far short of Old Testament prophecy in its failure to include the role of the compassionate Servant, suffering for others. Indeed, it pictures him as lording it over the Gentiles rather than as instructing and saving them.[1]

---

[1] R. A. Dyson, S. J. and A. Jones, *The Kingdom of Promise* (Westminster, Md.: Newman Press, 1957) pp. 131–133. A substantial portion of Psalm of Solomon 17 is reproduced in Manson, *Op. cit.*, pp. 26–27; cf. also Manson, *Ibid.*, p. 28 for an excerpt from Psalm of Solomon 18. The whole first chapter of Manson is very helpful in understanding Jewish messianic expectations. See also Milo Connick, *Jesus: the Man, the Mission and the Message* (Englewood Cliffs, N. J.: Prentice Hall, 1963) Chap. 17.

The Messianic Manifestation: Jesus' Entry Into Jerusalem
(Mark 11-12)

As Jesus rides into the city on an ass, he is greeted with shouts taken from Psalm 117:26—"Blessed is he who comes in the name of the Lord!" Now would this new Messia smash the Roman tyrants and scatter the foreign legions from Jerusalem! But Jesus had other ideas. The next day He curses a fig tree for not having born fruit—a symbol of the barren Jewish nation. And instead of cleansing Palestine of the Romans, He cleanses the Temple of its (Jewish) buyers and sellers— and from the court of the Gentiles at that! For this act the chief priests determine to "destroy" Him, and the following day Peter notices that the fig tree has withered up "from the roots." The cleansing episode plunges Jesus into five controversies with the Pharisees. (1) The source of His authority: Jesus refuses an answer to their request by a stinging, rhetorical question regarding John the Baptist's mission. (2) In proposing the parable of the vinedressers (adapted from Isa. 5:1-7), Jesus takes the initiative, showing that He expects no mercy at their hands. Again Psalm 117 is cited (in its typical meaning) to condemn the Jews. (3) The tribute query illustrates forcefully that citizens of God's kingdom likewise have duties to the earthly kingdom to which they pertain. (4) The objection raised by the Sadducees, who accepted only the Pentateuch and rejected the "Tradition of the Ancients," is shown to be based on a correct but incomplete interpretation of that part of the Scriptures which they did accept. Were Abraham, Isaac and Jacob not still "alive" and candidates for resurrection, Yahweh would have to have said, "I was the God of Abraham," etc. Skipping over the question about the greatest commandment—which seems to have come from a sincere Scribe—we find the final controversy involving the very essence of the Messia: (5) St. Matthew tells us (22: 46) that this question posed by Jesus to the Pharisees confounded and silenced them. For an adequate explanation, see the footnote in the Confraternity Version on Psalm 109:1. Jesus' renewed warning against the Scribes and the Pharisees is emphasized by the contrast which the widow's mite affords at the end of Chapter 12.

The Destruction of Jerusalem; A Type of the End of the World
(Mark 13)

Much unnecessary confusion has resulted from an artificial division of this discourse of Jesus and its application to two different events, viz., the fall of Jerusalem and the end of the world. Today the consensus of scholarly opinion is that the whole discourse refers literally to the former event and only typically to the Parousia. Christ's description constitutes a genuine prophecy, although some details probably have been added in retrospect to the Gospel accounts of Matthew and Luke. This prediction would have the effect of reassuring the Roman community for whom St. Mark wrote that the Master had foreseen the event which so decisively furthered the emergence of the Christian Church from the synagogue. Warned in advance, the Christians of Jerusalem fled across the Jordan to Pella and there found safety. The point to remember is that this is a moral rather than a dogmatic treatise: "Be on your guard! Be always ready for death!" This warning anticipates the persecution which would be meted out to the apostles by both Jews and Gentiles. Christ points to the "abomination of desolation," i.e., Antiochus Epiphanes' desecration of the Temple in 167 B.C., as a type of the approaching erection of Roman emblems within the Holy City two years before its destruction. The language describing the tribulations which were to accompany this cataclysm is borrowed from the Old Testament: Daniel 9:25–26 and 12:1; Isaia 13:6–16; Sophonia 1:14–15, etc. A number of false Messias actually did rise up, as Christ predicts, and precipitated the end of the City and the Temple.

The Coming of the Son of Man
(Mark 13:26)

This clear reference to Daniel 7:13–18 regarding the reception from the hands of God of the everlasting kingdom by a "son of man" (the "holy ones of the Most High" in v. 18) to replace *on this earth* all previous human dynasties *should be linked to the proclamation of the Gospel and the spread of the Christian Church, not to the second coming (Parousia) of Christ.* The language used here by St. Mark matches Old Testament descriptions of the "Day of the Lord" inaugurating the messianic era which would endure for an unspecified period of time. The corresponding New Testament term, "Day of the Son of Man," begins with His Resurrection and will be consummated by the Parousia. This interpretation is supported by the statement that "this generation will not pass away until all these things (the Resurrection and promulgation of the Church) have been accomplished (v. 30).[2] What we must keep in mind is that each fresh calamity is a miniature Parousia. "That day" (v. 32) is broad enough to include both type and antitype. Moreover, the divine timetable transcends the human knowledge of Christ; it is part of the mystery of the Kingdom. The discourse

---

[2] See Jesus' discourse on the coming of the Kingdom of God in Luke 17:20–37, which is distinct from his treatment of the destruction of Jerusalem in Chap. 21.

ends with an exhortation for vigilance on the part of Church leaders. All Christians, however, should profit from the lesson.

The Epistles to the Thessalonians and the Time of the Parousia

We have noted the fact that the early Christians seemed to be under the impression that the Parousia would occur within their own lifetime. Their Christian communism bore witness to this expectancy. That this was not an official doctrine of the Church is manifested in what were probably the first writings of the Greek New Testament: St. Paul's First and Second Epistles to the Thessalonians.[3] We shall formally introduce the author of these two epistles in Chapter VII, contenting ourselves at this point with a summary of the principal teachings contained in them.

The Church at Thessalonica had been established by St. Paul about 50 A.D. during his second missionary journey, and it was one of his most fervent groups of converts.[4] But a problem arose among them: when Christ returns in judgment at the Parousia, won't those Christians who are still alive—and hence not obliged to die—have an advantage over those who have already died and whose bodies have therefore corrupted? St. Paul answers in the negative, outlining the sequence of events at the end-time period: *1)* the dead (those "asleep") will rise first, with their bodies, *2)* then the bodies of the living shall likewise rise, *3)* finally, both groups "shall be caught up together . . . in the clouds to meet the Lord in the air, and so we shall ever be with the Lord" (4:15–17).[5]

The opening verses of II Thessalonians sound like a Mass-preface: St. Paul reiterates the central position of thanksgiving in Christian worship as already expressed in I Thessalonians 1:2 and 5:18. Then he turns to the Parousia again. This event will terrorize evil-doers "who do not know God, and who do not obey the Gospel . . . these will be punished with eternal ruin, away from the face of the Lord and the glory of his power . . ." (1:8–9). Because an enemy of his has forged a letter in his name to the effect that the "day of the Lord" is imminent (2:2), St. Paul offers a correction: The Parousia will be delayed until "the apostasy comes first, and the man of sin is revealed" (2:3). We do not know exactly to what he is referring; apparently he

---

[3] This excludes Matthew Aramaic. Cf. Monro, *Enjoying the New Testament*, p. 25. John 21:22–23 offers another antidote for this expectation of an immediate Parousia.

[4] I Thessalonians 1:3, 8; 2:13–14; 3:6. The decision of the Council of Jerusalem (to be treated in Chap. IX) seems to be reflected in 4:3–5.

[5] This is part of the passage which is used as the epistle in the Requiem Mass on the day of death or burial (4:13–18).

had previously explained the matter to the Thessalonians.[6] At any rate, the apostle concedes that "the mystery of iniquity is already at work," but is being "restrained" by some one (v. 7). Again the reference escapes us. It is useless to try to identify any past or present calamity with this reference as both Christ and St. Paul (who borrows much from his Master's apocalyptic terminology) assure us that the time will be unknown (Mark 13:32; I Thessalonians 5:2). In conclusion the reader should note in I Thessalonians 5:27 the antiquity of the custom of reading from an epistle at public worship. II Thessalonians 2:15 is a well known argument for tradition (cf. also II Cor. 11:2).

The Last "Passover": Messianic Banquet
(Mark 14:1–31)

By comparing all four Gospels it becomes probable that Jesus and the apostles celebrated the Passover at least twenty-four hours in advance. This arrangement permitted Him to die as the priests were slaughtering the paschal lambs in the Temple; besides, the Jews would never have carried out their decision to do away with Christ on the feast itself (which coincided that year with the Sabbath), and His death in such a case would have been an anticlimax. At any rate, it had all the characteristics of a Passover meal (14:16). The action of the woman identified by St. John as Mary, the sister of Martha and Lazarus, makes His death imperative. Jesus interprets the kindness as an embalming. M. Dibelius suggests that Mary intended it as a messianic anointing. The omission of this portion of the Gospel in the 1955 reform of the Holy Week liturgy appears enigmatic in the light of verse 9. St. John identifies the objector to this rite as Judas Iscariot, the "thief" (John 12:4–6), whose betrayal arrangements Mark describes at this juncture. The first detail of the meal recorded by St. Mark is Christ's prediction of the betrayal, but without mentioning any names. Again it is St. John who, after describing the deed as a fulfillment of Psalm 40:10, furnishes us with the identification tag via the episode of the dipping of the bread. St. Mark does not tell us at what point Judas left the assembly. Even with the help of the other Evangelists, it is difficult to say with certainty whether or not he partook of the Eucharist.

---

[6] This "man of sin" may be compared with John's "antichrists" in I John 2:18 (cf. also II John 7). We shall return to the topic of the second coming of Christ in conjunction with II Peter and the Apocalypse. As for the restraining influence of II Thessalonians 2:7, the Danish scholar J. Munck maintains that St. Paul thought it was his own preaching, and that the Parousia would take place as soon as he had evangelised the Gentiles! (Cf. W. D. Davies, *Christian Origins and Judaism* [Philadelphia: The Westminister Press, 1962] Chap. 8).

What happens next and is so casually described by St. Mark, verses 22–25, can only be understood in the context of the Passover rite of the Jews. Though much of the following correlation is conjecture, it illustrates that Jesus was transferring "the symbolism of the elements from the Exodus to his own death."[7]

PASCHAL MEAL	INSTITUTION OF THE EUCHARIST
1. Drinking from cup of blessed wine.	(Cf. Luke 22:17–18; then perhaps John 13:5).
2. Herbs dipped in bitter sauce; unleavened bread ("Matzah"). . .	Betrayal of Judas revealed. Then, "Jesus took bread, and blessing it, he broke and gave it to them, and said, 'Take; this is my body' " (14:22).
3. Lamb brought in; oration by father on the meaning of the Exodus	Jesus' death a baptism and cup (10:39; cf. also John 15:13).
4. Singing of the first part of the Hallel, Psalms 112–113:8.	
5. Second cup of wine.	
6. Lamb eaten	There is no mention of a lamb in Gospel.
7. Third cup of wine ("cup of benediction"); prayer of thanksgiving	"And taking a cup and giving thanks, he gave it to them, and they all drank of it; and he said to them, 'This is my blood of the new covenant, which is being shed for many' " (Mark 14:23–24).
8. Second part of the Hallel, 113:9—117.	
9. Fourth cup of wine ("cup of Elijah")	"Amen I say to you, that I will drink no more of the fruit of the vine, until that day when I shall drink it new in the kingdom of God" (14:25).
10. Symposium on the Exodus late into the night	Cf. John 14—17.
11. Singing of a hymn	"And after reciting a hymn, they went out to the Mount of Olives. And Jesus said to them, 'You will all be scandalized this night . . . But after I have risen, I will go before you into Galilee' " (Mark 14:26–28).

We may develop the analogy one step further. Just as the first Passover had been a dress rehearsal of the actual Exodus from Egypt on the morrow, so is Jesus' Eucharistic institution a prophetic symbol

[7] Wright and Fuller, *The Book the of Acts of God*, p. 279. For the order of ceremonies, see J. M. Osterreicher, *The Israel of God* (Englewood Cliffs, N. J.: Prentice Hall, 1963), Chap. 5.

of the separation of His body and blood on the cross a few hours later. And as the Exodus was the beginning of the Mosaic Covenant, the Eucharist inaugurates the new and eternal Covenant. To continue the quotation above from *The Book of the Acts of God:*

> The words 'body' and 'blood,' mentioned separately, indicate that it is his *death* which Jesus has specially in view. This death is to be accomplished for the 'many,' a phrase which recalls what is said of the servant's suffering in Isaiah 53:11–12 . . . The benefits which are to be conferred on all men by Jesus' death are defined as a 'covenant.' Now the inauguration of the New Covenant was an accepted feature of the coming reign of God since Jeremiah (31:31).[8]

Christ's declaration about next drinking wine with the apostles "in the kingdom of God" ("not . . . until the kingdom of God comes," Luke 22:18) refers to the post-Resurrection era, as already explained. Though they profess to be ready to die with Him, the apostles have not grasped the significance of His role as the suffering servant, as events proved.

St. Mark's Passion Narrative: The Servant Fulfills His Mission (Mark 14:31—16:20)

Gethsemani represents one of those disconcerting scenes in the life of Jesus in which the Gospel reader feels the full impact of His humanity: "My soul is sad, even unto death . . . Abba, Father . . . Remove this cup from me; yet, not what I will, but what thou willest." It is as true man that He fulfills the humiliating role of the servant. Peter is not spared by his faithful interpreter on this occasion (14:37). His triple denial has already been announced by the Master. The details of the Passion need not be labored over except insofar as they contain lessons. Here is St. Mark's schema.

1. THE ARREST. Only by help such as Judas gave them could the priests and Scribes have managed to apprehend Jesus without a tumult, by night. The betrayal goes off smoothly, the arrest is accomplished through a kiss, "that the Scriptures may be fulfilled" (14:50). As previously noted, verse 51 may be a first-hand account. All of the apostles flee; Peter alone (according to Mark) follows at a distance.

2. THE JEWISH TRIAL. St. Mark gathers all events of the Jewish trial into one narrative, in the "courtyard of the high priest" during the night. However, this does in no way exclude the possibility of an unofficial night trial (illegal under Rabbinic Law) before Annas,

---

[8] Wright and Fuller, *Op. cit.*, p. 277.

followed by the official trial before the actual high priest, Caiphas —the latter possibility alluded to in Mark 15:1.[9] Disagreement in the evidence presented, coupled with the silence of the prisoner, forces the high priest to try to make Christ incriminate Himself by asking Him point blank if He is the Messia, "the Son of the Blessed One" (thus avoiding the proper name of God). Jesus' Danielic declaration gives the judge what he is seeking; the trial is ended. Jesus is declared "liable to death," since the Jews could not pass a death sentence.[10] Verses 64–65 describe what was probably unofficial torturing of the prisoner. St. Mark, as all of the Evangelists, outlines the three denials of Peter, though the details vary. Mark concludes simply, "And he wept"; his repentance was immediate.

3. THE ROMAN TRIAL. In the succinct Markan account, the reader is left to surmise the shift in the charge against Jesus from blasphemy to the political arena. To Pilate's question, "Art thou the king of the Jews?" Jesus replies only to the extent of affirming that this is his (Pilate's) statement; otherwise He is silent. The procurator's efforts in Mark to save Him from the mob are feeble, consisting in the attempt to release Jesus instead of Barabbas, and demanding at one point in the proceedings, "Why, what evil has he done?" His only consolation after delivering Him up to be scourged and crucified is the inscription containing the official charge, "King of the Jews." St. Mark briefly describes the crowning with thorns and purple robe.

4. THE WAY OF THE CROSS. We learn only from Mark's Gospel that Simon of Cyrene, the "passer-by," was the father of Rufus and Alexander (cf. Rom. 16:13; the identification is not certain). The crucifixion itself is told with only the barest details: Jesus' refusal of the spiked drink to ease the pain; the division of His garments by lot; the challenge from the "chief priests and Scribes" (a favorite phrase of Mark) to come down from the cross "that we may see and believe" (15:32). Yet the Second Evangelist does have space to fill out the picture of the suffering servant from Isaia 53:12, "And he was reckoned among the wicked." Curiously, St. Mark has Jesus crucified at the third hour, but darkness fell over the earth only during the sixth to ninth hour—apparently incorporating two traditions into his text. The only explicit speech of Jesus from the cross recorded by Mark is the opening words of Psalm 21, "My God, my God, why hast thou forsaken me?"—another servant manifesto. The Jews still have Elias on their minds (v. 36).

---

[9] John 18 differentiates the hearing before Annas from that before Caiphas.

[10] But cf. the fate of St. Stephen in Acts 7:54ff. This will be considered later.

5. SERVANT AND SON: THE RESURRECTION. The loud cry of Jesus in verse 37 furnishes the final clue in St. Mark's account of His death to convince the centurion of the Evangelist's principal theme: this condemned man truly deserves the Gospel title of "Son of God." The last portion of Chapter 15 reveals the part played in the burial by a sincere believer, Joseph of Arimathea, who was "looking for the kingdom of God," and the pious women. The apocalyptic phenomena (the rending of the Temple veil in St. Mark, to which St. Matthew adds the resurrection of many dead persons) inform us that the Kingdom of God has come and the New Covenant is now realized. And though it was unexpected by the followers of Christ, His Resurrection is by no means an anticlimax in Mark's scheme, but the next eschatological step. It is generally agreed today that Mark 16:9–20 is an addition of the later Church; however, it is not therefore to be rejected as uninspired: since the passage is found in the Vulgate, it is a product of the Church under the "editorship" of Matthew, Mark, Luke, and John. Mark omits the baptismal formula found in Matthew and adds a detail of his own in verses 17–18, linking up the post-Pentecostal Church's activities with the ministry of Christ. The Ascension is the final vindication of Jesus as the true Son of God, in Whom are recapitulated the Servant and the Son of Man.[11]

Psalm 117: Blessed Is He Who Comes In The Name of The Lord . . . The Rejected Stone

On the three greatest feasts of the year, Passover, Pentecost, and Tabernacles, the Jews were accustomed to sing the "Great Hallel" consisting of Psalms 112 to 117. These six poems are a mixture of praise (hymn) and thanksgiving. The finale, Psalm 117, is predominantly an expression of national thanks for the restoration from Babylon and, it seems, in particular for the successful rebuilding of the walls of Jerusalem. Designed as a processional hymn to be chanted by alternate choirs, this psalm was perhaps first liturgically rendered at the feast of the dedication of the new walls (cf. II Esd. 12:27ff). This is the Holy Week hymn par excellence (with the exception of Ps. 21), quoted by the crowd on Palm Sunday (v. 26) and by Christ two days later (v. 22). The following brief analysis will help to indicate its profound significance.[12]

---

[11] This is the reasoned opinion of the eminent French form critic, Oscar Cullmann, and is largely based on the fact that Christ alone uses this title of Himself; the apostles never call Him by this name. See *Time Magazine* for April 14, 1961, p. 69.

[12] See C. J. Callan, O. P., *The New Psalter* (New York: J. P. Wagner, 1949), pp. 414–419.

Vv. 1–4: *An invitation to thanksgiving.* The "House of Israel" is the laity; the "house of Aaron" is the priests (clergy); "those who fear the Lord" are the proselytes (cf. Ps. 113:17–19).

5–18: *The motive for offering thanks.* The Lord has rescued the Jews from their enemies (Sanaballat, Tobias, the Arabians, Ammonites, and Azotians in II Esd. 4:7). It is better to trust in Him than in "princes," e.g., King Artaxerxes of Persia, who had commissioned Nehemia to rebuild the walls.

19–29: *The expression of thanks.* Realizing that the Lord has purified them by their recent ordeal which seemed to be destroying them (v. 18), the people carry on a colloquy (vv. 19, 21–23, 28–29) with the priests within the Temple enclosure (vv. 20, 24–27) as the former approach and enter its precincts. Verse 22 was written in reference to the rejection of the Jews by pagan empire builders; Christ shows that He is the antitype, rejected now by His own people. In later years as the people sang this psalm during Tabernacles, especially when verse 26 was being chanted, they would wave the leafy branches which they carried.

Suggested Readings

Bright, J., *The Kingdom of God*, Chap. 7.
Davis, *Theology for Today*, Chap. 19.
Dyson and Jones, *The Kingdom of Promise*, pp. 160–168.
Manson, *The Servant Messiah*, Chap. 5, 6.
Sloyan, *The Gospel of St. Mark* (New Testament Reading Guide Series, No. 2), p. 84–122.
Vawter, *I–II Thessalonians* (New Testament Reading Guide Series, No. 6), pp. 33–62.

For Further Study

1. Is there any additional indication that Christ united the roles of Servant and Son of Man in His person? Or perhaps there is evidence to discount this theme in St. Mark?
2. What significance is to be attached to the tearing of the veil of the Temple? Are we to take this in the proper literal sense?
3. What details in the passion account may be linked up with the role of Christ as victor over Satan, undoing the sin of the first Adam in Paradise?
4. Why did Judas make the decision to betray Christ? (His suicide is told in Matt. 27:3–10).
5. Is there any passage in the Markan passion account in which the author may well be revealing his identity?

Chapter V

St. Luke's Gospel (I): The Infancy Stories and Christian Universalism

READINGS: *Luke 1–9:50; Matthew 1–2; Magnificat, Benedictus, Nunc Dimittis. (Note: Luke 1:32–35, 44–45, 48; 3:38; 4:6, 21–23; 7:28–30, 47–50; 9:31; Matthew 1:22–25.)*

There is Luke, an Antiochene Syrian [a native of Antioch in Syria], a physician by profession, a disciple of the Apostles; but afterwards he was a companion of Paul until Paul's martyrdom. After serving the Lord unswervingly he fell asleep at eighty four years of age without wife or children in Boeotia [or 'Thebes the capital of Boeotia'] full of the Holy Spirit. Gospels had already been written by Matthew in Judea and by Mark in Rome, and Luke, inspired by the Holy Ghost, wrote this whole Gospel in the neighborhood of Achaea. In the preface he tells us that other [Gospels] had been written previously, and that it was necessary to provide the Gentile converts with an accurate account of the economy of salvation so that they should neither be distracted by the fables of the Jews nor miss the truth being deceived by heretical and vain imaginings . . .[1]

This ancient anti-Marcionite prologue to the Gospel of St. Luke summarizes nearly all that we know about the Third Evangelist from tradition, which had become fixed by about 150 A.D. Though addressed to an unknown Greek gentleman of some standing named Theophilus, this Gospel may well have been intended for a predominantly Gentile Christian community such as Achaea (Greece). This fact explains in part: *1)* the de-emphasis of strictly Jewish customs; and *2)* the universalist scope of St. Luke's work, stressing as it does the kindness of Jesus to all classes of men: "For the Son of Man came to seek and to save what was lost" (19:10). Charming and almost polished in style, it is the most literary of the Synoptics, less intended for liturgical use than to edify Christian readers. Yet it retains much of the original Semitic flavor found in Matthew and Mark, since its author deliberately strove to imitate the style of the Septuagint (Greek

---

[1] A. W. Wikenhauser, *New Testament Introduction* (New York: Herder and Herder, 1958), p. 205. It is possible that St. Luke came from Asia Minor where St. Paul met him, rather than from Antioch.

Old Testament).[2] St. Luke's Gospel has been aptly called the Gospel of Prayer (cf. 3:21, 6:12, 9:18), the Gospel of Women (8:3) and the Gospel of Pardons (7:47, 19:9, 23:43). In a word, St. Luke is the magnificent humanist.

St. Luke's Relationship to St. Paul's Ministry

Scripture itself bears witness to the long-standing tradition of St. Luke's association with St. Paul. Writing from Rome, the latter declares: "Luke, our most dear physician, and Demas send you greetings" (Col. 4:14); and from prison there, he tells us that "Luke only is with me" (II Tim. 4:10). It has even been conjectured—though without much evidence (cf. Feast of St. Luke, October 18)—that "the brother whose services to the gospel are praised in all the churches" (II Cor. 8:18) is a reference to St. Luke and his Gospel. Probably baptized by St. Paul, Luke accompanied him on his second missionary journey—as we learn from the sudden transition to "we" in Acts 16:10. This and other such "we" passages, as well as the style of the Acts, clearly indicate that the same person is the author of both the Third Gospel and its sequel, the Acts of the Apostles. About seventy-five words have been noted in the New Testament which are found exclusively in writings of Paul and Luke. Moreover, the latter is doctrinally close to St. Paul, particularly in his universal concept of salvation.[3]

St. Luke's Dependence on St. Mark

From Mark, St. Luke has borrowed not only the outline of the ministry, but about sixty percent of the former's 661 verses, making up approximately one-third of Luke's 1148 verses (the longest of the four Gospels). Notable instances of this borrowing are Luke 4:31–6:16; 8:4–9:50; 18:15–21:38. However, St. Luke is not a plagiarist, for he adapts and uses his materials, strategically omitting what is foreign to his purpose (e.g., the "liturgical" but anti-Pharisaical "greater omission," Mark 6:45–8:26). At the same time he includes from his proper sources much material not found in Mark, notably Luke 6:20–8:3 and 9:51–18:14—this latter section bearing the title of "the great insertion." Of the non-Markan verses in Luke, St. Matthew has some 325 verses; these are probably taken from an early Greek translation of Matthew Aramaic and from one or more collections of "Logia." St. Luke's pro-

---

[2] Cf. *La Sainte Bible . . . de Jerusalem* (Paris: Editions du Cerf, 1961), p. 1289.

[3] Note, for example, how St. Luke adds on Isaia 40:5, "and all mankind shall see the salvation of God" to the citation of the prophet by Matthew and Mark (cf. Luke 3:6).

fessional interest is betrayed in a number of passages, such as the guarded statement in 8:43 (cf. Mark 5:26). As we have already noted, it seems best to date the third Gospel just before the fall of Jerusalem in 70 A.D., although a later date is possible.

The Infancy Stories: Luke and Matthew Compared
(Luke 1-2, Matthew 1-2)

We might also call this the Gospel of Proclamations. St. Luke begins with the angel Gabriel's announcement to Zachary of the forthcoming birth of a boy to his superannuated wife, Elizabeth. Luke 1:13 reveals that these two descendants of Aaron had at one time prayed for an heir. However, they had long since given up hope, as Zachary's sinful doubt in verse 18 indicates. His punishment consisted in being struck dumb (and deaf also, according to 1:62) until John's birth. The sacred author next takes us to Nazareth, six months later. This time Gabriel is accorded a better reception. Though "troubled" at the "Angelic Salutation," Mary is reassured by the heavenly messenger, who declares that she is to become the mother of the Messia carefully identified by his Davidic royalty in 1:32. In 1:34 Mary is not demanding a sign as Zachary had done; rather, St. Luke is informing us by this question that Mary is a virgin. There is no evidence here that Mary had taken a vow of virginity, although many theologians suggest that she had at least the intention of remaining a virgin. Gabriel explains the divine plan: the Holy Spirit (frequently mentioned in St. Luke) will intervene to supply for the lack of human fatherhood (1:35).[4] Mary receives a sign for which she didn't ask and acquiesces in the proclamation: "Behold the handmaid (servant) of the Lord." We have been introduced to the Anawim. St. Luke *may* have heard this account from Our Lady herself.

Turning now to St. Matthew's Gospel, we find a very different approach to the mystery of the Incarnation. Whereas Luke was preoccupied with the hidden, divine origin of the Savior, Matthew concerns himself with the human, legal parentage of Christ. Out of respect for the mysterious pregnancy of his betrothed, the "just man" is willing to step aside and end their solemn engagement. But "an angel" manifests what his procedure is to be by means of a "dream": he is to provide legal parentage for the boy by giving Him his Davidic ancestry, i.e., by naming Him. The angel identifies the child as the Emmanuel of Isaia 7:14, stressing the name's etymology, "God with us." St. Joseph's obedience matches that of Mary; after she had

---

[4] Note "Trinitarian" reference: "Holy Spirit," "Most High," "Son of God": a later insight, as the mystery of the Trinity was not grasped until after Pentecost.

"brought forth her firstborn [and last] son . . . he called his name Jesus" (1:25).[5]

Theophanies begin immediately in both Gospels. Matthew 2 recounts the story of the Magi, an incident designed to manifest the future opposition which Jesus will face. The Gentile Magi (Arabian astronomers—or perhaps astrologers?) by humble trust gain access to the Messia Whom Herod's worldly wisdom overlooks in spite of the Scriptural heritage of the Jews. His "machinations only lead to the further realization of God's will, which triumphs despite human perversity and despite human power."[6] St. Matthew clearly portrays the star as miraculous; there is no point in trying to explain it as, for example, a triple conjunction of the planets Mars, Jupiter, and Saturn. The Evangelist further sees the return from Egypt by the infant Christ as an antitype of Osee 11:1.[7] On the basis of a normal birth rate, it is doubtful that more than twenty-five or thirty male babies perished at the hands of the infamous Herod—a small fraction of the blood-shed traceable to his neurotic temperament. The citation of Jeremia 31:15 in this connection is more an accommodation than a genuine spiritual sense. St. Joseph had apparently intended to take up residence in Bethlehem, the city of David his ancestor, but feared Herod's heir in Judea, Archelaus.

The association of the birth of Jesus with the death of King Herod by St. Matthew occasioned one of the most colossal blunders of history. About 527 A.D. (according to our present calendar), a Scythian monk named Denis the Little decided to transpose the dating of events from the beginning of the reign of a monarch (the custom still in vogue in his day) to an absolute standard based on the birthday of the Savior. His several errors, illustrated in the chart "Roman Era," resulted in a miscalculation of from five to seven years—so that we are actually living in the year c. 1970 instead of 1964 A.D. However, it is much easier to designate Christ's birth today as c. 6 B.C. in place of changing every other important date of history by a corresponding number of years. Denis erred in 1) *identifying the year of Herod's* death as the year of Christ's birth; and 2) in correlating said year

---

[5] The word *till* in Hebrew implies no subsequent reversal of procedure. "Firstborn" was a Jewish legal term designating the family heir and thus verifiable of an only son.

[6] David M. Stanley, S. J., *The Gospel of St. Matthew* (New Testament Reading Guide Series, No. 4 [Collegeville, Minn.: Liturgical Press, 1960], p. 13. Note that the "chief priests and Scribes" were able to come up with one right answer, Michea 5:1, 3.

[7] This isolated event must be considered as the use of a part for the whole: Jesus' whole life, death, and resurrection constitute the new and definitive Exodus. Cf. Philip King, "Matthew and the Epiphany," *Worship*, XXXVI (Jan. 1962), 89–95.

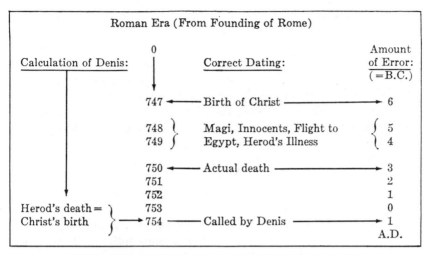

Roman Era (From Founding of Rome)		
Calculation of Denis:	0 ⟶ Correct Dating:	Amount of Error: (=B.C.)
	747 ⟵ Birth of Christ ⟶	6
	748 ⎱ Magi, Innocents, Flight to	⎱ 5
	749 ⎰ Egypt, Herod's Illness	⎰ 4
	750 ⟵ Actual death ⟶	3
	751	2
	752	1
Herod's death = ⎱	753	0
Christ's birth ⎰ ⟶	754 ── Called by Denis ⟶	1 A.D.

WHY OUR CALENDAR IS ABOUT 6 YEARS OFF

with the year 754 from the traditional date of the founding of Rome instead of 750 B.C. as it actually was; and *3)* dating Christ's birth as 1 A.D. instead of 0 A.D. Turning back now to St. Luke's account, we shall consider the first events of Jesus' earthly life schematically (Luke 1:39ff.).

1. THE VISITATION AND THE MAGNIFICAT. The leaping of the infant John in the womb of Elizabeth at Mary's greeting has suggested to theologians the cleansing of his soul of original sin (not an immaculate *conception* however; just an immaculate *birth*). Elizabeth completes the first half of the "Hail Mary" and assigns the reason for Mary's blessedness: faith. For her part, Mary uses a skeletal formula (cf. I Kings 2) to express her sentiments. Verse 48 is her unique proclamation, illustrating that her profound humility was matched by her magnanimity.

2. JOHN'S BIRTH unlooses his father's tongue; his first utterance on being cured of his dumbness is the canticle known as the "Benedictus." Verses 71 and 74 seem to smack of the popular, false messianic view; however, verses 75, 77–78 reassure us that Zachary, like Mary in her Magnificat, truly pertains to the Anawim. As in the case of the Magnificat, this hymn probably reproduces a popular song based on the Old Testament.

3. THE NATIVITY. The census information of Luke 2:1–2 has not been much help in accurately dating Christ's birth, as there was more than one census. At any rate, this event insured the birth of the Messia in Bethlehem in fulfillment of Michea 5:1. Mary's ability

to wrap her new-born son in swaddling clothes has occasioned many Fathers of the Church to conclude that hers was a painless childbirth—a conclusion in modern times challenged by more than one theologian.[8] Fr. Gerald Vann, O.P.,[9] sees the Child's appearance in the darkness of the stable (perhaps a cave) as a symbol of His "self-emptying"—a detail in harmony with the Markan Servant theme. At the same time, the Nativity represents God's descent to man, who cannot regain Paradise by his own unaided efforts (which were alleged as sufficient in the Greek mystery religions). The shepherds represent the homage of the Anawim, accompanied by an angelic theophany. "But Mary kept in mind all of these things, pondering them in her heart"—and perhaps revealing them to St. Luke in her old age.

4. THE CIRCUMCISION. Part of the Covenant which God made with Abraham, this rite constituted initiation into Judaism. It was performed at home by the father of the family on the eighth day (never anticipated), and was and is the occasion of the naming of the boy. By imposing the name Jesus, St. Joseph assumes legal parentage of the Child and designates Him the New Josue ("Savior").

5. PURIFICATION AND PRESENTATION. Leviticus 12 specifies that a woman contracts a legal impurity in giving birth to a child. Continuing for forty days after the birth of a boy, this uncleanness could be removed only by a sin offering (two turtledoves or pigeons in the case of poor people). If the child happened to be the couples' first boy, he had to be bought back from the Lord by an offering of five shekels (about two weeks' pay). These two rites are distinct and neither had to be performed in the Temple, though this was frequently the case: the mother would be purified at the entrance, then present the boy to the priest inside. In the case of Jesus, the prophecy of Simeon carries the motifs of universalism and future conflict. Verses 29–32 make up the canticle "Nunc Dimittis." Its dire sequel (vv. 34–35) will be fulfilled ultimately on Calvary.

6. THE FINDING IN THE TEMPLE. Just as Jesus' true greatness consists in His obedience to His heavenly Father first, so the true greatness of Mary and Joseph consists in the conformity of their wills with the plans of God, not in their physical relationship to Him. This axiom will be spelled out in Luke 8:19–21. The two obediences owed by Jesus (verses 49 and 51) insinuate His dual nature of God and man. Note Confraternity Version footnote on verse 52.

---

[8] A. Mitterer, for example. Cf. Kevin McNamara, ed., *Mother of the Redeemer* (New York: Sheed and Ward, 1960), pp. 124ff.

[9] Gerald Vann, O. P., *The Paradise Tree* (New York: Sheed and Ward, 1959) pp. 24, 27ff.

The Genealogies: Son of Adam vs. Son of Abraham
(Luke 3:23–38; Matthew 1:1–17)

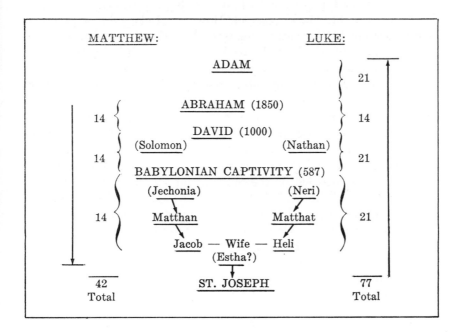

MATTHEW:		LUKE:
	ADAM	21
14	ABRAHAM (1850)	14
	DAVID (1000)	
14	(Solomon) — (Nathan)	21
	BABYLONIAN CAPTIVITY (587)	
	(Jechonia) — (Neri)	
14	Matthan — Matthat	21
	Jacob — Wife — Heli (Estha?)	
42 Total	ST. JOSEPH	77 Total

Skipping to the latter part of Luke 3 we come upon a literary genre familiar from the Old Testament: that art-form known as the geneaology. Nor are we to suppose that because it appears in the New Testament this genre is any more scientific. A comparative analysis of the genealogies in Luke and Matthew will quickly manifest the artificial nature of this form and at the same time expose the purpose of each. Note that Luke, who is writing for Greek converts to Christianity, portrays Jesus as son of Adam; Matthew, on the other hand, shows Him as son of Abraham from the Jewish standpoint. Both genealogies stress His Davidic ancestry. Regardless of the number of years covered, each section of the genealogies contains either 14 or 21 names (multiples of 7). Matthew prefers 14 because it is the numerical equivalent of the Hebrew consonants in the word *David* (D = 4, V = 6). It is difficult to reconcile the discrepancies between the two genealogies—especially the fact that Luke gives Heli as the father of St. Joseph, whereas Matthew gives Jacob. Perhaps they were cousins, each having been married to the same woman under the Levirate Law. Or Matthew may be giving us simply the official royal line traditionally linked with the Messia (see I Par. 3–4).

Baptism and Temptations of Jesus

At the beginning of Chapter 3, St. Luke orientates us somewhat both chronogically and politically.[10] John the Baptist is identified much the same as in St. Mark's Gospel. However, Luke adds a precis of John's message to the various classes of penitents, emphasizing the social nature of his teaching. John's baptism is not the Christian sacrament; from time immemorial such a rite had been used to signify moral cleansing. Hence, any effect resulting from it depended upon the sentiments of the recipient. Jesus' baptism by the Precursor (as He was "in prayer," v. 21) corresponds more to confirmation: it was His messianic anointing, preparing Him for public life. Further insights will emerge in our treatment of the Fourth Gospel account of this event. The formal assault against Satan's kingdom ensues immediately as Jesus "was led by the Spirit about the desert for forty days . . . being tempted the while by the devil" (4:1–2). Tested in the very areas in which the Jews had manifested their weakness in the desert during the forty years' wandering, Christ refuses to let Satan lead Him into appearing as the popular Messia: an economist, a political sovereign, a magician. All three biblical quotations used in His refutation are from the Book of Deuteronomy. Luke 4:6 is not an idle boast, but rather the wages of original sin.

The Galilean Ministry

St. Luke shows Jesus beginning His ministry in His home town of Nazareth. Because of the notable change of sentiment within verse 22 of Chapter 4, this narrative must represent two different visits (some exegetes say three). His rejection there results in the transferral of His headquarters to Capharnaum on the Sea of Galilee. At this point St. Luke begins to follow St. Mark very closely, so no special commentary is necessary. Luke inserts his brief report of the Sermon on the Mount (here the Sermon on the Plain) after the choice of the twelve apostles. The four beatitudes of Luke will be expanded to eight in Matthew. St. Luke lays down the golden rule in 6:31 and concentrates his remarks on the virtue of charity. In line with his Gentile interests, he reproduces a miracle not found in Mark, viz., the healing of the centurion's servant. The lesson is clear: faith in Christ is the essential condition, whether a man be Jew or Greek or Roman. The tender account of the cure of the son of the widow of Nain is reported exclusively by St. Luke. Luke does not stress secrecy as does Mark. Jesus answers the messenger from John the Baptist regarding His Messiaship with the passage from Isaia 35:5. Then he

---

[10] Luke 3:1—"Now in the fifteenth year of the reign of Tiberius Caesar" is about 27–29 A.D. Jesus would be 33–35 years old.

declares John the greatest prophet of the Old Testament (to which he pertains), yet less than "the least in the kingdom of God" (7:28). Here it is not individuals that are being compared, but institutions: the "kingdom of God" (New Testament) is superior to John (Old Testament). Note the title "Son of man" in verse 34. Jesus did not observe the (man-made) traditional fasts of the Pharisees on Monday and Thursday. In the account of the woman who anointed Christ's feet with her perfume, one notes the contrast in attitude between Jesus and Simon with regard to the woman's sins: this is the "Gospel of Pardons."

The Turning-Point
(Luke 9:51)

In Chapter 8 St. Luke again takes up the thread of Mark's Gospel, but with only one multiplication of loaves. After Peter's profession and the first prediction of the Passion, Jesus insists that His follower must "take up his cross daily" (9:23). The Transfiguration story has an interesting addition characteristic of Luke's special theme: we learn that Jesus was discussing His death, "which he was about to fulfill in Jerusalem." The Greek word used for death is *exodon*. At verse 51 we reach the turning point according to St. Luke: the beginning of His last trip to Jerusalem, the "New Exodus."

Suggested Readings

Hartdegen, *A Chronological Harmony of the Gospels*, pp. 3–6; 17–19.
Monro, *Enjoying the New Testament*, pp. 84–97.
Stuhlmueller, *The Gospel of St. Luke* (New Testament Reading Guide Series, No. 3), pp. 3–53.
Vann, *The Paradise Tree*, Chap. 2.
Wikenhauser, *New Testament Introduction*, pp. 200–221.

For Further Study

1. Can you recognize any Pauline doctrines in St. Luke's Gospel?
2. As a Gentile by birth, St. Luke might have been expected to be unfamiliar with the Old Testament. Was this actually the case?
3. What long treatise has been omitted by St. Luke because it would be unappealing to Gentile readers?
4. To what extent is *midrash* found in the infancy stories? (Cf. p. 88).
5. How was the date of Christmas (December 25) arrived at? (Cf. p. 212).
6. What three manifestations of Christ are commemorated in the liturgical feast of the Epiphany?

Chapter VI

St. Luke's Gospel (II): The Exodus of the New Adam

READINGS: *Luke 9:51–24; Psalm 30. (Note: Luke 9:51; 11:20, 27:28; 12:40–41, 50; 18:34; 22:18–20; 24:25–27.)*

Whatever his background, St. Luke had captured the central theme of the Old Testament. Realizing the significance of the Exodus in Jewish national and religious existence, and writing for a Gentile audience, he portrays Christ as accomplishing the new and definitive Exodus through this final journey to Jerusalem which will result in His passion and death, followed by the Resurrection. To get to the capital from Galilee, a Jew had either to leave Palestine (passing through Perea or going by boat on the Mediterranean) or else traverse Samaria. On this occasion the Samaritans manifest their habitual hostility; the Fourth Gospel, however, will present us with a different picture (John 4). This episode, together with the veiled reference in Luke 9:62 to III Kings 19:19–21 (q. v.), underscores the need of a familiarity with the Old Testament in order to appreciate the Gospels. In this whole "great insertion" the Evangelist "overlooks or erases historical or geographical details" in order to pursue his peculiar theme. Like St. Mark, Luke unloads much more material on his thin outline than the framework will bear; hence, we must avoid any attempt to pinpoint either chronologically or geographically every episode recounted.[1] Again it will be helpful to select a few key themes to guide our study. The parables in this section (9:51–18:14) which are peculiar to Luke will be treated separately.

The Following of Christ
(Luke 10 and Passim)

Although similar words are recorded in Mark 6:8–13, there is no reason why our Lord could not have applied this instruction to His disciples (the seventy-two—or seventy—"others") as well. Poverty is again laid down as a pre-requisite to the apostolate. Detachment has already been demanded in 9:57–62 even to the extent of leaving

---

[1] Cf. C. Stuhlmueller, *The Gospel of St. Luke* (New Testament Reading Guide Series [Collegeville, Minn.: Liturgical Press, 1960]), p. 56.

parents and letting "the dead bury the dead"—i.e., leaving the ordinary tasks of life to those who are not actively engaged in the apostolic way of life. (See also 14:26–35.)

The Conquest of Satan

Upon their return, these disciples joyfully report their success in working exorcisms; Jesus links this activity to His battle with Satan, but warns them not to become puffed up over this charism (10:20). This same connection of the coming of the kingdom with the conquest of the devil is clearly manifest to those conversant with the Old Testament in a later episode: "But if I cast out devils by the *finger of God,* then the kingdom of God has come upon you" (11:20). Here is a reference to Exodus 8:15. This episode ends with a solemn admonition that mere exorcism is not enough; positive cooperation with grace is likewise required. Disease is explicitly linked with diabolical dominion in 13:16.

The Wisdom Theme in St. Luke
(Luke 10:21–24, etc.)

Further evidence of the relationship between St. Luke and St. Paul appears in the prayer of Jesus recorded at this point. The worldly-wise (such as the Scribes and Pharisees) are unable to relish the message of Jesus. To their carnal prudence is contrasted the simple prudence of His loyal followers selected from the Anawim. Penetration of the good news is not the result of scribal exegesis but rather of a divine interior manifestation to those of good will. We may note here another recurrence by the Evangelist to a Wisdom concept in 13:1–5 and 13:22 ff. Like the author of the Book of Job, Christ rejects the old Deuteronomic principle which would measure virtue by temporal prosperity. Instead, Jesus praises not only asceticism but also voluntary poverty as royal avenues to God.

The Book of Sirach had formally identified true wisdom with the observance of the Law; Jesus now declares those blessed "who hear the word of God and keep it" (11:27). This quality sets souls into a closer relationship to Him than does consanguinity! Reading between the lines, we get a glimpse here of Mary's true greatness: not primarily in bearing Him, but in her perfect conformity to the will of God. Jesus on this occasion insinuates that His wisdom (i.e., teaching) is greater than even that of Solomon, and offers His unbelieving generation the sign of Jona—a sign which can be perceived only by the "lamp of the body," the sound eye of faith. Here we have a statement of Christ probably in its original context, but which St. Matthew inserts in his Sermon on the Mount (Matt. 6:22–23).

One of the commonest forms of wisdom teaching was the parable. Jesus used it extensively, and St. Luke has left us in this section a number of parables not found in the other Synoptics. The "parables of the kingdom" will be treated in conjunction with Matthew 13; the following table summarizes the message of the other principal parables as understood by the later Christian community (cf. our Chap. XIV, page 110, where we reproduce the form critics' attempt to get back to the "authentic" words of Jesus).

PARABLE	MESSAGE
1. The Good Samaritan (10:25–37).	A Christian evaluation of the concept of neighbor.
2. The Midnight Borrower (11:5–8). The Godless Judge (18:1–8).	} Persevere in prayer!
3. The Avaricious Farmer (12:13–21).	Attachment to wealth can be harmful to one's relationship with God.
4. The Unproducing Fig Tree (13:6–9). The Great Supper (14:15–24).	} The rejection of the "righteous" (Jews) in favor of "sinners" (Gentiles).
5. Building a Tower and Making War (14:28–35).	Before entering the service of Christ, one must be prepared to pay the full price.
6. The Lost Sheep and the Lost Coin (15:4–10).	Sinners are not dearer than saints, but nevertheless they are surprisingly precious to God.
7. The Prodigal Son (15:11–32).	We should not be envious because of God's great mercy to the apparently undeserving.
8. The Unjust Steward (16:1–13).	Worldly-minded people are often more shrewd about money than the followers of Christ about the kingdom of God (which is incompatible with avarice).
9. The Rich Man and Lazarus (16:19–31).	Not only that the lots of the poor-in-spirit will be reversed in the next life, but that those who pay no heed to ordinary graces will not be moved by miracles.
10. The Pharisee and Publican (18:9–14).	God welcomes the poor discouraged but repentant sinner before the proud self-confident individual.
11. The Parable of the Gold Pieces (19:11–27).	God reprobates those who place their security in a meticulous but mechanical observance of the law.

The Gospel of Prayer
(Luke 10:38 ff.)

More than any other Evangelist, St. Luke gives us a glimpse of the prayer-life of Christ (e.g., 11:1). This Third Gospel likewise contains a number of lessons on the value of prayer, beginning with the

Martha–Mary incident. Mary, the contemplative, is preferred to Martha, the active one. In entertaining her divine Guest, Mary shows that God must always come first, even in the heat of apostolic activity (cf. Mark 14:7). At some time or other Our Lord must have taught the apostles the Lord's Prayer. St. Luke places it at the beginning of Chapter 11 in a series of prayer-lessons; we shall consider it in detail with St. Matthew's Gospel. The climax of the lesson: God will be at least as generous as any human parent to his children. Indeed, the incomparable gift of the "Good Spirit" is bestowed only by Him (11:13). Our heavenly Father is not to be identified with the unwilling neighbor in the parable!

Blasphemous Opposition of the Pharisees
(Luke 11:14 ff.)

In attributing His miracles to Beelzebub ("Lord of Insects"), the Pharisees launched the vicious gossip campaign against Jesus which was to result eventually in His death. His presence among them has had the effect of an exorcism (as noted on page 51),[2] but they are leaving their house empty for the return of Satan by their failure to heed His teachings. A little later in the text (11:37), the dinner party at the home of one of the Pharisees provides Christ with an occasion to denounce their ugliness. The Pharisees are guilty of the formalism in worship condemned by the great prophets (Amos, Osee, Isaia, etc.) in attempting to define salvation in terms of mere human endeavor (keeping the Mosaic Law). And the Scribes' guilt consists in doctoring up the Law with excessive burdens for the people. Christ renews the evaluation of Ezechiel: the human race (and particularly the Jews) have been recalcitrant from the very beginning (Abel, Book of Genesis; Zacharia, II Paralipomenon, last in order of the books of the Hebrew Bible). The unproducing fig tree in 13:6–9 is a figure of the Jewish nation: a more humane judgment than the cursed fig tree of Mark 11:12–14! And so the Pharisees and lawyers began "setting traps for him and plotting to seize upon something out of his mouth, that they might accuse him" (11:54).

Although Christ's denunciation of the Pharisees is milder in St. Luke than in St. Matthew, it is persistent. More than once He excoriates their own inconsistency regarding Sabbath observance (13:15; 14:5). The parable of the Pharisee and the Publican is directed against their conceited prayer life (18:9ff.). Their treachery in attempting to lure Him from Galilee into Jerusalem (under the pretext that Herod, Tetrarch of Galilee, "wants to kill thee"—13:31) in

---

[2] Cf. J. Leclercq, O.S.B., "The Finger of God," *Worship*, XXXVI:7 (June–July 1962), 426–437.

order that they themselves may seize Him leads Jesus to a preliminary prediction of Jerusalem's impending fate. The parables of the Great Supper and Prodigal Son are clearly meant for them; their avarice is the target of the parable of the Rich Man and Lazarus, introduced by the scathing rebuke of 16:15.

The Coming of the Kingdom: Realized Eschatology

One of the most baffling and misunderstood concepts in the New Testament centers around the meaning of the term, "coming of the Kingdom of God" (17:20). We have already alluded to the tragic error of the eschatological school of New Testament interpretation at the beginning of Chapter II. It should be noted here that whereas the borrowed Greek term "parousia" (arrival, return: used in ancient times to describe the formal visit of a sovereign) designates Christ's second coming at the end of the world, the term "eschatological" (from *eschatos*: remote, latest) refers not only to the second coming and general judgment, but also to the *times preceding these events*. Indeed, the eschatological period began with the Resurrection of Jesus and the promulgation of Christianity on Pentecost Sunday. We may, in fact, see its preparation in the preaching of John the Baptist, according to the pronouncement of Christ in Luke 16:16.[3] To develop this theme, four texts must be examined:

1. LUKE 12. In this whole chapter Christ is clearly referring to His "coming" to each individual at the hour of death (e.g., vv. 5, 20). The Kingdom of God comes with Jesus, and He is handing it over to His "little flock" to spread throughout the land (vv. 32ff.). He warns not only the apostles but everyone to be on their guard (vv. 41ff.); the inauguration of the kingdom will involve great difficulties and trials (vv. 49ff.), and will exact His own death ("baptism" in v. 50) and cause divisions within families.

2. LUKE 17:20–36. Being questioned by the Pharisees as to the time of the Kingdom's coming, Jesus replies, "The kingdom of God is within you" (17:21). In this context, the best interpretation of the phrase seems to be this: The Kingdom of God does not consist essentially in external religious observances (as practiced by the Pharisees), but in an internal good disposition.[4]

3. LUKE 21. We have already examined the parallel eschatological discourse in St. Mark's Gospel. The same apocalyptic imagery (vv. 25–26) is borrowed from Daniel and Isaia to portend the destruction of Jerusalem; it refers to the end of the world *typologically*.

---

[3] A sign of the inauguration of the Kingdom is Christ's abolition of divorce with hope of remarriage, immediately following in verse 18. A new order is beginning!

[4] Cf. Richard Sneed, "The Kingdom of God is within You (Luke 17:21)," *The Catholic Biblical Quarterly*, XXIV:4 (Oct., 1962), 363–382.

Verses 20, 24 suggest an eye-witness account (hence the alternative dating of this Gospel after 70 A.D. but this conclusion is by no means demanded by the context). The future rehabilitation of the Jews is suggested in verse 24b. The word "redemption" found in verse 28 is proper to St. Paul, and is used only in this one place in the Gospels[5] Verses 34–36 strongly suggest I Thessalonians 5:18–24 —more evidence of the connection between St. Luke and St. Paul.

4. LUKE 22. There are three different references to the Kingdom in this chapter, two of them in conjunction with the Eucharist. Putting together verses 17–18, Jesus seems to be saying that the Passover will be fulfilled in the Kingdom's (i.e., Church's) messianic banquet (the Eucharist).[6] The third reference is similar to these two: in verses 29–30 (after alluding to His role as the Servant, verse 27), Jesus promises that their endurance of trials for His sake will earn them a share in His messianic banquet—again the Church, not heaven.

St. Luke's Passion Account
(Luke 22–24)

It will suffice here simply to note the more important texts proper to Luke's account of the Passion, since we have already covered the basic outline of the Passion in St. Mark.

Luke 22

V. 19: Rather than "blessed" as in Matthew and Mark, Luke has Jesus say "gave thanks"; this is likewise St. Paul's term in I Corinthians 11:24, in conjunction with which we shall analyze the Eucharistic institution.

31–32: St. Peter's denial is attributed to Satan's intervention; his primacy is presupposed in verse 32. Only Luke mentions Jesus as looking at Peter (verse 61).

35–38: These verses balance off 10:4; they will have some material needs as the Church develops.

43–44: Only St. Luke (some texts) mentions the comforting angel in the garden, whereas only Matthew and Mark had mentioned an angel after the three temptations (but cf. Luke 4:13). We would expect the physician to be the one to report that the sweat "became as drops of blood," not precisely that He sweated blood.

---

[5] This term probably refers to the future emancipation of the Christian Church from Jewish opposition with the destruction of the Temple.

[6] Cf. Stanley, *The Gospel of St. Matthew*, p. 83; and F. X. Durrwell, *The Resurrection: A Biblical Study* (New York: Sheed and Ward, 1960) Chap. 5, especially pp. 152–153. This whole question will be reopened in conjunction with the Acts of the Apostles and St. Matthew's Gospel.

48–49, 51, 53: *Luke portrays Christ as being in perfect command of the situation:* He rebukes Judas' kiss (verse 48); He asks the soldiers to "bear with" the impetuous disciples as they start to use their swords, and heals the ear of the servant (verses 49, 51); He indicts their cowardice in seizing Him in the dark (verse 53). Note Christ taking the initiative in verses 67–68.

Luke 23

Vv. 8–12: The appearance of Jesus before Herod fits in logically with 9:7–9; the prisoner refuses to satisfy the tetrarch's morbid curiosity.

25: St. Luke contrasts Christ and Barabbas to show the enormity of the injustice being done—just as he has already listed three declarations of Jesus' innocence by Pilate (verses 4, 15–16, 22), who nevertheless offers to "chastise" (scourge) Him to appease the mob.

27–31: Report of the "daughters of Jerusalem" lamenting over Jesus, including a contrast between the innocent ("the green wood"—Himself) and the guilty ("the dry [wood]").

34, 40–43: The first word from the cross, forgiveness of His enemies, and the forgiveness of the repentant thief: hence Luke's is the Gospel of Pardons. "Paradise" is the term Jesus uses for His other-worldly kingdom.

46: The quotation from Psalm 30; see below.

48: Luke's report of the centurion's eulogy calls Christ a "just man" rather than "Son of God" in Matthew and Mark. Luke also notes a general consternation on the part of the bystanders in "beating their breasts," and absolves Joseph of Arimathea from all guilt in the trial (verse 51).

Luke 24

Vv. 5, 7–11: St. Luke speaks of "two men" in "dazzling raiment"; St. Matthew says it was an angel, and that he rolled back the stone amidst an earthquake and terrified the guards; St. Mark describes "a young man . . . clothed in white." Luke also links up the Resurrection with Christ' promise and has "them" remember His words. The names of the women do not agree in the Synoptics. Luke has the Eleven treat their story as nonsense.

13–32: Only St. Luke reports this episode in full; Mark makes only a brief reference to it (Mark 16:12). The location of Emmaus is uncertain, as also the identity of the two disciples, whose hopes had apparently been momentarily aroused by the women's report and then dashed by Christ's failure to appear to the menfolk. It is disputed whether or not the breaking of bread which caused their recognition was the Eucharist. Their fault lay in neglecting to penetrate the messianic prophecies!

34, 42: An apparent parallel to John 20:19–23, this passage notes the Lord's appearance to Simon (verse 34) and his *eating before the Eleven* on Easter evening to convince them of the reality of His Resurrection (v. 42).

50, 53: Luke places the Ascension near Bethany, and leaves the little band worshipping in the Temple. Faithful to his theme to the very end, the Evangelist underscores the religious symbolism of the city of Jerusalem. He has carefully omitted the appearances of Jesus in Galilee. The apostle's final instructions are to preach "repentance and the remission of sins . . . in his name to *all the nations, beginning from Jerusalem.*" They, the official "witnesses" of these events, are to "wait here *in the city,* until you are clothed with power from on high" (verses 47–49). These verses form an important bridge between the third Gospel and Luke's other work, the Acts of the Apostles (cf. Acts 1:4–5). The Exodus to Jerusalem has ended in victory. The Resurrection inaugurates the kingdom, but it also presupposes Jesus' death.[7]

Psalm 30: The Ideal Prayer in Times of Depression

This complex poem contains elements of petition, thanksgiving, and confidence; it is best classed as a Psalm of Lament. Verses 8–19 are reminiscent of Jeremia; older commentators considered the psalm as David's prayer for deliverance from Saul in the wilderness of Maon (cf. I Kings 23:24–26). The use of verse 6 by Christ from the cross would seem to justify its classification as a messianic psalm in the typical sense; the psalmist is the ideal sufferer as he exclaims: "Into your hands I commend my spirit. . . . you will redeem me. . . ."

---

[7] Durrwell, *Op. Cit.,* pp. 6–10, gives a concise summary from the Catholic viewpoint.

Suggested Readings

Orchard, *A Catholic Commentary on Holy Scripture,* cols. 768–775.

Stuhlmueller, *The Gospel of St. Luke* (New Testament Reading Guide, No. 3), pp. 54–93.

Wright and Fuller, *The Book of the Acts of God,* pp. 287–299: A Protestant statement of the significance of the Resurrection, linking up St. Luke's Gospel with the Acts.

For Further Study

1. What references can you find to the fact that Jesus "is going up to Jerusalem" after 9:51?
2. What passages can you find which suggest that St. Luke is a master of the ascetical and mystical life?
3. What lessons are contained in St. Luke's parables?
4. Does St. Luke consider the "coming of the Kingdom" as proximate or remote?
5. What value does St. Luke attach to the Resurrection?
6. How much time actually elapsed between the Resurrection and the Ascension? (Compare Luke 24 with Acts 1:3.)

Chapter VII

Acts (II) and Corinthians: The Conversion of Saul and the Baptism of Wisdom

READINGS: *Acts 6–9; I Corinthians 1–10:13; II Corinthians 3, 10–12; Galatians 1; "Hymn" to Wisdom, I Corinthians 1:17–2:16. (Note: Acts 7:47–50; I Corinthians 7:3, 5, 9, 15; 10:1–11.)*

Returning to the Acts of the Apostles, we are confronted with the story of the rapid spread of Christianity under the manifest operation of the Holy Spirit. The first five chapters (previously assigned) portray the apostolic activity of the post-Pentecostal community. The coming of the Spirit completed the Passion-Resurrection-Ascension cycle by effecting among them an *awareness of the presence of the messianic era:* the kingdom of God has at last come on this earth. It is not, then, to be identified with the *second* coming of Christ, but rather with His *first* coming. The miracles wrought by the apostles, especially Peter, the ecstatic tongues, and the ability to speak foreign languages, all furnish living testimony to the arrival of the "Day of the Lord" foreseen by the prophets.[1] The Petrine manifesto in 2:36 shows that the Holy Spirit eventually effected the additional *awareness of the divinity of Chris*t hitherto realized only imperfectly (if at all), and contains a reference to the Gentiles which was equally veiled.

> Therefore, let all the house of Israel know most assuredly that *God has made both Lord and Christ,* this Jesus who you crucified . . . For to you is the promise and to your children and to *all who are far off,* even to all whom the Lord our God calls to himself. (2:36, 39)

Persecution and the Martyrdom of St. Stephen: First Break with Jewry

(Acts 6–8)

In Chapters 6 and 7 of Acts we find the Church meeting what seemed to be its first setback: the martyrdom of St. Stephen, followed by the outbreak of a vicious persecution of the Christian community.

---

[1] St. Peter quotes apocalyptic imagery from Joel 3. Note Acts 5:12–16.

The laying on of hands in 6:6 to create an order of almoners emphasizes that unity of worship was carried into the material order through the common possession of property.[2] All seven of the new ministers are "Hellenists," i.e., Greek-speaking Jews born outside of Palestine and using a Greek translation of the Scriptures. A number of this group had already embraced Christianity. Their activities included preaching and healing as well as taking care of destitute widows. It was St. Stephen's inspired preaching and adeptness at disputation that got him into trouble with the local leaders.

In his speech before the Sanhedrin, St. Stephen betrays a penetrating insight into the distinctive character of Christianity. It is the first attempt to supply a theology of history for the new religion, and it rivals the work of the Chronicler in breadth of vision. It is actually a history of the *rejections* by the Jews of their divinely commissioned agents of salvation: first Joseph, then Moses (twice rejected—first as a prince of Egypt, "mighty in his words and in his deeds," then as official lawgiver), and finally of Christ, the New Moses. Throughout the speech he stresses the universalism of true Judaism, particularly in his de-emphasis of the Temple. In this connection, the wisdom of Solomon is reprobated by negation: St. Stephen does not even mention this quality of the Temple-builder; in fact, he "implies that the less said of Solomon, the better."[3] The New Wisdom proclaimed by St. Stephen is destined to find one of its most fervent propagators in his most avid persecutor, Saul of Tarsis. In the meantime, the persecution gives impetus to the spread of the Church into Samaria under the direction of the budding hierarchy (8:14–17; see *Liturgical Interlude* on p. 76).

The Conversion of Saul: Life and Works
(Acts 9; II Corinthians, 10–12; Galatians 1)

The story of the conversion of the great apostle St. Paul is too well known to belabor. It was his distinction to pass abruptly from persecutor of the Church to ardent apologist—and to merit the appella-

---

[2] As the forerunner of the diaconate in the later Church, this order emphasizes the role of Church ministers as one of service to the faithful, not simply that of administration. Cf. Matthew 23:2–12 and the article, "Restoring the Diaconate" in *Herder Correspondence*, I:1 (Jan. 1964), pp. 13–18.

[3] Neal M. Flanagan, *The Acts of the Apostles* (New Testament Reading Guide, No. 5 [Collegeville, Minn.: Liturgical Press, 1960] p. 30. Note Acts 7:22, 47–50. This is reminiscent of Jeremia's de-emphasis of the Ark of the Covenant in Jeremia 3:16 and of the Temple in 7:4. Some exegetes think the Hellenists were an anti-temple sect; see D. J. Selby, *Toward the Understanding of St. Paul* (Englewood Cliffs, N. J.: Prentice–Hall, 1962), p. 158, ft. 39.

tion "apostle."[4] The poignant words of the "voice" asking him, "Saul, Saul, why does thou persecute ME?" (Acts 9:4), must have left an indelible orientation on Saul, who afterwards became the outstanding propagator of Christianity as a vicarious existence. Piecing together the biographical clues of this intrepid apostle from New Testament writings can be rewarding, *even though many of the dates are uncertain.*[5] It is interesting to compare the conversion of St. Paul with Daniel 10. The chart on the next page summarizes what information we can glean about his life.

I Corinthians and the Baptism of Wisdom
(I Corinthians 1:17–2:16)

Pagan wisdom literature underwent a drastic reorientation at the hands of Jewish scribes before finding its way into the Old Testament. Purged of their naturalistic and purely utilitarian tendencies, the axioms of the sages were adapted to fit the Deuteronomic principle of submission to the will of Yahweh, particularly as embodied in the Torah. Progressively refined by the authors of the Books of Job, Proverbs, Ecclesiastes, Sirach and Wisdom, this genre had come to embrace even the concept of the redemptive value of personal and national suffering. Yet, this accretion lacked depth; in the hour of its big decision, Israel failed to identify the suffering Servant of Yahweh with the triumphant Son of Man. The truth broke through only after Pentecost, for Jewish messianism was incomplete and fragmentary. The New Testament fulfillment of necessity *included a sublime transformation of traditional molds in the very process of their fulfillment.*[6] This facet is illustrated in the deacon Philip's inspired interpretation of Isaia 53 in Acts 8: without hesitation he supplies the link missing from rabbinic exegesis.

Thus the final transformation, the "baptism" of wisdom, fell to the lot of the early Christian apologists, foremost among whom is St. Paul. Having established the Church at the prosperous Greek city of

---

[4] At least three different usages of the term "apostle" can be observed in the New Testament: *a)* simply for "messenger," as in II Corinthians 8:23; *b)* as specially commissioned Church officers, as in I Corinthians 12:28 and Romans 16:7; *c)* in the restricted sense as one of the original Twelve chosen by Jesus. It is in this last meaning that Acts usually employs the word (cf. Selby, *Ibid.,* pp. 168–169).

[5] Cf. Kathryn Sullivan, *St. Paul's Epistles to the Philippians, Ephesians, Colossians, Philemon* (New Testament Reading Guide No. 9 [Collegeville, Minn.: Liturgical Press, 1960.])

[6] Cf. John L. McKenzie, S. J., "Messianism and the College Teacher of Sacred Doctrine," *Proceedings of the Sixth Annual Meeting of the Society of Catholic College Teachers of Sacred Doctrine,* 1960, pp. 34–53.

LIFE AND WRITINGS OF ST. PAUL IN THE CONTEXT OF OTHER NEW TESTAMENT EVENTS

Timeline axis: 0 · 20 · 40 · 50 · 60 · 70 · 80 · 90 · 100

EMPEROR	PALESTINIAN KINGS, PROCURATORS	DATE	EVENTS	SOURCE	WRITINGS
30—AUGUSTUS	HEROD THE GREAT, 37–4 B.C.	6 B.C.	BIRTH OF JESUS		
—A.D.—	ARCHELAUS (Judea and Samaria); HEROD ANTIPAS (Galilee and Perea); PHILIP (Iturea, Tra-chonitis, &)	5 A.D.	BIRTH OF SAUL		
14—TIBERIUS	Coponius, Ambibulus, A. Rufus, V. Gratus, Pontius Pilate, 26–36	20	Paul at Rabbinic school in Jerusalem	Gal. 1:14	
		27	Preaching of Baptist / PASSION OF CHRIST		
37—CALIGULA		34? / 35?	Death of Stephen / Conversion of Saul / —To Arabia 3 years / —Back to Damascus / —15 days in Jerusalem / Paul retires to Tarsus	Acts 7 / Acts 9 / Gal. 1:17 / Acts 9: 23–30 / II Cor. 11:32–12:9	
	These two territories to Agrippa	39–43	—his visions		
41—CLAUDIUS	Herod of Chalcis; AGRIPPA I, 41–44	42	James Greater killed	Acts 12:2	
		43–44	Paul preaches: Antioch	Acts 13	
		45–49	1st MISSIONARY TRIP (Cyprus, Asia Minor)	Acts 13–14	
	Agrippa II of Chalcis	49	COUNCIL OF JERUSALEM	Acts 15:6	
(51–52 Gallio in Greece)		50–53	2nd MISSIONARY TRIP (Thess., Athens, Corinth)	Acts 15:36f.	I–II Thess.
	Antoninus Felix 52–60	53–57	3rd MISSIONARY TRIP (Ephesus, Corinth)	Acts 18:23—21:26	Galatians, Philip., I Cor.
		55	—Imprisoned at Ephes.?		
		57?	—Winter in Corinth	Acts 20:2	Rom., II Cor.
	Porcius Festus, 60–62	58–60	Paul imprisoned at Caesarea: his appeal	Acts 21–26	James? Philem., Col., Eph.
	Albinus, 62–64	61–63	Prisoner at Rome	Acts 27–28	I Pet.
	G. Florus, 64–65	62	Death of James Less		I Tim., Titus
		63	Paul free: Spain?	Rom. 15:28	II Tim.
64—FIRST PERSECUTIONS OF CHRISTIANS		64		Philem. 22 / Tit. 3:12	St. MARK
		66	"Pastoral" Epistles		LUKE, ACTS
68—GALBA, and	Jewish revolt	67	Martyrdom of Sts. Peter and Paul, Rome		
69—VESPASIAN	Christians flee to Pella	70	CHRISTIANITY AN HIERARCHICAL RELIGION CLEARLY DISENGAGED FROM THE SYNAGOGUE		Jude?
79—TITUS	DESTRUCTION OF JERUSALEM				
81—DOMITIAN	NON-BIBLICAL WORKS: Works of Josephus / DIDACHE	90?	John exiled: Patmos		MATTHEW
91–93—SECOND PERSECUTION		96?			II Peter? Hebrews? Apocalypse 1, 2, 3, John
96—NERVA	Letters of St. Clement / "Pastor of Hermas"	100	Death of St. John		St. John
98—TRAJAN	Letters of St. Ignatius	c. 107			
117—HADRIAN	Jerusalem becomes "Aelia Capitolina"	135			

Corinth in the days when Gallio was Roman pro-consul there, he wrote a letter back to his new converts from Ephesus after completing that missionary journey (his second). Aimed at halting the formation of cliques among them (cf. 1:12–13), and at warning them against certain immoral practices characteristic of the big city, I Corinthians ranks as one of Paul's four "great epistles" along with II Corinthians, Romans, and Galatians. As in the case of the latter, its doctrine stands midway in development between I–II Thessalonians and the Captivity Epistles. Just as Philip had invoked the New Wisdom in helping the Ethiopian eunuch, so Paul now turns to this same source in directing his neophytes.

After asserting the supra-natural character of true wisdom (God's plan of human salvation revealed in Christ), St. Paul gets to the heart of the matter: the Christian mystery lies in the crucifixion of Christ— the paradoxical exaltation-through-humiliation theme, "to the Jews indeed a stumbling-block and to the Gentiles foolishness, but to those who are called, both Jews and Greeks, Christ, the power and the wisdom of God" (1:23–24). The Holy Spirit is the exclusive vehicle of this wisdom, creating in its recipient "the mind of Christ" which is opposed to the mind of the "sensual man." The implications of this profound analogy will be explored in a later chapter. The pivotal truth which emerges at this level is the transcendent nature of Christianity, pointing up the indispensable role of faith. This is precisely what was lacked by "the rulers of this world . . . for had they known it, they would never have crucified the Lord of glory" (2:8). We have already alluded to this theme in the previous chapter in connection with Luke 10:21–24. In adjudging those who have built badly on this foundation (Christ), St. Paul concludes that though their work will burn, they themselves "will be saved, yet so as through fire." Although this is not a direct reference to purgatory, some of the Fathers of the Church saw here a basis for that doctrine.

Marriage Re-Visited by the New Wisdom: The Dignity of Virginity
(I Corinthians 5–7)

In redressing sins of the flesh, St. Paul invokes the new concept of matrimony characteristic of the messianic age. After urging excommunication in the case of an egregious offender (cf. 5:5, 9—implying a lost epistle!), the saint accentuates the positive by declaring that among Christians there are as many temples as there are bodies of the faithful: "your members are the temple of the Holy Spirit, who is in you . . . you are not your own" (6:19). This thought leads Paul to clarify further the nature of the sacramental contract of marriage by means of two distinctions: *1)* Far from being unwholesome, marriage

63

is a genuine "gift from God" for those called to that state which not only permits but even demands the use of sex under pain of injustice upon the request of either partner (7:3–7). For some individuals, marriage is actually expedient as a safeguard against "burning," i.e., concupiscence (verse 9). *2)* Yet, within the Christian framework, sex and marriage itself occupy ancillary roles. In proof of this, St. Paul lays down the famous "Pauline Privilege" (7:15) whereby a convert to Christianity may put aside an "unbelieving" (unbaptized) spouse and remarry a Christian, provided that the unbelieving spouse refuses to live peacefully with the baptized party and "departs" (deserts the home). The messianic reorientation of matrimony is further illustrated by Paul's almost revolutionary adjudication of virginity, which was generally shunned by ancient peoples—including the Jews.[7] Having reiterated Christ's reprobation of divorce in 7:10–11, he brings the Osean marriage symbolism to its fulfillment in II Corinthians 11:2 by extending it to the union between Christ and His Church.

Shadow Versus Reality: Type Yielding to Antitype
(I Corinthians 10:1–11; II Corinthians 3)

A final theme demands our attention: typology, of which St. Paul is the master. Taking the Exodus and desert-period as his primary analogue, he shows us more "realized eschatology."[8] But the saint rises above a purely allegorical approach to the subject; he synthesizes the signification brilliantly by letting the Exodus as a whole stand for Christian baptism, and the nourishment furnished in the desert (manna, water) proclaim the Eucharist; for "all these things happened to them (the Israelites) as a type, and they were written for our correction, upon whom the final age of the world has come" (10:11). In II Corinthians 3:7ff., the apostle hints at the mysterious incompleteness of Hebrew revelation whose transcendent fulfillment its recipients missed. However, this lack of comprehension ("veil") was not entirely inculpable: "Yes, down to this very day, when Moses is read, the veil covers their hearts; but when they turn in repentance to God, the veil will be taken away" (verses 15–16).[9]

In this same Second Epistle to the Corinthians we are given a precious insight into the character of the saint, who apparently was

---

[7] Cf. I Corinthians 7:25ff., and note warning against mixed marriages in 7:39 and II Corinthians 6:14–18. Notable exceptions to the shunning of virginity were the celibate Essenes among the Jews and the Vestal Virgins among the pagan Romans.

[8] See table of types and antitypes in *God's Kingdom in the Old Testament,* Chap. XVIII.

[9] These passages constitute the Epistles for the ninth and twelfth Sundays after Pentecost.

of small stature (cf. 10:10). He sounds almost as though he had an inferiority complex (10:12, 11:1, 5). Suffering has been his royal road to sanctity climaxing in infused contemplation. His visions recounted in 12:2ff. constitute a distinct font of revelation, forming part of his authentic apostolic witness. His message to the Corinthians—and to the Church at large—will be continued in the next chapter.

Suggested Readings

Bouyer, *The Meaning of Sacred Scripture,* Chap. 17.

Bullough, *St. Paul and Apostolic Writings,* especially pp. 43, 50–51.

Flanagan, *The Acts of the Apostles* (New Testament Reading Guide, No. 5), pp. 25–39.

L. H. Grollenberg, O.P., *Shorter Atlas of the Bible* (London: Thomas Nelson and Sons, 1956) p. 152. Compare this chronology of the Pauline Epistles with that of Protestant scholars, e.g., Key and Young, *Understanding the New Testament,* pp. 474–475; also, Wright and Fuller, *Book of the Acts of God,* pp. 321–323.

Lucien Legrand, *The Biblical Doctrine of Virginity* (New York: Sheed and Ward, 1963).

Monro, *Enjoying the New Testament,* pp. 53–57; 196–197. Chronology of New Testament books.

Claude Peifer, O.S.B., *First Corinthians, Second Corinthians* (Collegeville, Minn.: New Testament Reading Guide Series, No. 8 1960), *passim.*

Stanley, "From Kingdom to Church," *Theological Studies* XVI (1955), 1–29.

Vawter, *Introduction to the Pauline Epistles,* pp. 3–32. Read in conjunction with the author's *I–II Thessalonians* (New Testament Reading Guide, No. 6).

For Further Study

1. Was there any precedent for St. Stephen's statement about the Temple (Acts 7:48)?
2. What implications do you see in Acts 9:4?
3. Give an example of how a knowledge of the literary history of the New Testament aids exegesis.
4. In what ways is Jesus the "New Israel"?
5. How does virginity fit in with messianism?

St. Paul and Corinthians (II): The Eucharist, Christ's "Mystical" Body, the Resurrection

READINGS: *I Corinthians 10:14—16:24; II Corinthians 4–6; Romans 12–15; "Hymn" to Charity, I Corinthians 13. (Note: Acts 2:42–47; 4:32–37; I Corinthians 10:15–17; 11:17–34; 12:12–13; 15 [all]).*

And they continued steadfastly in the teaching of the apostles and in the communion of the breaking of the bread and in the prayers. (Acts 2:42)

This scene borrowed from the Acts of the Apostles brings into focus the bonds which united the early Christian Church: *1) common instruction* received from the apostles (assuring unity of faith); *2) the breaking of bread,* i.e., the Eucharist;[1] and *3) prayer*—apparently the gift of tongues (to be discussed later). It is the second of these bonds which will be treated first, viz., the breaking of bread.

Eucharist and Agape
(I Corinthians 10–11)

Among Semites eating was and still is a solemn act rich in symbolism. To invite another man to eat with him is the Oriental way of expressing fellowship. Even today an Arabian sheik would not think of asking an enemy to dine at his table. St. Paul makes use of this fact to show the intimate union which the Eucharist effects not only with Christ but with one's fellow Christians who eat at the same sacrificial table. The terms "sharing" of blood and "partaking" of the body are translations of the same Greek word, *koinonia* (fellowship). This is the cue for introducing his famous analogy between the Christ-union and the members of the human body (verse 17); the saint will return to this concept in Chapter 12. By way of corollary, a stern warning against eating food offered to idols follows: this passage seems to reflect the decision of the Council of Jerusalem which we shall treat in the next chapter. Note the freedom of conscience advocated by St. Paul. Like the Mosaic Law, however, Christianity transforms every

---

[1] Fr. Raymond Orlett gives evidence for this identification of the breaking of bread with the Eucharist in *The Bible Today,* I:2 (November 1962), "The Breaking of Bread in Acts," pp. 109–113.

area of life into worship: "Therefore, whether you eat or drink, or do anything else, do all for the glory of God" (verse 31).

Chapter 11 begins an apparent digression on female attire. Drawing on the theology of woman as the helpmate of man expressed in Genesis, St. Paul emphatically insists that it is proper for a woman to appear in church only with her head covered, "as a sign of authority over her head (and) because of the angels" (verse 10). Later, in Chapter 14, he debars women from any preaching activity in divine worship.

After this brief bit of liturgical protocol, the apostle returns to the Eucharist in laying down regulations for the Agape or Love-feast customary at the time. This was a communal supper late in the evening which served as a kind of vigil and preparation for Mass, which would follow in the early hours of the day (cf. Acts 20:7). Instead of promoting a spirit of fellowship and unity among the participants, St. Paul notes that the Agape rather introduces factions. Well-to-do Christians were expected to provide for their poorer brethren; instead, the former ate and drank to excess in small cliques while the latter went hungry. His suggestion in verses 21 and 34 was heeded by later Church authorities; by the end of the fourth century the Agape had disappeared.

From his stock of personal revelations the apostle reproduces an authentic account of the institution of the Eucharist by Christ at the Last Supper. A footnote on 11:20–22 in the Confraternity Version summarizes his teaching in this passage. What is noteworthy is the addition of the words ". . . do this in remembrance of me" in both verses 24 and 25.[2] There is a similar phrase in verse 26 identifying the Eucharist with Calvary. St. Paul's statement about eating and drinking judgment to oneself (verse 29) is strong evidence that he was not speaking metaphorically, but is bearing witness to the doctrine of the Real Presence. With those who were abusing the Agape in mind, he even assigns sickness and death as penalties for such crimes (cf. footnote on verse 30 in the Confraternity Version).

The Endowments of the "Body of Christ": Charismatic Gifts
(I Corinthians 12, 14; Romans 12–15)

In beginning a treatise on the "spiritual gifts" prevalent in the early Church St. Paul is not changing the subject; he is following a carefully worked-out plan. Portraying these gifts as manifestations of the Spirit, he enumerates nine charisms (gratuitous powers) given for the

---

[2] This same phrase occurs, understandably, in Luke 22:19. These words have (or already had) found their way into the consecration of the Mass. Their implications with regard to the institution of Holy Orders will be considered later.

building-up of the Church rather than for the good of the possessors. They are graces only in a loose sense, and can be given even to sinners (though ordinarily they are not). In Chapter 14 the saint offers a detailed explanation and evaluation of some of them. The following table offers a brief description of the charisms and "hierarchical functions" mentioned in 12:28. There is no strict correspondence between the two lists.

CHARISMATIC GIFTS	HIERARCHICAL FUNCTIONS
1. WISDOM: Speculative insights into the mysteries of faith with which to aid others.	
2. KNOWLEDGE: Practical judgments with regard to more fundamental matters of faith.	1. APOSTLES: Church leaders, especially missionaries.
	2. PROPHETS: inspired preachers.
3. FAITH: Great confidence in God inspiring one to accomplish difficult feats.	3. TEACHERS: catechists? (Note priority given to apostolate).
4. HEALING: A corporate work of mercy.	4. MIRACLE-WORKERS.
5. MIRACLES: Signs of the messianic age.	5. HEALERS.
6. PROPHECY: Inspired, intelligible utterances.	6. ALMONERS (deacons?).
	7. ADMINISTRATORS.
7. DISTINGUISHING OF SPIRITS: Ability to evaluate charisms in others.	8. POSSESSORS OF ECSTATIC TONGUES.
8. GIFT OF TONGUES: Power to make ecstatic (but unintelligible) utterances.	
9. INTERPRETATION OF TONGUES: Power to explain the meaning of tongues (No. 8).	

At this point the apostle reveals his hand; he conceives of the Christian Church at Corinth after the manner of an organism, viz., the human body. Just as its various parts—however different their functions—are held together by the same skeleton and vivified by the same life-principle, so it is with the Christians of Corinth.[3] The Holy Spirit is their common "soul" uniting each member to Christ and, through Him, to each other. Initiation into this union is accomplished through baptism:

> For as the body is one and has many members, and all the members of the body, many as they are, form one body, so also is it with Christ. FOR IN ONE SPIRIT WE WERE ALL BAPTIZED INTO ONE BODY, whether Jews or Gentiles, whether slave or free .... (12:12–13).[4]

[3] Saint Paul will broaden this concept by extending it to the universal Church in Collossians and Ephesians. Here it is applied only at the local level.

[4] The passage is one of the most well-known of Pauline texts.

Most scholars distinguish two phases of development in this Pauline metaphor. The first stage is that outlined in Corinthians and Romans, with the full-blown concept appearing later in Ephesians and Colossians. Here in I Corinthians and also in Romans 12, we find the body-concept used to stress: *a)* the notion of unity-within-diversity divinely appointed for the attainment of the Church's goal (hence those who possess charismatic gifts must use them for the good of the whole "body"); *b)* the source of life is the same in all: the Holy Spirit, the body's "soul"; *c)* Christ is the central support of the whole, for each member—regardless of race or condition—enjoys unity and equality with other members to the degree in which he is united to Christ.

Without dismissing the term "body" as a *mere* metaphor, we should note that St. Paul sees the unity it denotes as an effect of the Eucharist.[5] We shall return to this metaphor in treating his Epistles to the Ephesians and Colossians, where the saint adds the notes of Christ's headship, the Church as His *pleroma* or fullness, and the note of universality. Even now is it not evident that the apostle is indicating the fulfillment of that intimacy with Yahweh presaged by Osee, foreshadowed in Canticles, and predicted in Jeremia 31:33–34? Is not the Mystical Body the transcendent realization of the *hesed* of such tender poems as Psalm 102? This same development of the charisms and hierarchical functions is found in Romans 12. In both I Corinthians 13 and Romans 13:8–10 we find the same corollary of this doctrine in the importance assigned to the virtue of *charity:* St. Paul equates this virtue to the ensemble of all other virtues, for which charity must supply the motivation.[6] We pass now from charisms to *personal* virtue.

St. Paul's Hymn to Charity
(I Corinthians 13)

Any attempt at paraphrasing the great apostle's "more excellent way" of charity ("Agape" is the Greek term used) is bound to sound flat. Here is the royal charter of intimacy with Christ and the unique source of unity among His members. "Agape" is the essence of holiness (which is godliness), the shortcut to sanctity. Its way is open to Jew, Gentile, and slave. Like the Servant of Yahweh, it "bears with all things, believes all things, hopes all things, endures all things"; it is truly the "mind of Christ," the atmosphere of Christianity—even when given such a disarming title as sanctifying grace.

---

[5] Originally the terms "mystery" and "mystical" denoted a sacrament, particularly the Eucharist. The phrase "Mystical Body" is not Saint Paul's, but a later development to differentiate Christ's physical and Eucharistic presence from His presence in the body of the faithful.

[6] The medieval Scholastics will call charity the "form" of all the other virtues.

Christ's Resurrection, the Cause of Christian Life
(I Corinthians 15)

Returning to his revelations, St. Paul strikes another key theme: the Resurrection of Christ. Citing an otherwise unreported incident in which the risen Savior appeared to more than five hundred people (v. 6), the apostle undertakes to refute those Greeks who found the doctrine of the resurrection of the body hard to accept—perhaps because of the Platonic one-sided emphasis on the superiority of the soul over the body:

> For if the dead do not rise, neither has Christ risen; and if Christ has not risen, vain is your faith, for you are still in your sins. Hence they also who have fallen asleep in Christ have perished. If with this life only in view we have had hope in Christ, we are of all men the most to be pitied. (Vv. 16–17)

In making this declaration, St. Paul is not content to let the Resurrection serve merely as an apologetical tool; he is affirming the dependence of the whole Christian way of life on this great mystery. His line of argument is the solidarity of the human race via the two Adams: the First (earthy) Adam brought death on his progeny by sin; the Second (heavenly) Adam, Who is Christ and Who enjoys a similar corporateness with our race, has by His Resurrection from the dead restored life to His "members" (cf. vv. 22–23, 45–49). The full restoration of (glorified) bodily life will occur only at the Parousia, since it is at the end of the timetable: "And the last enemy to be destroyed will be death . . . then comes the end, when he delivers the kingdom to God the Father" (vv. 26, 24).[7] Filling in the picture sketched in I Thessalonians 4:15–17 (cf. Chap. IV), St. Paul declares that the risen body will be abruptly different from the decayed body coming out of the grave: as different as the plant is from the seed which produced it (vv. 35–44), for it will be spiritualized. Then, in verses 50–55, he clarifies the transformation which had only been suggested in Thessalonians: *all* bodies, whether of the living or the dead, will be changed from *corruptible* to *incorruptible* flesh (according to the best reading; be sure to see footnote on 15:51).

The question naturally arises at this point, "Will *all* of the effects of Christ's Resurrection be deferred until the Parousia? Does not HIS victory over death make a difference even now to those who share the life of His Body?" The saint has an answer.

---

[7] Even this deferred premium seems to have been the occasion of certain pagans' acceptance of baptism in the hope of seeing their loved ones in the general resurrection. This seems to be the best interpretation of verse 29 (Peifer, *First Corinthians* [Collegeville, Minn.: Liturgical Press, 1960], pp. 56–57.)

Christ's Resurrection and "Realized Eschatology"
in II Corinthians 4–6

Apparently St. Paul's First Epistle to the Corinthians healed the factions in that community. However, a new crisis arose when certain Jewish Christians began to attack the authority of the saint so that he had to make a quick visit there to put down the turmoil. Though it is difficult to reconstruct the situation, it seems that some "offender" on this occasion "caused grief" to St. Paul (II Cor. 2:5) and that the latter wrote another (now lost) letter, severe in tone, to correct the situation. Judging from II Corinthians 2:12–15 and 7:5–7, we may conclude that it had its intended effect. Later on he again wrote to the Corinthians from Macedonia (Philippi?) to cement his authority over them: this would be II Corinthians. A good portion of this intensely emotional letter is apologetical, pleading for harmony and having little logical arrangement.

After devoting most of the first three chapters to a defense of his ministry, St. Paul speaks of death as an active principle in human existence: ". . . always bearing about in our body the dying of Jesus, so that the life also of Jesus may be made manifest in our bodily frame. For we the living are constantly being handed over to death for Jesus' sake, that the life also of Jesus may be made manifest in our mortal frame" (4:10–11). The *death to which Paul is referring is the death of Jesus* (and he has his own sufferings for the sake of the Gospel in mind); our own bodily dissolution (the "decaying outer man" of v. 16) is, in itself, negative and inefficacious, a result of sin (cf. Rom. 7:7–25). Durrwell puts it in this way:

> . . . death in itself is simply the conclusion of life according to the flesh, the supreme affirmation of the presence of sin, the ultimate failure of man's weakness. It is not a triumphant liberation or even an escape; death does not do away with death.[8]

After reasserting the corporate nature of Christ's death and Resurrection in man's behalf (5:15), the saint emphatically affirms a positive, *present* effect of His Resurrection in each Christian: "So that henceforth we know no one according to the flesh. And even though we have known Christ according to the flesh, yet now we know him so no longer. If then any man is in Christ, he is a new creature; the former things have passed away; behold, they are made new!" (vv. 16–17) Just as the Kingdom of God has already come in Christ's Resurrection, so also has the gift of immortality begun to take hold on fallen man through the very same miracle. The final stage of God's

---

[8] Durrwell, *Op. cit.*, p. 53.

plan is now being run off; here is another case of *realized eschatology* which forms such an important element in both St. John and St. Paul.

St. Paul concludes Chapter 5 with a strong statement in saying that God made Christ "to be sin" for our sakes; it is stated more carefully in Romans 8:3. In the next chapter the apostle returns to another facet of realized eschatology: marriage in the New Order. Because of the intimate relation of the Christian with Christ, mixed marriages (i.e., with pagans) are strictly forbidden, "for you are the temple of the living God" (v. 16). For St. Paul the body-metaphor has become the cornerstone of every phase of Christian life.

Suggested Readings

Bouyer, *The Meaning of Sacred Scripture,* Chap. 18.
Bullough, *St. Paul and Apostolic Writings,* pp. 99–128 (I–II Corinthians); 149–153 (Romans).
Davis, *Theology for Today,* Chap. 15; *Liturgy and Doctrine,* Chap. 2.
Ellard, *Christian Life and Worship,* Chap. 7.
Monro, *Enjoying the New Testament,* pp. 54–57.
Peifer, *First Corinthians, Second Corinthians.*

For Further Study

1. What is the relationship between Christ's physical, sacramental, and Mystical Body?
2. To what extent has Original Justice been restored to mankind via realized eschatology?
3. Is there any evidence in these readings for *lay* apostolic activity? (Cf. I Corinthians 16:15ff.)

Chapter IX

Acts (III) and Galatians: "Christians," The Council of Jerusalem, and The Mosaic Law

READINGS: *Acts 10–23; Galatians 2–5. (Note: Acts 11:18; 13:35; 14:22; 15:1, 28–29; 20:7; 21:21; Galatians 2:16; 3:1–29.)*

Peter's Vision and the Church's Mission to the Gentiles

(Acts 10–12)

Our attention now shifts from St. Paul to the activities of St. Peter as recorded in the Acts of the Apostles. The repetitious treatment of the two visions, one to Cornelius and the other to Peter, indicates their importance in the early Church. Two themes are tied in with the vision of Peter: a reiteration of the abrogation of Jewish dietary laws (cf. Mark 7:19), and a command to begin the evangelization of the Gentiles. The extent to which their legal separatism had curtailed association of Jews with Gentiles is spelled out in 10:28. In his instruction of Cornelius, St. Peter reproduces the primitive, basic outline of the oral Gospel (vv. 37–43). In the scene which follows (known as the "Pentecost of the Gentiles"), we have an instance of God acting outside of the sacraments. After due explanation, the Jewish Christians at Jerusalem accept the divine will: "Therefore to the Gentiles also God has given repentance unto life" (11:18).[1] Note the association of the remission of sins with the sacrament of baptism, here contrasted with the baptism of the Precursor.

Apart from Philip's mission to the Samaritans (who were actually half Jewish), the spread of Christianity to Antioch in Syria represents the first large-scale approach of the Church to Gentile peoples. It is noteworthy that evangelization was the work of *all* Christians, not just of apostles (11:20); Barnabas, a native Cypriot and Levite introduced

---

[1] In view of this delayed awareness of the Gentile mission (surely Christ told them), it seems probable that recognition of Christ's *divinity* (not messiaship, which the Resurrection manifested) by the apostles was also delayed for some time after Pentecost. It would take a period of serious reflection before the "obstacles" of Jewish monotheism and the divine transcendence would permit their Old Testament mentality to assimilate the mystery of the Trinity.

in Acts 4:36, is sent to supervise their work and heartily approves it. It is these non-Jewish converts who are first known as "Christians." The presence in the Church of genuine prophets is attested to by Agabus, who foretells the great famine.[2] This detail, together with the account of the martyrdom of James the Greater at the hands of Herod (Agrippa I, grandson of Herod the Great), enables us to date these events about 40–42 A.D. The reception of St. Peter at the home of "Mary, the mother of John who was surnamed Mark," after his miraculous escape from Agrippa's clutches introduces us to the Evangelist whose Gospel we have already considered (Chap. III–IV).

St. Paul's First Missionary Journey: Cyprus and Asia Minor

(Acts 13–14)

It was the keen insight of Barnabas which recognized in Paul the makings of a Gentile proselytizer, thus rescuing him from retirement (11:25). The two of them are "set apart" by the presbyters of Antioch for missionary work.[3] Stopping off at the island of Cyprus, they preach first to the Jews in their synagogues. However, their first recorded convert is a Gentile, the proconsul Sergius Paulus. Continuing the journey, they sail to Perge on the coast of Asia Minor (now Turkey). Here Mark deserts them, thereby incurring the ill-feeling of St. Paul (cf. 15:38). At Antioch in the province of Pisidia Paul delivers a discourse similar to that of St. Peter in Acts 2; both sermons make reference to Psalm 15 in a messianic context. In Acts 13:39 he clearly states *that faith in Christ has replaced the Mosaic Law* (but does not outlaw observance of the latter). Upon meeting opposition from their Jewish brethren, Paul and Barnabas turn to the Gentiles and reap a rich harvest. At this point the opposition turns into a persecution which follows them from town to town. At Lystra the pagan populace begins by attempting to offer sacrifice to Barnabas ("Jupiter") and Paul ("Mercury"), but ends up by stoning Paul after the envious Jews from Antioch and Iconium poison their minds. Acts 14:22 informs us that it was the custom to appoint presbyters (elders) over each new church. Jerusalem, however, still is looked upon as the "mother" church, as the next episode illustrates.

---

[2] It was this crisis or a similar one which occasioned the collection mentioned by St. Paul in II Corinthians 8–9, a concrete example of Christian charity.

[3] The accompanying laying-on of hands may have been episcopal consecration (cf. Confraternity Version footnote); Paul and Barnabas are called *apostles* for the first time in 14:4 and 14:13. The Greek word translated "ministering" in 13:2 is the one from which we derive the term "liturgy." It will occur again in the Epistle to the Hebrews.

The Council of Jerusalem and Its Two Decrees: A Catholic Manifesto

(Acts 15)

Following the treatment of the topic in the Jerusalem Bible,[4] we can see in this chapter two distinct decisions of the Christian authorities at Jerusalem—very possibly handed down at different times. St. Luke has recorded them in a composite account, and we cannot be sure of the exact sequence of events. The following solution is probable:

1. St. Paul's first missionary journey not only resulted in the conversion of many Gentiles, but also posed a problem: must these Gentile converts observe the Mosaic Law? Converts from Judaism were doing so, and the Pharisees among them insisted that this obligation likewise pertained to converts from paganism (15:5). The controversy bursts into the open when the saint arrives in Jerusalem after his first missionary journey, c. 49 A.D. Turning now to Galatians 2:1–10 we find what seems to be a parallel account to Acts 15:1–12. The former shows how acute the issue had become and indicates an amicable settlement in favor of the Gentile converts. Indeed, Galatians 2:10 reflects Acts 15:10–11: these are *not* to be burdened with the obligation of observing the Mosaic ordinances—including circumcision. The decision is handed down by St. Peter, who bases it on the Cornelius incident described in Acts 10. Paul and Barnabas are pleased: no restrictions have been placed on their ministry to the Gentiles.

2. Going back to Galatians 2:11–14, we discover the background of the second question which must be decided. Those converts to Christianity brought up in the strict observance of the Mosaic Law found it very difficult to mix with Gentile Christians who violated the "Noachic" Covenant (Gen. 9:4–7) which the rabbis considered to be binding on all men: the prohibition against drinking blood and eating animals which had been strangled (because the blood would still be in them). In addition, it was especially offensive to a Jew to see someone at the same table eating food which had been sacrificed to idols, and also to see these Gentile converts have marital relations with close relatives (cf. Lev. 18:6–18 and I Cor. 5:1). We find St. Peter in the Galatians passage going even further on the occasion of a visit to Antioch and withdrawing completely from Gentile converts for fear of offending Jewish Christians. St. Paul rebukes him for his squeamishness, but Peter has a point and the

---

[4] *La Sainte Bible*, p. 1458, footnote m. Some notes of Fr. Raymond Brown, S.S., have also been very helpful.

matter comes up for discussion in Jerusalem. It may have been the same occasion as the other decision, with the "Bishop" of Jerusalem, St. James (known for his Jewish leanings) interjecting an amendment;[5] more likely, however, it was a later occasion. At any rate, this second decree promulgating the "hold-overs" from the Mosaic Covenant represents a *disciplinary* matter rather than a doctrinal issue. Its restricted local coverage manifests this: it is to be promulgated in "Antioch, Syria, and Cilicia" (v. 23). St. James mentions it to St. Paul upon the latter's return to Jerusalem after his third missionary journey and he observes it (Acts 21:25ff.), though not with very happy results. In due time these hold-overs became obsolete—as did the observance of the Mosaic Law itself by Jewish converts. The "catholic" character of the Church is gradually emerging.

St. Paul's Second Missionary Journey: Macedonia and Greece (Acts 15:36—18:22)

Refusing to let Mark go with him, St. Paul pairs off with Silas, while Barnabas takes Mark (his cousin). At Lystra Paul adds Timothy to his party; in circumcising him, Paul is simply doing what his Gentile father should have done, since Timothy's mother was a practicing Jewess (cf. II Tim. 1:5). Acts 16:6 shows the manifest intervention of the Holy Spirit in their work (cf. also 15:28). It is in response to this guidance that the little group sets out for Macedonia. It is clear from the first of the "we" passages of the book that its author, St. Luke, has also joined them (cf. the "they" in 16:40; Luke apparently stayed on).

Passing over the details of the journey, we shall note only the important doctrinal points. At Athens (dedicated to Athena) Paul tries a philosophical approach which meets with ridicule and sneers. The saint abandons this method in future sermons (cf. I Cor. 1:17ff.). Medieval Christianity has confused Dionysius the Areopagite with the French St. Denis. At Corinth Paul meets with considerable success. He is joined by two militant "lay" apostles, Aquila and Priscilla, and writes his two Epistles to the Thessalonians. Note in 18:18 that he still practices Mosaic observances. He returns home (Antioch) via Jerusalem after a three-year absence.

Liturgical Interlude: Sacraments in the Early Church

In the procedure followed by Peter and John in Acts 8:15–17 we can detect a growing awareness of the distinction between baptism and confirmation. That Christian baptism was also distinct from the

---

[5] This is the opinion expressed in Louis F. Hartman, *Encyclopedic Dictionary of the Bible* (New York: McGraw-Hill Book Co., 1963), col. 431. These four observances were required of aliens living among Jews (cf. Lev. 17).

Precursor's rite is made clear in Acts 18:25 (the case of the eloquent Apollos) and 19:2–6. For several centuries confirmation was conferred along with baptism; this practice is still observed in the Eastern Church. Scholars see possible evidence for infant baptism in the conversion of whole *families* (cf. Acts 16:15, 33; 21:5–6).[6] Note the origin of the word *simony* in 8:18–24.

The Eucharist has been treated at length in the previous chapter. In Acts 20:7 we note that the "breaking of bread" took place on the first day of the week: *Sunday has replaced Saturday as the Christian Sabbath* (although devout Jewish Christians continued to frequent the synagogue on Saturday). As for Holy Orders, we find forerunners of the sacramental rite in the inauguration of the "deacons" in Acts 6:6, the Jewish "exorcists" in 19:13, and the charismatic gifts discussed in the last chapter. The laying-on of hands occurs frequently, e.g., 8:17, 13:3. "Presbyters" are mentioned several times as part of the hierarchy (11:30, 14:22, 15:4). Finally, in 20:28–31 we see St. Paul referring to the leaders of the church of Ephesus as "bishops," whose task is to "rule the Church of God."[7] The sacraments will be treated in greater detail in conjunction with St. John's Gospel. Acts 19:12 suggests the use of relics.

Third Missionary Journey: Does the Mosaic Law Bind Jewish Christians?
(Acts 18:23—21:40)

After a short time at Antioch, St. Paul sets out on his last missionary effort, which covered much the same territory as the previous one. His two years at Ephesus produced much fruit, and was the occasion of the writing of First Corinthians, and perhaps of the imprisonment during which he wrote Philippians. The avarice of the Ephesian silversmiths forces him to move on to Macedonia, followed by visits to Troas and Miletus. A touching farewell address is delivered by the saint to the presbyters of Ephesus at the latter city, foreshadowing his arrest in Jerusalem. This foreboding is corroborated by the prophet Agabus (21:11).

That the Council of Jerusalem had not settled completely the status of the Mosaic Law in the Christian community becomes evident as soon as Paul sets foot in Jerusalem. Whether or not he is correctly quoted in 21:21, this statement is a logical conclusion of his teaching as well as of the decision of the Council. At best, the Mosaic Law was

---

[6] See the fine summary in Orchard, *A Catholic Commentary on Holy Scripture,* col. 820.

[7] It would be premature to read into presbyter (elder) the equivalent of priest, and into episkopos (from *epi-skope,* overseer), the equivalent of bishop. In this passage in Acts, presbyters are called *episkopoi* (cf. page 136 below).

now a work of supererogation; however, St. Paul had never forbidden its observance by Jewish Christians—even those living among Gentiles. His efforts to placate the "Judaizers" (Jews who were attempting to force the Mosaic Law on Christians as though necessary for salvation) by joining in the observance of a Nazirite vow according to Numbers 6 boomerangs, giving his enemies an occasion to claim (falsely) that he had committed the capital offense of "bringing Gentiles into the temple" (21:28). Only the timely arrival of the Roman tribune with his soldiers saves Paul from being beaten to death. It is obvious that further attempts to compromise with Jewish zealots is no longer feasible, and that the "Way" will soon have to make a complete break with Judaism. We find him addressing to his adversaries words calculated to allay their suspicions. But their reaction at the mere mention of the phrase "Go . . . to the Gentiles" in Acts 22:21 shows to what extent their universalist mission had receded into the background. Only Paul's declaration to the centurion that he is a Roman citizen saves him from torture. His subsequent defense before the Sanhedrin consists of an *ad hominem* argument directed to the Pharisees, whose support he wins by proclaiming his hope in the Messia and in the ressurection of the dead (23:8). As the apostle may have foreseen, another violent dispute breaks out—this time between the Pharisees and the Sadducees, "who say that there is no resurrection, and that there are no angels or spirits"—and again the soldiers have to intervene. Paul receives another divine assurance in a vision, which commands him to bear witness not only in Jerusalem but also in Rome (23:11; cf. 18:9).

Galatians and the Binding-Power of the Mosaic Law
(Galatians 2–5)

We have already appealed to Galatians for biographical material on St. Paul (Chap. VII). Now we shall employ this letter according to its main purpose: to prevent those Galatians[8] who have been converted to Christianity from Jewry from succumbing to the false doctrine of the Judaizers. We see here and in the corresponding passages in Romans the mature doctrine of St. Paul regarding the nature of the Mosaic Law, going beyond the decision reached at the Council of Jerusalem. The date, place of origin, and precise destination of Galatians are uncertain. We suggest the date as c. 54 A.D.

---

[8] Galatians were a Gallic race who migrated from the area around the Danube River to Galatia in the strict sense (now part of modern Turkey) sometime after 300 B.C. The "Judaizers" were, according to the most common opinion, *Jewish* Christians. Professor Munck has attempted to prove that they were zealous *Gentile* converts of St. Paul. (Cf. Davies, *Christian Origins and Judaism,* Chap. VIII.)

After citing his refusal to circumcise the pagan Titus before baptizing him (in line with the official decision), St. Paul rebukes Peter for not having the courage to follow out this decision in a comparable situation (2:11–14), as we have just noted. Then Paul states his position plainly: "But we know that man is not justified by the works of the Law, but by the faith of Jesus Christ" (2:16). He goes even further in 3:1–5, calling them foolish for going back to the Mosaic observances. Some of his arguments for the inefficacy of the Old Law can be summarized as follows:[9]

1. Abraham was saved by faith in the promise by God of future blessing in Genesis 12:3. Since this promise was given 430 years before the Mosaic Law, his justification could not have come from the latter, as illustrated in the following chart.

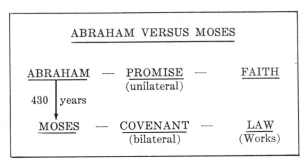

2. Christ became "a curse" under the Law in dying on a gibbet (Deut. 21:23); that is, He placed an action which put Himself outside the Law in order to rescue Christians from the Law. Their dissociation from the Law flows from the fact that in baptism they "have put on Christ" (3:27; cf. 2:16–21; 3:10–14).
3. The Law was only an "intermediary" or "tutor" between God and the Promise (Christ) possessed by faith (3:19–26). Moreover, the Old Law is to the New Law what Ismael was to Isaac (4:21–31; cf. also Rom. 4:13–17).

Paul's conclusion, duplicated in Romans 4–5, is that "You who would be justified in the Law are estranged from Christ; you have fallen away from grace" (Gal. 5:4). The final blow forcing a clean break between Christianity and Jewry will be the destruction of Jerusalem. We shall discuss the implications of the replacement of the Old Law in the next chapter. Galatians 5 returns to a specifically Christian

---

[9] This passage was treated in Chap. XV of Hopkins, *Gods Kingdom in the Old Testament;* cf. also Chap. IX of the same work. St. Thomas gives a dogmatic summary of the binding power of the Mosaic Law in the *Summa Theologica,* IaIIae, Q. 103, Art. 4.

theme: charity, whereby one rises above the flesh and walks in the Spirit. Verses 22–23 enumerate the fruits of the Spirit in opposition to the "works of the flesh" (19–21).[10]

Suggested Readings

Ahern, *The Epistles to the Galatians and to the Romans* (New Testament Reading Guide, No. 7), pp. 3–30.

Bullough, *The Church in the New Testament, passim*

————, *St. Paul and Apostolic Writings,* pp. 152–166; see p. 159 for date of Galatians.

Davis, *Theology for Today,* Chap. 3.

Flanagan, *The Acts of the Apostles* (New Testament Reading Guide, No. 5), pp. 40–84.

Hasseveldt, *The Church, A Divine Mystery,* pp. 68–83.

Monro, *Enjoying the New Testament,* pp. 48–52.

Orchard, *A Catholic Commentary on Holy Scripture,* col. 832c–841e.

For Further Study

1. What development takes place in the Christian community's consciousness of its destiny in Acts 10–21? What event is comparable to St. Stephen's martyrdom?
2. Why did St. Paul's mention of the resurrection of the dead (17:32) evoke a sneer from the Athenians?
3. What is the best text you can find for evidence of the Christ-union in Galatians?
4. When did the Mosaic Law become not only "dead" but "deadly" (i.e., sinful)?
5. What is the difference between "justification" and "sanctification?" What is the role of faith in each process? Of works?

---

[10] Three of the twelve fruits of the Holy Spirit found in the Latin Vulgate and the English Douay–Rheims Version are missing from the Confraternity translation (which here has been made to conform to the Greek text): long-suffering, mildness, and chastity. (Cf. *Summa Theologica,* IaIIae, Q. 70, Art. 2.)

Chapter X

Acts (IV) and Romans: Original Sin, Predestinaton, and the Salvation of the Jews

READINGS: *Acts 24–28; Romans 1–11; Galatians 6; James 2; Psalm 13. (Note: Acts 26:23; 28:28; Romans 1:20; 3:8–26; 6:3–11; 8:28–30; 11:23–26; James 2:22.)*

The Jewish conspiracy against Paul which necessitated his removal to Caesarea at the end of Acts 23 reveals the magnitude of the bitterness towards his efforts in behalf of the Gentiles. In his defense before the governor, Felix, he again identifies his cause with the doctrine of the resurrection of the dead. But a few days later he alarms Felix and his third wife, Drusilla, by speaking of justice and chastity; had he instead been willing to bribe the governor, he could have obtained release (cf. 24:25). Festus, the successor of Felix, proves to be a more responsible man, yet too weak in the face of Jewish pressure to release Paul. When the governor suggests that Paul be returned to Jerusalem for trial, the apostle sees through the plot of his enemies and appeals to Caesar. In order to find a way out of the situation, Festus consults King Agrippa II, who had succeeded to a portion of the kingdom of his father in 53 A.D. Agrippa is moved by Paul's defense and exposition of Christianity, especially the doctrine of the Resurrection; however, his incestuous union with his sister Bernice makes him an unlikely candidate for conversion. Although St. Paul's innocence is again admitted, he is put on board a ship for Rome to make his appeal to Caesar.

St. Paul's Exodus to Rome: The Catholicity of the Christian Church
(Acts 27–28)

The "we" of 27:2 assures us that St. Luke was an eyewitness of this trip which is described in such minute detail. These details illustrate the manifest intervention of God in Paul's behalf as he turns out to be the savior of the group. His reputation has preceded him, and everywhere the boat stops along the Italian coast he is greeted by the "brethren" (fellow Christians). Upon arriving at Rome, Paul follows his usual custom of preaching first to the Jews, as he is under house arrest with permission to receive visitors. As a group they reject Christianity, bringing upon themselves severe words from the saint, who then turns to the Gentiles. It was during this two-year imprisonment that he also wrote the "Captivity" epistles: Philemon, Colossians and Ephesians.[1] St. Luke does not describe his release; the purpose of Acts has been accomplished: the Kingdom of God has been transferred from Jerusalem (where Christ had established it at His Resurrection) to Rome, headquarters of the Empire. Rejected by Israel, the "Way" is now proclaimed to the world through the powerful vehicle of Roman civilization (cf. Rom. 15:18–21).

The Epistle to the Romans: The Theology of Salvation

Three years before he arrived in Rome (i.e., 57 or 58 A.D.), while still in Corinth, St. Paul addressed a letter to that Church before he had ever visited it. This letter is no doubt one of the reasons why the saint was so well received there. It is a well thought-out statement of the fundamental nature of human salvation reflecting his experiences with the Galatian church. Duplications have already been noted in the overlapping of Romans 4–5 with the Epistle to the Galatians, and of Romans 12–14 with I–II Corinthians. St. Paul's central theme is that *salvation is God's work, not man's;* he develops it by outlining the terms of salvation for pagans, Jews, and Christians. Note that he terms himself an apostle in verse 1. He is employing an early Christian creed in verses 2–4 (cf. Acts 2:32–33 and 13:33–34).

Pagan vs. Jew, Natural Law vs. Mosaic Law
(Romans 1–3)

This epistle is not calculated to inflate the ego of the Jews, although St. Paul is careful to avoid direct offense. From the beginning of time, he insists, the way of salvation has been open to all mankind, who can know God through His effects in nature:[2]

> For since the creation of the world his invisible attributes are clearly seen—his everlasting power also and divinity—being understood through the things that are made (1:20).

Even pagans, then, are without excuse in practicing idolatry whereby "they have changed the glory of the incorruptible God for an image made like to corruptible man" (1:23). St. Paul traces all human perversions to this cardinal sin, thus reproducing a theme of the Book of

---

[1] As we noted in the previous chapter, Philippians was probably written during an unrecorded captivity at Ephesus.

[2] The Vatican Council cited this text in defining that man can know God through reason alone (cf. John F. Clarkson, *The Church Teaches* [St. Louis, Mo.: B. Herder Book Co., 1955], No. 58).

Wisdom.[3] Pagans should not be judged according to the Law, because God will not hold them responsible for it; their norm is the natural law applied according to their consciences (2:12–16), and they have the opportunity of attaining eternal life (2:7).

Turning his attention to the Jews, St. Paul points out that the true Jew is not simply one who has been circumcised, but one who follows the Mosaic Law. The good pagan who substantially lives up to the Law—even without realizing it—is more of a Jew than circumcised sinners. It would seem then, argues the saint rhetorically at the beginning of the third chapter, that there is little profit to be had in obeying the precepts of the Law if one can be saved without it. In fact St. Paul had even been accused (falsely, as he declares in 3:8) of teaching that the end justifies the means in human behavior. He answers his own rhetorical question: the Mosaic Law was necessary in the wake of original sin to keep alive an awareness of evil, the ability to recognize sin (3:20). In line with the Confraternity Version footnotes on 3:20–21 and 4:3, we must make the all-important distinction between *justification* (initial infusion of sanctifying grace in the soul which cannot be merited) and *sanctification* (the use of God's grace to perform good works and thus to merit). Both of these steps are necessary for salvation. Justification is the free gift of God; under both Old and New Covenants, it comes through faith, not good works, since it is God's act in the soul of man: this is St. Paul's special point. In such strong passages as Romans 3:20–26 he is not denying the efficacy of works in the sanctification of man, even under the Old Testament. St. Paul himself emphasizes good works as essential to salvation in Galatians 6:7–10 and II Corinthians 5:10. A good commentary on Romans 3 is the Epistle of St. James—especially 2:14–26, which should be read at this juncture.

Original Sin and Human Solidarity: Adam vs. Christ
(Romans 4–7)

Romans clearly teaches the doctrine of Original Sin, citing Psalm 13 in 3:10–12. As we now turn to Romans 5:12–14, we note the saint resuming the theme of our solidarity in Adam already treated in I Corinthians 15:20ff. In this connection, Fr. Stanilaus Lyonnet's observation is worth noting. He does not think the conjunction "because" in 5:12 brings out what he sees in the passage, so he corrects the verse as follows: "Therefore as through one man sin entered into the world and through sin death, and thus death has passed unto all men *in view of the fact that* all (adults) have sinned . . ." This reading sees each human adult as ratifying through his own actual sin the

---

[3] Cf. Hopkins, *God's Kingdom in the Old Testament*, Chap. 14 for references.

guilt of Adam's original sin, and thus makes men's personal sins a *condition* for acquiring the latter's guilt.[4]

As we continue reading Romans 5 and pass into Chapter 6, we see him again appealing to the corporate nature of humanity to explain the nature of salvation: mankind died in the Old Adam, but has been raised up in Christ, the New Adam. St. Paul is telling us that *salvation is not directly the product of good works, but rather of our incorporation into Christ (which faith along with good works effects)*. And in the next chapter he declares:

> Therefore, my brethren, you also, through the body of Christ, have been made to die to the Law, so as to belong to another who has risen from the dead, in order that we may bring forth fruit unto God. For when we were in the flesh, the sinful passions, which were aroused by the Law, were at work in our members so that they brought forth fruit unto death. But now we have been set free from the Law, having died to that by which we were held down, so that we may serve in a new spirit and not according to the outworn letter (Romans 7:4-6).

The effects of this incorporation into Christ are not all immediately realized, however, for they are impeded by the "flesh." Yet, many scholars today insist that the Pauline concept of the faithful as constituting the Body of Christ is real and ontological, not simply metaphorical.[5] The last two sentences quoted above recapitulate a basic Semitic notion frequently employed by St. Paul. The Semite tends to view man as a whole; the term often used for the "self" or person in the New Testament is the Greek word *soma* (usually translated "body"). In Romans 8 the apostle sees this mortal body as a battleground in the struggle between flesh *(sarx)* and spirit *(pneuma)*. More often than not in St. Paul, flesh denotes man's lower nature with its evil tendencies, the "Old Adam." Spirit, on the other hand, signifies man's good impulses, coming from God. These impulses must be obeyed if man is to overcome the flesh and obtain salvation. The victory of the spirit has already been won by Christ, the Head; all that remains is that this victory be disseminated throughout His members, the Church. The identity between Head and members becomes man-

---

[4] Cf. Stanilaus Lyonnet "Original Sin and Romans 5:12-14," *Theology Digest,* V:1. (Winter, 1957), 54-57; 63; also his commentary on this passage in *La Sainte Bible . . . de Jerusalem,* p. 1497.

[5] See Fr. Barnabas Ahern's two excellent articles: "The Christian's Union with the Body of Christ in Corinthians, Galatians, and Romans", *The Catholic Biblical Quarterly,* XXIII:3 (July 1961), 199-209, and "The Spirit of Christ in the Christian," *New Horizons,* pp. 145-157. Also cf. two articles in *The Bible Today:* G. T. Montague, S.M., "Paul's Teaching on Being and Becoming" (Nov. 1962) 79-85, and Sister John Mary Lane, S.N.J.M., "The Body of Christ in I Corinthians" (Feb. 1964) 650-655.

ifest to the degree in which the latter have put to death the works of the flesh by allowing the spirit to gain the ascendancy. New Testament revelation reaches its climax in linking up this good spirit in man with the Holy Spirit. (Cf. Romans 8:9–17.)[6]

Meditating on these texts and on Romans 6:14 in particular, Fr. Lyonnet concludes that Christians are freed not only from the Mosaic Law but from ALL law. His reasoning is that law is an external norm; as such, its function is to curb the weakness of the flesh. But one who lives by the Spirit has an internal principle placing him above the law. Such a one will, in fact, do all the things prescribed by the law through the higher motive of love. This observation is certainly valid, provided one realizes that in many (if not most) Christians the Spirit has not won out completely, and the flesh still exerts a very strong influence on their lives.[7] In the meantime, the Christian manifests a kind of "split personality" as he struggles to "put to death the deeds of the flesh" (8:13) with the aid of both law and Spirit. At any rate, St. Paul assures us that not only mankind but all creation is destined to "be delivered from its slavery to corruption into the freedom of the glory of the sons of God" (8:21). This consideration leads him into the topic of predestination.

Predestination and the Ultimate Fate of the Jews
(Romans 8:28—11:36)

In the beautiful passage, Romans 8:28–30, St. Paul unmistakably teaches the doctrine of predestination; it is his teaching which the Catholic Church has made her own on this subject. If it is remembered that God wills the salvation of every human soul (within the framework of His own glory, which is primary), that He offers sufficient grace to all, and finally, that predestination is only to heaven and not to hell, this doctrine can be a great consolation rather than a nightmare. Predestination is simply a *special case of divine providence, guaranteeing that certain chosen souls will earn eternal life.* Only by deliberate sin can any soul become "reprobated" to hell.[8]

---

[6] Davies, *Christian Origins and Judaism*, Chap. 7, points out a parallel use of flesh and spirit in the Dead Sea Scrolls.

[7] See his article, "St. Paul: Liberty and Law," *Theology Digest*, XI:1 (Spring 1963), pp. 12–18, and Fr. Ahern's, "The Lord's Freedman," pp. 19–20. Fr. G. T. Montague has an article touching all of these themes: "The Idea of Progress in the Early Church," *The Bible Today* (Feb. 1964), 630–642.

[8] References to Church definitions are given in the suggested readings at the end of this chapter. It must be remembered that many souls are consigned to limbo also. Watch all Confraternity Version footnotes, e.g., on 9:13 and 9:17. Many headaches will be avoided if predestination is regarded as a *guaranteed minimum* of persons to be saved, even though the mystery remains.

St. Paul lists the following steps in the process of predestination.

1. FOREKNOWN. From all eternity God has a specific idea of the individuals who will be created to manifest His mercy in the Beatific Vision.
2. PREDESTINED. By a positive free choice (e.g., Jacob in Romans 9:13), He ordains these souls to be saved in His plan. This is to be realized by making them "conformed to the image of His Son," i.e., through His Body, the Church.
3. CALLED. In due time, God creates these souls and offers them His grace.
4. JUSTIFIED. The predestined soul freely accepts God's initial grace by faith.
5. GLORIFIED. Predestined souls are "glorified" by the life of sanctifying grace here on earth, and enabled to merit truly eternal salvation.

That this doctrine is one of the great mysteries of faith is nowhere more apparent than in the concrete case which St. Paul uses to exemplify it: the salvation of the Jewish race. Chosen by God, they have rejected this grace in rejecting Christianity as a people. However, because "the gifts and the call of God are without repentance" (11: 29), i.e., God's plan is not to be frustrated in the end, "a partial blindness only has befallen Israel, until the full number of the Gentiles should enter (the Church), and thus all Israel should be saved" (11:25–26). He explains the return of the Jews by the striking metaphor of the olive tree. Israel is represented by the natural branches of an olive tree which have been broken off and replaced by artificial branches (the Gentiles). Now, if God is able to make these "wild" branches grow on the cultivated tree, "how much more shall these, the natural branches, be grafted into their own olive tree!" (11:24) God has used the sin of the Jews as the occasion of the salvation of the Gentiles; yet, "if their offense is the riches of the world, and their decline the riches of the Gentiles, how much more their full number!" (11:12) In other words, the repentance and conversion of Israel before the End will constitute one of the most glorious chapters in salvation history. The famous doxology at the end of Chapter 11 pays tribute to the magnificence of the divine Wisdom.

Psalm 13: The Depths of Human Perversity
(A Psalm of Lament)

We do not know what great evil the Psalmist had in mind in painting such a sorrowful picture of humanity; the Deluge, the Tower of Babel, Sodom, and the Egyptian oppression have been suggested. At any rate, this poem does reflect the ravages of Original Sin on the human race. Psalm 52 is a duplicate of this one.

Original Sin, Predestination, and the Salvation of the Jews

Suggested Readings

Ahern, *The Epistles to the Galatians and to the Romans* (New Testament Reading Guide Series, No. 7), pp. 31–77.

Bullough, *St. Paul and Apostolic Writings*, pp. 128–152.

Clarkson, *The Church Teaches*, par. 565–567 (on justification by faith); 548–549 (on predestination).

Davis, *Theology for Today*, Chap. 10, 11.

Denziger, H., *Enchiridion Symbolorum*, par. 321–322 (definition of predestination by the Council of Valence in 855; this was not an Ecumenical Council.)

Flanagan, *The Acts of the Apostles* (New Testament Reading Guide Series, No. 5), pp. 84–105.

Monro, *Enjoying the New Testament*, pp. 77–83.

For Further Study

1. What evidences does the New Testament supply with regard to the observance of the Mosaic Law by Christians? Did St. Paul himself continue any observances?
2. What seems to have been the main reason for Jewish refusal of the Gospel? How did their monotheism figure in the picture?
3. How many deaths does a Christian have to undergo to attain salvation? Explain.
4. Is there any likelihood of doctrinal cooperation between Saints Peter and Paul in Rome? (Cf. Margaret T. Monro, *Enjoying the New Testament*, p. 78.)
5. What light does St. Paul's doctrine of "life-in-Christ" throw on predestination? How does the Catholic view of predestination differ from that of John Calvin?

Chapter XI

The Gospel of St. Matthew (I):
The Beatitudes and
The New Morality

READINGS: *Matthew 3—5:15; Isaia 61; Psalms 71, 112; Stanley, The Gospel of St. Matthew (1963 ed.), pp. 3–37. (Note: Matthew 3:11; 4:1–11, 19; 5:3–14.)*

Chapters 1 and 2 of St. Matthew's Gospel have already been treated with St. Luke's infancy account in Chapter V of this work. By way of review, the student is referred to Fr. Stanley's excellent introduction and commentary on this section in the "New Testament Reading Guide Series" noted above, which supplies valuable insights not only to Matthew but also the Gospels in general. In answer to Question 4 raised on page 49 in this text, and by way of supplement, a few words should be devoted to the *midrashic* element to be found in the New Testament—particularly in St. Matthew's Gospel.

In explaining some of the more mysterious passages in Luke 1–2 and Matthew 1–2, certain exegetes (e.g., Fr. Stanley, *Opus cit.*, p. 13) suggest that the sacred author took a nucleus of historical truth and then proceeded to embellish it with details modeled on Old Testament accounts. The star of Bethlehem in the Magi story, for instance, *may* have been suggested by the sacred author of Numbers 24:17 (Balaam's oracle); the massacre of the Holy Innocents harks back to Jeremia 31:15; the flight into Egypt is referred to Osee 11:1. Some modern exegetes see *midrashic* elements added in order to portray Christ as the New Moses (S. Munoz-Iglesias) or the New Jacob (Myles Bourke).[1] Such scholarly researches are still too new to permit a final evaluation. They surely have good foundation in reality; however, the warning of the Holy Office of June 20, 1961 against calling into question the objective existence of certain events and sayings in the life of Christ must be kept carefully in mind. In brief, the authentic historical nucleus of these accounts has not yet been accurately isolated and perhaps never will be.

---

[1] For a concise statement of some of these *midrashic* approaches, see *Current Scripture Notes*, II, No. 4, pp. 15–16 (with basic references to other articles) and III, No. 1, pp. 1–2. Midrash in Wisdom 11, 13–19 is treated in *God's Kingdom in the Old Testament*, Chap. XIV. Cf. also *Theology Digest*, (Winter 1961), pp. 15–25.

St. Matthew and His Gospel

There is a general agreement in the mind of Catholic scholars that "Levi, the son of Alpheus" (Mark 2:14) is the same person as the Matthew in Matthew 9:9. What is not certain is whether the Alpheus in the Markan passage is the same as the father of the Apostle James in Mark 3:18.[2] Even less certain is the pious tradition that has St. Matthew, after preaching in Judea, undertake missionary work in Ethiopia and there suffer a glorious martyrdom for refusing to marry the king's daughter, Iphigenia, because of a vow of virginity which he had taken. As a custom accountant at Capharnaum, Levi acquired a mania for orderly, logical exposition, a flare for numbers, and the odium of his fellow Jews (who placed him in the category of "publicans"—tax-gatherers). Thus, we find in his Gospel one of two genealogies furnished by the Evangelists; a neglect of time intervals and the telescoping of related events (e.g., the Sermon on the Mount); doubling of individuals (compare Matthew 20:30 with Mark 10:46). Other "standard" Semitic stylistic peculiarities are characteristic of this Gospel: parallelism and antithesis (cf. 5:40–42); and the bunching of separated events by the use of a categorical term placed at the beginning and again at the end of the topic. This is known as "inclusion"; an example is the use of the term "works" in 11:2 and 11:19 to include many activities.[3] Note, finally, the careful avoidance of the term "God" in such phrases as "The Kingdom of heaven."

Turning to the Gospel of Matthew, we have recourse once again to Papias (c. 130 A.D.): "Matthew put together in the Hebrew (i.e., Aramaic) language the discourses (Logia) and each one translated them as best he could."[4] This statement together with other testimonies forms the basis of the constant Catholic tradition that St. Matthew wrote a primitive work in Aramaic centered around the sayings (Logia) of Jesus before 50 A.D. After providing the basis for a number

---

[2] Cf. Matthew 10:4 and Luke 6:15–16; this information will be consolidated in a chart in Chap. XIII. See also the "black sheep" theory in Monro, *Enjoying the New Testament*, pp. 112–113.

[3] See page 107, footnote 7.

[4] Eusebius, *Ecclesiastical History*, III 39, 16. The Biblical Commission's decision of 1911 affirming the substantial identity of the Aramaic and Greek versions has been broadly interpreted in recent decades. This was substantiated quasi-officially by a statement of late secretary of the Pontifical Biblical Commission, Fr. Athanasius Miller, O.S.B.: "However, as long as these decrees propose views which are neither immediately nor mediately connected with truths of faith and morals, it goes without saying that the scholar may pursue his research with complete freedom and may utilize the results of his research, provided always that he defers to the supreme teaching authority of the Church" (*Catholic Biblical Quarterly*, XVIII:1 [Jan. 1956], 24). Fr. Jacques Dupont further clarifies the implications of this statement when he points out that questions of authorship, date of composition, and integrity are not inseparably linked with biblical inerrancy (cf. his article "Apropos du nouvel Enchiridion Biblicum," *Revue Biblique*, LXII [1955], 418).

of "gospels," it was finally translated and elaborated by Matthew or some one else in the Greek language. We have already conjectured that this, our canonical Matthew, originated after the fall of Jerusalem in 70 A.D.—perhaps about the year 80. Although ignored by Protestant critics (they prefer the "Q" document) and frequently challenged in Catholic circles, the existence of a now lost Matthew Aramaic does help to explain a strange dualism detectable in our extant Greek version:

	ARAMAIC VERSION	OUR GREEK VERSION
1. Audience for whom written:	Jewish Christians of Palestine.	Converts from paganism (Christians of Antioch?).
2. Purpose of the Gospel:	To show that Christ is "Emmanuel," the Messia.	Expected (Davidic) Kingdom is the Christian Church.
3. Medium of demonstration:	Fulfillment of Old Testament prophecies.	Jesus' Five Discourses (all stress universality).

In our study, we shall have to keep both views in mind, realizing that the final product (Matthew Greek) still reflects its Aramaic core. Fr. Stanley summarizes the Evangelist's plan under three themes:

(1) There is Matthew's personal conception of Jesus Christ as "Emmanuel" ("with us is God"). Its expression forms an "inclusion" which stamps the character of the whole book. At the outset, Matthew explains the sacred Name (1:23); at the very end of his Gospel he reminds his readers that it is through his Church that the glorified Emmanuel makes good his final promise, "I am with you all the time until the end of the world" (28:20). (2) Matthew proposes to demonstrate that Old Testament prophecy has been fulfilled in Jesus' earthly career in a divine way which quite transcends the earthly expectations of his Jewish contemporaries, with the tragic result that they reject him as their Messiah and hand him over to the pagans for execution. Thus God's plan for the pagan's salvation is effected: they replace "the wicked and perverse generation" in the Kingdom. (3) Matthew finally wishes to show that Jesus' words and deeds in Galilee and Jerusalem are so many steps in establishing that "Kingdom of heaven" in this world, which for Matthew means the Christian Church . . . [this] phrase . . . has replaced the more traditional "God's Kingdom" (i.e., sovereignty), [and] suggests that Matthew habitually thinks of the divine dominion as actualized in the Church.[5]

---

[5] Stanley, *The Gospel of St. Matthew* (Collegeville, Minn.: 1960 ed.), pp. 6–7, 9. Elsewhere the 1963 revision is cited in this book.

Let us not forget, in pointing out the peculiarities of Matthew's Gospel, that he has much in common with the other two Synoptics, Mark and Luke.[6] In the words of Fr. MacKenzie, the Synoptics "are the crystallization, in three different forms, of the oral teaching carried on in the different centers of the primitive Church by missionaries, teachers, or oral evangelists. The foundation of all of it is the recollections and testimony of the apostles (and, for the Infancy narratives, of some others)."[7] All of the developments in salvation history recorded in the Acts of the Apostles are presupposed in St. Matthew's Gospel.

Christ's Baptism and Temptations in St. Matthew

(Matthew 3-4)

Matthew 3:3 refers the reader to the prophet Isaia. In Isaia 40:3, it is the *preparation* which is to be found in the desert (Babylon), not the voice. Moreover, John the Baptist (whom Matthew depicts after the manner of Elias) uses the kind of apocalyptic language characteristic of the passage in Malachia (refiner's fire, fuller's lye). Both Matthew and Luke go beyond the Markan account in severely rebuking the Pharisees and Sadducees (whose names Luke omits for his Gentile audience); St. Luke alone records John's advice to the "laity": observe properly the duties of your state in life (Luke 3:10–14). Confessing his own inadequacy, John declares that his baptism is to that of "him who is coming after me" as water is to fire. The sacramental implications of this statement will be taken up in connection with the Fourth Gospel. The proximity of the kingdom of heaven announced by John is borne out by the baptismal theophany over Christ; as in Mark and Luke, Jesus is identified with the Servant of Yahweh with the help of Psalm 2:7.

Having been duly anointed, Christ proceeds to the enemy's den; the overtones of Genesis 3:15 reach a climax in the desert. Like the forty days spent by Moses on Sinai followed by his forty-day penitential prostration because of the Golden Calf episode, and like the forty-day trek of Elias to the same mountain, the New Moses–Elias battles with Satan for forty days, behaving as the Jews should have behaved during their forty years in the wilderness. We have already linked up the temptations with three aspects of the popular messianic view (p. 48); now we can proceed one step further and see the crisis mirrored in three great prophets.

---

[6] Review, p. 20–21 on the synoptic problem and the formation of the Gospels.

[7] MacKenzie, *Introduction to the New Testament* (New Testament Reading Guide Series, No. 1 [Collegeville, Minn.: Liturgical Press], p. 25.) We shall give an outline of the five discourses proper to Matthew in the next chapter.

TEMPTATION OF CHRIST	POPULAR MESSIANIC VIEW	PROPHET
1. Turn stones into bread! (Here the miraculous element is secondary.)	Naturalistic: The Kingdom will be an economic paradise.	Isaia: God is transcendent, supernatural.
2. Throw yourself down from the Temple! (The miracle is the key.)	Magical, automatic: The Kingdom will come miraculously.	Osee: Salvation via merciful punishment.
3. Fall down and worship me, and I will give you the kingdoms of the world! (Cf. Luke 4:6.)	Political: Looking toward a Jewish national state.	Amos: Messianic era will have universal dimensions.

As Fr. Stanley notes[8] the three temptations are toward sensuality, presumption, and idolatry; or one might also see here the vices of gluttony, vanity, and avarice. In quoting the Book of Deuteronomy against the devil on each occasion, Jesus gives the Deuteronomic Principle its correct orientation: "Not by bread alone does man live, but by every word that comes forth from the mouth of God." The truth dimly perceived by Ecclesiastes, Job, and Tobias now comes out into the open. The prosperity promised in Deuteronomy 28 and the success guaranteed to Josue (Josue 1:5ff.) for keeping the Law were never meant to be the *motive* of obedience, nor was the keeping of the *letter* of the Law meant to be an end in itself: all was to be subordinated to the love and service of God, even though it meant starvation.

Identifying His mission with that announced by John, Jesus repeats his message: "Repent, for the kingdom of heaven is at hand" (4:17). His settling at Capharnaum hints at His rejection by the Nazarenes (cf. 13:57). The calling of the disciples anticipates a theme to be treated in the next chapter. His miracles serve as His messianic credentials. The cures identify Him as Servant of Yahweh, the exorcisms are part of the combat with Satan, as are also the healings: "the diseases and infirmities of men are the ransom-price of sin, they belong to the kingdom of evil."[9]

The Sermon on the Mount and the New "Morality" (Matthew 5:1–16)

A clear instance of Matthew's logical rather than chronological arrangement of material begins with the Sermon on the Mount in

---

[8] *Op. cit.*, p. 33.
[9] L. Cerfaux, *The Four Gospels* (Westminster, Md.: Newman Press, 1960), p. 3. H. C. Key and F. W. Young, *Understanding the New Testament* (Englewood Cliffs, N. J.: Prentice-Hall, 1957), pp. 57–58.

Chapter 5 (Luke places it after the choice of the Twelve some time later, Luke 6:20). Because of the crowds attracted by His message, Jesus is constrained to declare the nature of the kingdom He preaches. What He offers is neither a new code of ethics, nor an extension of the Mosaic Code: He demands a total commitment to the will of God. In the words of Wright and Fuller,

> Jesus does not offer a complete system of ethics. He propounds no list of ideals or virtues which a man can go away and cultivate by himself. What he offers is a series of illustrations of what the demand of God involves in concrete circumstances.[10]

St. Thomas makes the same point in placing the beatitudes in the category of *acts* rather than *virtues*—presupposing, of course, the existence of corresponding virtues in the soul.[11] It would be impossible to give a detailed commentary on each beatitude, as the implications of each one are too vast; we shall have to content ourselves with a few suggested lines of development borrowed from the Old Testament.

THE BEATITUDES: THE CHARTER OF THE KINGDOM OF GOD (Review: Isaia 61 and Psalm 71)				
BEATITUDE	OLD TESTAMENT BACKGROUND	INCLUDES	EXCLUDES	REWARD
POOR IN SPIRIT (Soph. 2:3; Isa. 61)	Seekers of God's will; the faithful	Humble Detached	Conceited Avaricious	Belonging to God's pasture (Isa. 14:30)
MEEK (Num. 12:3; Sir. 28:3)	Positive acceptance of suffering (Tob. 3:21)	Tranquil Patient	Aggressive Unpleasant	Palestine, symbol of blessing (Ps. 36:11)
MOURNERS (Ps. 125:5)	Purged remnant; the "Good Figs" (Jer. 24:5)	Contrite Long-suffering	Unrepentant Rebellious	Messianic consolation (Isa. 61:2-3)
HUNGERERS AFTER JUSTICE (Ps. 57)	Zeal for righteousness and God's word (Amos 8:11)	Militant Dedicated	Complacent Uncommitted	Realization of all ideals (Ps. 71:1-2)
MERCIFUL (Sir. 28:1-7)	The prophetic role (cf. Isa. 35:3-5)	Compassionate Forgiving	Hardened Revengeful	Price of divine forgiveness! (Sir. 28:4)
CLEAN OF HEART (Ps. 14; Ps. 23:4)	Blameless, single-purposed life	Guileless Chaste	Double-minded Lustful	Sight of God = intimacy (Deut. 34:10)
PEACEMAKERS (Sir. 28:8; Ps. 33:15)	Peace = summation of messianism (Ps. 71:7; Isa. 9:5)	Gentle Conciliatory	Violent Divisive	Adoptive sonship (cf. Ex. 4:22)
PERSECUTED (Isa. 53; Ps. 21)	Servant of Yahweh; the ideal sufferer	Principled Loyal	Compromising Fickle	Exaltation-through-humiliation (Isa. 53:12)

[10] Wright and Fuller, *Op. Cit.*, p. 270.

[11] *Summa Theologica*, IaIIae, Q. 69, Art. 1. They are the highest acts of the Gifts of the Holy Spirit.

These are the perfections required of all of the members of the new kingdom; the beatitudes represent a Christian manifesto. What follows in 5:13–16, however, is addressed to His disciples. They must first of all *be better* (salt) than their neighbor in order to *edify* (light) by good example: not precisely *"in order that* they may see your good works," but *"with the result that"* they may do so and therein glorify "your Father in heaven" (v. 16). The injunctions which follow are all implied in these eight principles. St. Luke, concentrating on the notion of "Anawim," has fewer; they approximate numbers 1, 3, 4, 8 (Luke 6:20–26), with corresponding "woes."[12]

In declaring practitioners of the beatitudes "blessed" (happy), Christ is underscoring the actuality of the Kingdom of Heaven. The Kingdom has already come for the poor in spirit and the persecuted: "For theirs IS the kingdom of heaven." The rewards promised are, on one plane, truly the immediate results of the corresponding dispositions, for happiness consists in a current relationship with God. At the same time the use of the future tense in the other six beatitudes warns us that their fulfillment is incomplete and must await fruition on a second, higher plane. Membership in the new People of God offers the first, messianic level of reward, but only in the next life will the "happy ones" attain perfect beatitude. In a word, the beatitudes and their effects are a basic expression of Christianity in its various facets: a way of life, not an accumulation of merits.

Psalm 112: Hymn to the Lord for His Care of the Anawim

As the first psalm of the Great Hallel, this poem was probably recited by Christ and the apostles at the Last Supper. Like the Canticle of Anna (from which verses 7–8 are borrowed), it assures us of God's special care for the pious poor. It represents an intermediate stage of religious development when temporal rewards still played a predominant role in Jewish aspirations.

Suggested Readings

MacKenzie, *Introduction to the New Testament* (New Testament Reading Guide Series, No. 1), pp. 22–24.
Monro, *Enjoying the New Testament,* pp. 111–120.
Robinson, Carol Jackson, "Eight Keys to the Kingdom" (a series of articles on the Beatitudes), *Ave Maria* (March 3–April 21, 1962).
Sheen, *Life of Christ,* Chapters 3 (Temptations) and 11 (Beatitudes).
Wikenhauser, *New Testament Introduction,* pp. 175–199.

---

[12] Fr. R. E. Brown shows the contrast between the *sociological* emphasis of St. Luke on the actually poor, and St. Matthew's emphasis on the *spiritual* quality of detachment, in "The Beatitudes according to St. Luke," *The Voice of St. Mary's Seminary,* XXXVIII:4 (Feb. 1961), 8ff.

The Beatitudes and The New Morality

1. Why do you suppose that *Levi* is called *Matthew* aften he joins the apostles?
2. Which episodes in St. Matthew's infancy account seem to have been influenced by *midrashic* additions?
3. Are there any details of the temptations which need not be taken historically?
4. In what sense should we interpret the reference to Osee 11:1? Jeremia 31:15? What do these "types" teach us about typology?
5. According to Matthew, who saw the heavens open and the dove descend at Jesus' baptism? Was it a public manifestation?

Chapter XII

Matthew (II): The Old Law Versus The New Law: The Lord's Prayer

READINGS: *Matthew 5:17–7:28; James 1, 3–5. (Note: Matthew 5:17–18; 6:9–15; James 5:14–15).*

Before proceeding any further, it is imperative that the material treated be placed in context with reference to the five discourses of St. Matthew's Gospel. Not only is this a convenient method of dividing his work; it is the inner structure which gives meaning to the contents of the book. The following outline has been adapted from Fr. Stanley's *The Gospel of St. Matthew.*

Division of St. Matthew's Gospel According to the Five Discourses

PROLOGUE: The credentials of the Messia—(1–2).

1) Descendant of Abraham (1:2), Tribe of Juda (1:3), House of David (1:6).
2) Emmanuel (1:23).
3) The new Josue ("Jesus," 1:21), sent even to Gentiles (2:11).
4) The New Moses, sought as an Infant by the hostile Herod (2:16).
5) The New Israel, leaving Egypt (2:15, 21).
6) A "Nazarene" (2:26).

I. *FOUNDATIONS OF THE KINGDOM: The Sermon on the Mount* (3–7).

1) The Beatitudes: special appeal to the Anawim (cf. Isa. 61).
2) Fulfillment: from Old Testament to New Testament.

II. *MISSIONARY CHARACTER OF THE KINGDOM: The Apostolic Instruction* (8–10).

    1) The new Kingdom to be apostolic, not hereditary.

    2) Miracles, sign of the presence of the Kingdom.

    3) Persecution to be expected.

III. *THE KINGDOM A TRANSCENDENT, SUPERNATURAL ORGANISM: Parables of the Kingdom, which is a present reality* (11–13).

    1) Future of the Kingdom guaranteed; the violent will take it by storm.

    2) Membership demands being the brother of Jesus in the Spirit, not in the flesh (12:48–50).

    3) But evil members will not be cast out, rather they will be transformed.

IV. *THE KINGDOM A COMMUNITY GOVERNED BY A "HIERARCHY," ANIMATED BY CHARITY: The Christian Virtues* (14–18)

    1) Two accounts of the multiplication of loaves: Eucharist, bond of unity, foreshadowed.

    2) Peter's primacy foretold.

    3) Virtues: child-like simplicity, good example, fraternal correction, forgiveness.

V. *UNIVERSALITY OF THE KINGDOM: Denunciation of Pharisees, Destruction of Jerusalem* (19–25): Separation of Christian Church from synagogue.

EPILOGUE: THE NEW COVENANT IN CHRIST'S BLOOD: The Eucharist supersedes the Passover (26–28).

Foundations of the Kingdom: The First Discourse

In the previous chapter we began the study of the first discourse, the Sermon on the Mount. After enunciating the beatitudes, Jesus launches into a comparison of the New Covenant, which He is establishing, with the Old Covenant. As the model Pedagogue, He goes from the more known to the less known. Because of the nature of this section (pure discourse modeled after the Wisdom books), it seems best to analyze it in outline form, backtracking to the beginning of the Sermon on the Mount for the sake of integrity.

SERMON ON THE MOUNT: THE NEW SINAI

REFERENCE IN MATTHEW:	OUTLINE	EXEGESIS:
	I. PERFECTION REQUIRED OF MEMBERS OF THE KINGDOM	
5:3–12	A. ALL MEMBERS: the eight beatitudes.	
	B. Perfection required of APOSTLES:	
5:13	1. Higher degree: salt.	
5:14–15	2. Good example: light.	
	II. RELATION OF THE NEW LAW TO THE OLD	
	A. IN GENERAL:	
5:17–19	1. New Law is the fulfillment of the Old according to the three classes of precept in the Law.	CEREMONIAL PRECEPTS: Replaced by Christian sacraments. JUDICIAL PRECEPTS: Replaced by Christian charity. MORAL PRECEPTS: Retained, but re-interpreted and extended.
5:20	2. Greater interior perfection required (more than Scribes' and Pharisees' formalism).	
	B. IN PARTICULAR: Re-interpretation and extension of Moral Precepts:	
5:22	1. Fifth Commandment extended to . . .	a. Anger b. Name-calling c. Cursing ("fool" means "damnable")
5:23–24	a. Offender barred from worship.	
5:25–26	b. Go more than half way!	
5:27–28	2. Sixth Commandment extended to . . .	Thoughts and looks
5:29–30		Avoidance of all occasions
5:31–32		Exclusion of divorce [1]
5:33–37	3. Second Commandment extended to . .	No unnecessary oaths
5:38–42	4. Law of Talion abrogated	Replace justice with charity!
5:43–47	5. Love of neighbor extended to	Even enemies: learn to love! (Cf. Prov. 25:21)

5:48	C. MANNER IN WHICH GOOD WORKS ARE TO BE PERFORMED:	Perfectly: this is a command.
6:1		Unostentatiously
6:2–4	1. Almsgiving	Without "sounding a trumpet"
6:5–8	2. Prayer	Negatively: pray in secret.
6:9–15		Positively: the Lord's Prayer
6:16–18	3. Fasting	("anoint thy head.")

III. VIRTUES EMPHASIZED BY CHRIST

6:19–21	A. Kind of treasure to put efforts into . . .	Place your security in heaven.
6:22–23	B. Care of the "eye"	Have a pure intention.
6:24	C. A true dilemma	Serve *either* God *or* money.
6:25–34	D. Precautions for the future	Anxiety reprobated. (Antithesis of "secularism")
7:1–5	E. Fifth Commandment further extended to	Rash judgments condemned.
7:6	F. Admonitions regarding piety	Treat holy things reverently.
7:7–11		Have confidence in prayer.
7:12	G. How to treat others (charity)	The "golden rule"

IV. EXHORTATIONS

7:13–14	A. Way of salvation	"Narrow," i.e., difficult
7:15–20	B. How to discern false prophets	Judge them by their actions.
7:21–27	C. Nature of good works	Required along with faith!

---

[1] In restoring marriage to its primitive perfection, Christ clearly outlaws all divorce which implies any possibility of remarriage (cf. Luke 16:18; I Cor. 7:10–11, 39–40). The footnote on Matthew 5:32 in the Confraternity Version gives the traditional interpretation of the phrase, "save on account of immorality." Recent exegetes have suggested that the phrase may be a reference to marriage with close relatives contracted by Gentile converts and forbidden by the Council of Jerusalem in Acts 15:29. In this event, Matthew would be giving an interpolation for his *Syrian* audience comparable to the Markan prohibition of divorce by *Roman* wives (Mark 10:11). Cf. Stanley, *Op. Cit.*, p. 40.

The Epistle of St. James: A "Commentary" on the Sermon on the Mount

(James 1, 3–5)

This is the first of the "Catholic" Epistles, i.e., those not addressed to a determined audience, but apparently intended for the Church in general. Seven of the New Testament letters are in this category. The epistle in question is a moral exhortation similar to the Wisdom literature of the Old Testament; it gives strong support to good works along with faith (Chap. 2, previously assigned). It was written most probably by James the Less, the "Bishop" of Jerusalem, and reflects a primitive state of Christianity (e.g., 2:1).[2] Many exegetes place its date of composition before the Council of Jerusalem (in the 40's); we have taken the date c. 62. One of the deuterocanonical works of the New Testament (some early Fathers thought it was pseudepigraphic), it was for a time rejected by certain Protestant reformers because of its emphasis on good works. However, today it is generally accepted as canonical.

Even a casual reading will convince the student that this work is remarkably similar to the Sermon on the Mount. A few examples will suffice: "Double-minded man" in James 1:8 suggests Matthew 6:22–23;[3] frequent references to the "poor" (2:5) and "lowly" (1:9) smack of the first beatitude. Other beatitudes are reflected in James 1:12, 1:21; 4:4, 6, 8, 9; 5:1. We find rash judgment condemned in 4:11, oaths forbidden in 5:12 in Matthew's own words; and fraternal correction (cf. Matthew 18:15–18) enjoined in James 5:19–20. Finally, there is an important text with reference to Last Anointing in 5:14–15.

The Our Father: A Prayer for the Present and the Future

St. Luke has the Apostles asking Jesus to teach them how to pray (Luke 11:1), whereas Matthew puts the Lord's Prayer into the Sermon on the Mount. At any rate, Christ has given us more a model than a formula. The explanation given here brings out the eschatological overtones as well as day-to-day needs.

1. *Our Father.* Christ's coming has set mankind into a new relationship with God—genuine sonship far beyond the adoption of the Jews in Exodus 4:22. This intimate sonship was promised for the messianic age (the reward of peacemakers; see also Sir. 51:10; Luke 6:35).

---

[2] The identity of this James will be treated in the next chapter.

[3] By "double-minded" St. James means *vacillating between Christ and the world,* wavering in faith. This term will be considered later in connection with the *Pastor of Hermas.*

2. *Who art in heaven.* This phrase expresses the divine transcendence. It also points to what will be our home at the end of the ages.
3. *Hallowed by Thy Name.* The New Testament retains the close association between the person and the name characteristic of the Old Covenant; hence, for God's name to be hallowed is for His Person to be sanctified before men. His name is to be universally hallowed before the end of time (cf. Ez. 36:22–23).
4. *Thy kingdom come.* This is a corollary of the previous petition. Christ has begun the reign of God on earth by His death and Resurrection; the work must go on and spread throughout the earth until God is undisputed King (cf. Ez. 20:33; Zach. 14:9; Dan. 7:13–18, etc.).
5. *Thy will be done on earth as it is in heaven.* This explains how God's kingdom is to come eventually. It demands looking beyond the present day and working for the restoration of all human institutions in Christ, not just individual conformity to His will.
6. *Give us this day our daily bread.* This is, indeed, a request for our immediate needs. However, there is strong evidence that the Greek word goes beyond material needs and refers to a "supersubstantial" bread—suggesting the Eucharist. To eat bread together is a sign of the coming of the messianic kingdom.
7. *And forgive us our trespasses as we forgive those who trespass against us.* This envisages personal pardon from God, but it also looks to that general remission of sins which will presage the end of time. Our forgiveness by God is contingent upon our forgiveness of our neighbor (cf. Sir. 28:2).
8. *And lead us not into temptation.* We pray not to be relieved of all temptation, but rather to be able to overcome it (Jas. 1:13). Daily tests are the stuff of salvation; but what the petition especially looks toward is the cosmic battle between God and Satan at the end-time (Eph. 6:12–13; Apoc. 3:10). God will keep us from the Evil One if we are faithful to Him (John 17:15), and begin to prepare now.
9. *But deliver us from evil.* The final assault of the devil on the Kingdom of God and His children.[4]

Suggested Readings

Brown, Raymond, "The Pater Noster as an Eschatological Prayer" in *Theological Studies,* XXII:2 (June, 1961), 175–208; the same article is condensed in *Theology Digest,* X:1 (Winter, 1962), 3–10.
Cyril of Jerusalem, *Mystagogical Catachesis No. 5* (See Appendix, pp. 227–228). This commentary on the Lord's Prayer will be considered with a later chapter.

---

[4] Raymond Brown, "The Pater Noster as an Eschatological Prayer," *Theological Studies,* XXII:2 (June, 1961), 175–208.

Maly, *The Epistles of Saints James, Jude, Peter* (New Testament Reading Guide Series, No. 12), pp. 3–24.
Monro, *Enjoying the New Testament*, pp. 98–103.
Stanley, *The Gospel of St. Matthew* (New Testament Reading Guide Series, No. 4), pp. 38–48.
Wikenhauser, *New Testament Introduction*, pp. 473–487.

For Further Study

1. In general, what is the relationship between the Old and New Testaments, according to Christ's teaching in the Sermon on the Mount?
2. What Old Testament evidence can you cite for the seriousness of calling some one a "fool"?
3. Why is divorce related to the *sixth* commandment? Oaths to the *second?*
4. Could James the Greater have written the Epistle of James? How many *James'* were there?
5. What picture do you get about James from reading his epistle?
6. Are you convinced that the Lord's Prayer is eschatological?

Chapter XIII

Matthew (III): Second, Third Discourses: Missionary and Transcendent Nature of The Kingdom

READINGS: *Matthew 8–15; Psalm 144. (Note: Matthew 8:17; 10:1–5, 10, 34–39; 12:24, 32, 36, 46–50; 13:54–58 and parables.)*

In this chapter we shall consider the second and third discourses of Christ, together with the connecting material. Departing somewhat from Fr. Stanley's procedure, we are taking Chapters 8–9 and 11–12 with the "Apostolic Instruction" (Chap. 10, Second Discourse) and Chapters 14–15 with the "Parables of the Kingdom" (Chap. 13, Third Discourse). In the First Discourse, the Sermon on the Mount, Jesus appeared as the great Teacher and Legislator. St. Matthew now portrays Him as the Miracle-Worker establishing His messianic claims and documenting the arrival of the Kingdom of God. Paralleling this theme is the growing opposition of His enemies and their vicious gossip campaign calculated to nullify His influence with the people.

Miracles, Pharisaic Opposition, Realized Eschatology
(Matthew 8–9:34)

The beginning of this section contains another example of the logical arrangement of St. Matthew's Gospel in the bunching of miracle stories. Both the leper and the centurion illustrate the insistence of Christ on faith as a prerequisite to the working of a miracle. He Himself marvels at the faith of the centurion, who has given us the words, "Domine, non sum dignus ut intres sub tectum meum" (8:8). The cure of this Gentile's servant was the exception rather than the rule; it does not vitiate 10:5. The healing of Peter's mother-in-law tells us that the future head of the Church was a married man. St. Matthew's citation from the fourth Servant Song of Isaia in 8:17 throws more light on this recurring theme: Jesus has become the Servant *in order to identify Himself with the poor and the oppressed whose cause He is championing.* He is living the Sermon on the Mount. And we find Him calling Himself "Son of Man" in 8:20.

The requirements of discipleship are indicated in two succinct logia in 8:18–22. The storm on the lake in the following passage reveals how poorly the disciples' faith compares with that of the centurion. It is interesting to note the ambivalent use to which the Church is able to put the storm episode (read also St. Mark's eyewitness account, Mark 4:35–40). As the Gospel text for the Fourth Sunday after the Epiphany, it has an Epiphany motif—the manifestation of divinity. But when it is used to fill in for one of the final Sundays after Pentecost, it takes on a Parousial connotation.[1] In the Gerasa incident, Jesus manifests His power over devils and brutes as He permits the demons to enter the swine (8:32). Surely the riddance of the countryside of this diabolical influence was adequate compensation for the loss of the animals!

Not only does the forgiveness of the paralytic's sins at the beginning of Chapter 9 suggest (at least to *us*) the divinity of Christ, but it also announces the beginning of the messianic age. The prophets had foretold the Day of the Lord as one of judgment and the remission of sins (cf. Isa. 4:4, 40:2; Luke 1:77). As Fr. Stanley puts it, Christ's

> . . . healing work is allied to His fight against sin. The correct meaning of 'Jesus, seeing their faith' is only discovered in the Marcan narrative, thanks to Matthew's abbreviation. The restoration of man's physical powers is an external symbol of the unseen forgiveness of his sins (See Mark 2:1–12).[2]

The first note of protest from "the Scribes" is recorded in 9:2.

The call of Levi (Matthew?) manifests Christ's policy is dealing with "sinners": He is only too happy to associate Himself with those who are *repentant* of their misdeeds, but He will have nothing to do with hardened sinners (such as the Scribes and the Pharisees who persecute Him) except to warn them of their evil ways. His quotation from Osee in 9:13 "suggests the primacy of fraternal love over the formalities of code and cult."[3] The battle with the religious formalists has begun in earnest! Further friction arises over the refusal of Jesus to observe the Monday and Thursday fast prescribed by the "Tradition of the Ancients." He subtly suggests the advent of the messianic era by means of three metaphors: "bridegroom" (the wedding feast was a symbol of the day of salvation—cf. Apoc. 19:7, 9); the need of a whole new "garment" (cf. Heb. 1:10–12); and "new wine" in "fresh skins."

St. Matthew continues to enumerate the Master's miracles: the resuscitation of a "ruler's" daughter (Jairus: cf. Mark 5:23), the cure

---

[1] See Parsch, *The Church's Year of Grace* (Collegeville, Minn.: The Liturgical Press, 1957–1959) Vol. 1, pp. 337–344; Vol. V, pp. 122–124.

[2] Stanley, *Op. cit.*, p. 52.

[3] *Ibid.*

of the woman with a hemorrhage (for whom Mark has Jesus "looking around") and of "two" blind men (perhaps the same incident as 20: 29–34—i.e., Bartimeus), and the expulsion of a devil. This last miracle unlooses the Pharisaic calumny (9:34). Unable to match His miracles, emulate His rhetoric, or refute His doctrine, these degenerate successors of the Hasidim (cf. I Mach. 2:42) declare: "By the prince of devils he casts out devils."

The Apostolic Instruction

(Second Discourse: Matthew 10; also 11)

Two more messianic references bring Chapter 9 to a close: the "sheep without a shepherd" and the "harvest" in verses 36–37, and serve to introduce the second great discourse. St. Matthew places the naming of the Twelve at this juncture, whereas Mark and Luke locate the choice just before the Sermon on the Mount. Their special dignity seems to consist in accompanying Him constantly, preaching, and working miracles (cf. Mark 3:13ff.). Actually, we can distinguish three "calls" issued to the Twelve: *1)* the transferral of allegiance of John (the Son of Zebedee?) and Andrew from the Baptist to Jesus on a part-time basis (cf. John 1:35ff); *2)* their becoming "fishers of men", i.e., giving up their occupations to follow Jesus full-time (Matt. 4:19); and *3)* their elevation to apostleship. They are given the following instruction before being sent forth on their first "mission":[4]

1. *Preach to the Jews first,* preparing them by spiritual and corporal works of mercy to receive the Good News (perhaps an echo of Matthew Aramaic?).

2. *Poverty is indispensable to the apostolate:* Take no excess baggage, and let the people support you.

3. *Be prudent and guileless, and courageous in persecution,* for "If they have called the master of the house Beezlebub, how much more those of his household!" (10:25).

This instruction, as Fr. Stanley points out, clearly shows a later adaptation by the Christian community; as we have previously stated, the Gospels are testimonies of the early Church, not primarily biographies of Christ! The mention of "governors and kings" in verse 18 supposes the spread of Christianity beyond Palestine, and the mention of "the Gentiles" in the following verse presupposes Peter's vision in Acts 10. Verse 20 suggests Pentecost as accomplished (cf. Luke 12:12), and verse 23 probably refers to the destruction of Jerusalem,

---

[4] The instruction to the "seventy-two (or seventy) others" in Luke 10 reflects this same message; it may have been the same occasion, or perhaps the discourse was repeated.

thus pointing to 70–80 A.D. as the date of composition of this Gospel. Finally, verses 26–27 seem to indicate a rather universal preaching of the Good News whose aftermath is described in apocalyptic terms in verses 34–39. The lot of the Apostles will be that of Christ Himself: to fulfill the role of the Servant of Yahweh, even unto martyrdom. Indeed, the Apostles have replaced the prophets of the Old Testament (v. 41).

THE APOSTOLIC COLLEGE

(See Matt. 10:2–4; Mark 3:16–19; Luke 6:14–16; Acts 1:13)

NAME	OTHER DESIGNATION	FATHER	TEXTS	REMARKS
Peter	Simon; Cephas (Kephas, Petros)	Jona	Matt. 4:18 John 1:42	Brother of Andrew
James the Greater	"Son of Thunder"	Zebedee (and Salome)	Matt. 4:22 Matt. 27:56	Brother of John
John (the Evangelist)	"Son of Thunder" (Mark 3:17)	Zebedee (and Salome)	John 1:35? Matt. 4:21	Brother of James the Greater
Andrew		Jona	Matt. 4:18	Brother of Peter
Philip			John 1:43	Called by Christ
Bartholomew	Nathanael ? (Identification not certain)	Tolomai	John 1:45 John 21:2	(If Nathanael)—an "Israelite without guile"
Matthew	(Probably) Levi . . . . . . "The publican" (Matt. 10:3)	Alph(a)eus ?	Mark 2:14 Matt. 9:9	Tax-collector, Evangelist (?)
James[5] (Luke 6:16)	Otherwise unknown	Alph(a)eus	Mark 3:18	Probably NOT the brother of Jude
Thaddeus[6] (Mark 3:18)	Same as Jude, (son) of . . . ("Lebbaeus," Matt. 10:4)?	James ?	Luke 6:16 John 14:22	Not the brother of James (above)
Thomas	"Didymus" ("Twin")		John 20:24	
Simon	"Cananean" ("Zealot")		Luke 6:15 Matt. 10:4	
Judas		Simon	Matt. 10:4 John 13:26	From town of Kerioth?

[5] It is very unlikely that James, son of Alphaeus, is the same person as James the Less who was the leader of the Jerusalem Church and (probably) author of the epistle and cousin of Jesus.

[6] There were probably two Judes besides the Iscariot: *a)* one of the Twelve; and *b)* the brother of James of Jerusalem (and cousin of Jesus). It is not certain that Jude the Apostle is the same as Thadd(a)eus (Mark 3:18), since some good manuscripts of Matthew 10:4 give the name "Lebbaeus." Moreover, "Jude the brother of James" in Luke 6:16 and Acts 1:13 is an unlikely translation.

In Chapter 11 John the Baptist is revealed as the greatest prophet of the Old Testament. Many persons, following his advice, have been forcing their way into the New Kingdom. In fact, Jesus identifies John as the "Elias who was to come" (cf. Mal. 3:23 and Sir. 48:10) before the Day of the Lord, and demonstrates the inconsistency of the Jews in rejecting both John and Himself by means of a short parable. The passage ends by closing the inclusion with the term "works."[7] Chapter 14 tells of the death of the intrepid Baptist through the vile connivance of Herodias and her daughter, Salome.

Hardening of the Pharisaic Opposition: Sins Against the Holy Spirit (Matthew 12)

The two incidents at the beginning of Chapter 12 show to what extent the Pharisees had distorted the Mosaic observances by their "Tradition of the Ancients." Plucking a few ears of grain was construed as "harvesting," while Jesus' cure of the withered hand was considered to be exercising the office of a physician: neither activity, therefore, could be performed on the Sabbath. Christ restores the Sabbath to its proper function in verse 8. The cure moves St. Matthew to identify Him once more as the Servant of Yahweh in a lengthy quotation from Isaia 42. A new exorcism occasions the renewal of the Pharisaical charge that Jesus is in league with Satan. Christ refutes this blasphemous calumny by a dialectical argument in which He reaffirms the actual presence of the Kingdom of God in their midst (v. 28), and brands their behavior as one of the unforgivable sins against the Spirit of God. This category represents sins of malice (i.e., bad will): attributing the works of God to the power of Satan.[8] It is "unforgivable" in the sense that it is unlikely (but not impossible) that the sinner will ever have the proper disposition for pardon, since this would require a complete change of attitude on his part. Christ's parting shot (vv. 36–37) expands His condemnation of Pharisaical gossip into a general principle (see Confraternity Version footnote on these verses).

---

[7] The same Greek word, *erga*, is employed in both 11:2 and 11:19 to bind up the intervening material. The central idea is: Christ, the True Wisdom, is vindicated by His Works (cf. 7:19); they are acceptable to John, but not to "this generation." Corozain and Bethsaida are cursed for not accepting His works, while the "little ones" in 11:25 who do accept them are refreshed by Christ's revelation of His Father. In 11:19, *erga* is translated "children."

[8] St. Thomas expands the category of "sins against the Holy Spirit" to include six species: despair, presumption, resistance to the truth, envy of graces given to another, a determination to die impenitent, and obstinacy in vice (*Summa Theologica*, IIaIIae, Q. 14, Art. 2).

The principal sign-value of the reference to Jona (as Fr. Lagrange points out) is not the three days in the belly of the fish, but rather the preaching of penance (which is the point of Luke 11:29–32). The warning that follows serves as a fitting introduction to Chapter 13 (the parables of the Kingdom). Christ is telling His hearers that the present moment is a time of crisis demanding an all-important decision on their part. He, the New Solomon, is come with the True Wisdom capable of exorcising men's souls. Failure to heed His words will leave them prey to repossession by seven devils (i.e., much worse evils). Salvation will not be meted out according to any hereditary claims; in fact, not even his own mother and "brethren" (i.e., cousins) enjoy special privilege in God's Kingdom, for their only genuine claim to merit lies in their conformity to the will of God. In saying this, Jesus is setting forth the Virgin Mary's greatest title to glory. (See the breviary homily of St. John Chrysostom for the vigil of the Assumption.)

The Parables of the Kingdom (Third Discourse: Matthew 13:1–52) and Other Logia

One of the greatest impacts of modern form criticism has been made in a re-understanding of our Lord's parables. What we have in the Gospels is an application of these parables by the Christian community "to its own actual situation, characterized by the Gentile environment, the Gentile mission, and the delay of the Parousia; in terms of this situation the Church interpreted and expanded the parables."[9] Often those sayings which Christ addressed to His opponents or to the crowds in a concrete setting were generalized by an allegorical or hortatory elaboration. Sometimes this generalization was the result of collecting and fusing two similes, metaphors, or parables, and adding new settings to them. This is not in any way to diminish the notion of biblical inspiration; rather, it is simply a reaffirmation of the fact that the New Testament is not primarily a biography of Christ but the early Church's testimonial of faith in Him and His mission. Yet, in considering these vignettes of the Kingdom of Heaven

---

[9] Joachim Jeremias, *The Parables of Jesus* (London: SMC Press, 1954), p. 88. This is a digest of his "seven laws of transformation" of parables by the early Church. Cf. also pp. 9–19 and 159 (especially footnote 11 on p. 12), and C. H. Dodd, *The Parables of the Kingdom* (New York: Charles Scribners' Sons, 1961), Chap. 1. Matt. 13:11 is part of this psychology of re-interpretation in the light of later opposition to the Gospel, especially on the part of the Jews.

presented in Chapter 13, we should remember that it is the *gospel* meaning which is inspired, not the reconstructed "original" meaning provided by form criticism. This latter simply adds to our understanding of the gospel meaning. Moreover, current Semitic studies tend to disprove the basic principle of the man who initiated the de-allegorizing trend, Adolph Julicher. In a work published in 1888–89, this scholar maintained that the allegorical features of the parables *must* have been added by the later Church because they are too sophisticated for the Semitic style of Jesus' preaching. While it is true that a parable is a story which, *taken as a whole,* teaches a lesson, it was not beyond Semitic usage to insert allegorical features.[10]

An excellent example is the reinterpretation of the parable of the Sower and the Seed in verses 36–43. This interpretation adapts it for use as "an exhortation to converts" by concentrating attention on the importance of a good disposition on the part of those who hear the Word of God. Thus, the parable is enlarged to include allegorical features. Its original meaning is seen when we compare it with the parables of the Mustard Seed, the Leaven, and the Growing Seed (Mark 4:26–29): Christ is simply assuring His hearers that *the Kingdom of God is already present in their midst, and that it will continue to grow in stature until its eschatological fulfillment in spite of the difficulties it faces* (birds, rocky ground, scorching sun, and thorns). The mustard seed and the leaven point to ultimate triumph of the Kingdom (for Matthew, the Christian Church) in spite of an insignificant beginning, and Mark's parable of the hidden growth of the seed implies that its spread is a divine rather than a human accomplishment. The chart below is an attempt to synthesize what is valid in the form criticism of the parables and sayings of Jesus, together with the use which the primitive community made of them through the Synoptic Gospels. The reader will note that a parable from Matthew 13 is used to illustrate each general category suggested by the form critics. The last column also gives a few examples of variant Gospel interpretations of the same parable (see pp. 52 and 120–121).

---

[10] Fr. Raymond Brown's conclusion is apropos here: "The reapplication of this explanation in the Gospels to the situation of the primitive Church simply reflects the continued validity of Jesus' teaching in the minds of his followers. Their word (the gospel) was, after all, the extension of his word; therefore it encountered a similar fate. Such a rooting of the parable in Jesus' ministry and words is, we believe, far more plausible than the theory of spontaneous introduction of allegory by the Church" (*Novum Testamentum,* Vol. 5, Fasc. 1 [1962], "Parable and Allegory Reconsidered"). Cf. also his *The Parables of the Gospel* (Glenn Rock, N. J.: Paulist Press Doctrinal Pamphlet Series, 1963), 31 pp.

GENERAL CATEGORY	PARABLES, SAYINGS	REFER-ENCE	APPLIED MEANINGS
1–THE DIVINE AS-SURANCE: God's reign will eventually prevail !	a–THE MUSTARD SEED and THE LEAVEN	Matt. 13:31 } Matt. 13:33 {	To explain the meager re-sponse to Jesus' Galilean ministry?
	b–The Growing Seed	Mark 4:26	A divine work!
2–COST OF THE KINGDOM: —total dedication demanded of followers.	a–TREASURE AND PEARL	Matt. 13:44	Effort required to possess it!
	b–The Tower-Builder	Luke 14:28	Discipleship demands re-nunciation.
	c–The Wedding Garment	Matt. 22:11	The Kingdom DOES make demands.
3–CHALLENGE OF THE KINGDOM: —de-mands a personal deci-ion; (reflecting, perhaps, the delayed Parousia).	a–SOWER AND THE SEED	Matt. 13:3	Problems of primitive Church?[11]
	b–Rich Man and Lazarus	Luke 16:19	"You can't take it with you."
	c–Unjust Steward	Luke 16:1	Prudence; detachment from money
	d–Gold Pieces (cf. 6e)	Luke 19:11	Delay of Parousia (Arch-elaus?)
	e–The Good Samaritan	Luke 10:45	Concept of neighbor ex-tended.
4–NEWNESS OF THE KINGDOM: —in con-trast to Judaism	a–PRUDENT HOUSE-HOLDER	Matt. 13:52	(Matthew?) Suggests continuity.
	b–Wineskins and Patch	Matt. 9:16	Suggests eventual break.
	c–The Unscandalized	Matt. 11:6	Jesus is not the popular Messia.
5–INCLUSIVENESS OF THE KINGDOM: the divine mercy toward "outcasts" exceeds human standards.	a–WHEAT AND WEEDS	Matt. 13:24	Not a "society of the per-fect"
	b–Lost Sheep (and Coin)	Luke 15:1	Sinners (fallen-aways in Matt. 18)
	c–Prodigal Son	Luke 15:11	Wayward Jews
	d–Pharisee and Publican	Luke 18:9	Outcasts
	e–The Marriage Feast	Matt. 22:1	Gentiles (2c above is distinct)
	f–Laborers in Vineyard	Matt. 20:1	Transcendence of God's mercy
6–CRISIS OF THE KINGDOM: —God's reign, begun in Jesus' ministry, serves as a pre-liminary judgment on men's decisions (realized eschatology).	a–PROPHET AT HOME b–Children in Market	Matt. 13:57 } Matt. 11:16 {	Jaundiced eyes fail to recognize true messianic works (cf. p. 107, footnote 7.)
	c–On Settling Disputes	Luke 12:58	In Matt. 5:25 = forgive-ness[12]
	d–Evil Vinedressers	Matt. 21:33	Jewish leaders reprobated.
	e–Ten Virgins; Talents	Matt. 25	Imminence of judgment (cf. 3d)
	f–The Cursed Fig Tree	Matt. 21:18	A Prophecy-in-act (cf. Luke 13:6)
7–CLIMAX OF THE KINGDOM: —final judgment will come only at the end (unrealized eschatology).	a–THE NET	Matt. 13:47	
	b–Sheep and the Goats	Matt. 25:31	"Realized discipleship."
	c–Two Kinds of Servants	Matt. 24:45	Particular judgment?
	d–The Twelve Thrones	Matt. 19:28	Prophets of the New Age

[11] Verse 22 suggests a situation like the deception of Ananias and Saphira in Acts 5:1ff. (Cf. Stanley, *The Gospel of St. Matthew*, p. 71.)

[12] Matthew tends to soften Luke's eschatological orientation by turning Jesus' statements into moral exhortations applicable to the Christian community; but cf. 3d and 6e.

As a whole, the parables in Matthew 13 serve to announce to men that the Kingdom of God is a present reality on the earth through the ministry of Jesus. But it does not yet exist in its perfect state; this will come about only at the Parousia:

> With Jesus the reign of God has become present in an initial, provisional manner. With his Parousia it will be completely realized. In the meantime the faithful are in a situation similar to that of those who heard Jesus. They are summoned to a personal decision, to be made here and now in the whole religious and moral attitude. This explanation includes a reference to the early Church's pastoral methods, in which it employed the material of tradition for catechesis and preaching.[13]

Miracle of the Loaves and Fishes and Abrogation of the Dietary Laws
(Matthew 13:53–15)

Although such analyses as the one above are not, perhaps, definitive, they do show the existential orientation which Jesus gave to the Kingdom of God. St. Matthew was writing in the wake of organized Jewish persecution of the "Way" when it had become apparent that the Kingdom would have to be institutionalized in the form of a Church in order to survive and carry out its work of transforming citizens of the world into citizens of the Kingdom of Heaven. A type of this transformation of men is contained in the miracle of the loaves and fishes (14:13ff. and 15:32ff. may well represent one incident duplicated). Jesus' walking on the water and Peter's feeble attempt to imitate Him presage the promise of primacy in Matthew 16:18–19. And His statement in 15:11 will be interpreted by the Christian community as the abrogation of the kosher laws which had been so critical in Jewish worship. This declaration hardens the opposition of Christ's enemies; henceforth He will concentrate on the formation of His apostolic band. Even his own townspeople spurn Him (cf. Matt. 13:53–58). We see Him migrating into pagan territory in the cure of the Canaanite's daughter (15:21ff). Again faith evokes a miracle.

Psalm 144: The Kingdom of God and Compassion for the Lowly

This eschatological hymn extols the greatness of God and expresses confidence in His enduring kingdom: "Your kingdom is a kingdom for all ages, and your dominion endures through all generations" (v. 13). The second half of the poem *identifies the coming of God's king-*

---

[13] Rudolph Schnackenburg, *God's Rule and Kingdom* (New York: Herder and Herder, 1963), pp. 151–152. This whole section (pp. 143–159) contains penetrating insights on the parables. Note also the warning against too close an identification between Kingdom and Church which is quoted on p. 130 of this text.

dom with relief of the poor and the needy (vv. 14, 19). Similar thoughts are expressed in Psalm 145:7–10. Both psalms remind us of the Lord's Prayer.

Suggested Readings

Connick, *Jesus, the Man, the Mission and the Message,* Chap. 14.
Dodd, *The Parables of the Kingdom,* especially Chap. 1.
Dyson and Jones, *The Kingdom of Promise,* pp. 176–190.
Jeremias, *The Parables of Jesus,* Chap. 3 contains a summary. The works of Dodd
    and Jeremias are Protestant classics on the parables.
Stanley, *The Gospel of St. Matthew,* pp. 48–80.

For Further Study

1. What does Matthew understand by the term "Kingdom of God"? How is it to come?
2. What general characteristics of the Kingdom do the parables in Matthew 13 reveal?
3. How was sickness regarded by the contemporaries of Jesus? Were they wrong?

Chapter XIV

Matthew (IV): Fourth, Fifth Discourses: The Hierarchical and Universal Church

READINGS: *Matthew 16–25; Psalm 116. (Note: Matthew 16:16–28; 17:12, 20; 18:3, 6, 8, 15–18; 19: 11:12, 21; 22:21, 40, 44; 24:30–31; 25:34–35; Isaia 22:22; Zacharia 12:10—13:9.)*

Peter's Profession and the Promise of His Primacy in the Church

(Matthew 16:1–20)

Chapter 16 is the climax of St. Matthew's Gospel; here he shows the Kingdom's prophetic transformation from a synagogue into a hierarchical organism resting on Peter as its foundation-rock. The "leaven" of the Pharisees (whom Peter replaces and to whom Christ again denies a sign "from heaven": note pun on the weather) forces Jesus to take His disciples into retirement above Lake Huleh in Philip's territory.[1] The popular opinions which His question evokes regarding the messianic expectation shows that virtually the only point of general agreement was that the Messia would be a prophet (Deut. 18:15). Although the profession of Simon Bar-Jona was certainly an act of faith, it was probably not as profound as Matthew makes it. Comparing the latter's account with those of Mark and Luke, scholars suggest that St. Matthew has telescoped several developments into both Peter's and Christ's words:

1) Although "Son of God" in the Synoptics usually does imply merely adoptive sonship, the addition of the term "living" and Christ's laudatory acknowledgement contain overtones of divinity; yet, in 16:23, Peter's faith is shown to be still very imperfect since he still entertains the popular, "devilish" messianic view. It is more reasonable to take Mark and Luke as our guides here and to conclude that only belief in Christ's messiaship is being confessed.

---

[1] The mention of two multiplications of loaves may well be simply a "kind of cross-reference by Matthew to HIS two accounts of this mircale" (Stanley, *The Gospel of St. Matthew*, p. 80).

2) According to John 1:42, Simon's name was changed to Peter ("Cephas" in Aramaic) at his first calling. But Matthew strategically locates it in conjunction with a reference to his office as chief of apostles; this seems more logical.

3) Matthew's account of the primacy here is in the future tense: hence, a *promise*. Luke suggests its *fulfillment* at the Last Supper (22:32), while John puts it after the Resurrection (21:17). Thus, Matthew's composite picture seems to have joined Peter's post-Resurrectional faith to the promise of primacy.

The interrogation of the apostles, the change of name, the reference to the "keys of the kingdom" and "binding and loosing," and the impotence of the cosmic forces of evil against the Kingdom (to which a guarantee of Christ's abiding presence will be added in 28:20) all enhance the solemnity of the occasion.[2] Moreover, they suggest quite forcefully that the evangelist is reading back into the episode events which were actually later developments in the hierarchical structure of the Church. This "structure" will be documented in our Chapter XVII when we consider the Pastoral Epistles.

TOPIC	WIDESPREAD PROTESTANT VIEWPOINT	CATHOLIC VIEWPOINT
1. Petrine Primacy	Applicable to the historical Peter but not continued in the Church.	Handed down via succession of the Bishops of Rome.
2. The "Ekklesia" (Church)	A gathering of men joined by a spiritual "fellowship."	An organism animated by the Holy Spirit: Body of Christ.
3. Presence of Christ in the Eucharist	Commemorative; or at most, real but non-substantial ("consubstantiation").	Actual, real ("ontological").
4. Sacrifice	The Lord's Supper the commemoration of an unrepeatable event.	The Mass a renewal of Calvary (Heb. 10:14 *vs.* I. Cor. 10).
5. Sacraments	Basically signs and symbols, but possessing a certain dynamism.	Divine actions (though hidden under symbols).
6. Revelation	The written word of Scripture, self-manifesting.	Scripture as contained in the Church's memory (Tradition).
7. Justification	Justification still confused with salvation.	Genuine, ontological removal of sin from the soul.
8. Incarnation	The "act of God in Christ."	A substantial assumption of flesh via "hypostatic union."
9. Grace	The act of God in US.	Participation in God's life.
10. The Virgin Mary	The mother of Jesus.	"Theotokos": mother of God.

[2] Fr. Stanley sees here a basis for the doctrines of purgatory and indulgences.

At this point it is interesting to compare the Catholic interpretation of this passage in Matthew with that of contemporary Protestantism. In his penetrating analysis of Professor Oscar Cullmann's study,[3] Fr. Charles Journet provides the material for an extended comparison. Beginning with Prof. Cullmann's contention that, although "the saying in Matthew 16:17ff. is genuine," nevertheless "what is said of Peter as the Rock refers only to him, the historical apostle; he represents once for all the earthly foundation," Fr. Journet projects the analogy into other areas. What is contained in the chart on the previous page is my own adaptation and synthesis.[4]

The picture painted by this chart will be misleading without two qualifications: *a)* Protestant denominations vary widely in their beliefs, and no single schema can do justice to all of them; *b)* it is impossible in so brief a list to take into full account all modern trends in the various areas of theology cited above, especially in view of the fact that most Protestant groups have moved notably away from a number of the tenets of "classical Protestantism" (cf. Chap. XXVI).

The Cross, Road to Glory
(Matthew 16:21–17:26)

The three predictions of the passion and death occur in all of the Synoptics, but they fall on deaf ears. In each instance the topic serves as the occasion for laying down the conditions of discipleship: "For he who would save his life will lose it; but he who loses his life for my sake will find it. For what does it profit a man if he gain the whole world, but suffer the loss of his own soul?" (vv. 25–26). The "coming" of the Son of Man in 16:28 is a reference to the destruction of Jerusalem. Here is another case of realized eschatology: Matthew *may* have already witnessed this event.

The Transfiguration was an anticipation of the glorification which was to follow His death. For a few fleeting moments the three apostles are given a glimpse of His role as *Lord* in stark contrast to His normal role as *Servant*. The vision identifies Him as "Son of God" in the company of Moses and Elias (Law and Prophecy).[5] But this glorification is premature; the true hour of glory will be only after He has died on the Cross. Peter—dubbed "Satan" by Christ in 16:23—still doesn't understand: he wants to build three tabernacles to perpetuate the event! He and the others are not yet ready to face the ordeal of

---

[3] Oscar Cullmann, *Peter, Disciple, Apostle, Martyr: A Historical Study* (Philadelphia: The Westminster Press, 1953), 252 pp.

[4] Cf. Charles Journet, *The Primacy of Peter* (Westminster, Md.: Newman Press, 1954), especially pp. 1–49. The quotation in the previous sentence is from p. 5.

[5] For a recent insight on the delicate topic of Jesus and the Beatific Vision, see Jean Galot's article, "The Knowledge and Consciousness of Christ," *Theology Digest*, XII:1 (Spring 1964) 48–52, and the subsequent article by Karl Rahner.

the passion. Their need of self-denial and mortification rather than sensible consolation is illustrated by Christ's dictum in 17:20, "But this kind (of devil) can be cast out only by prayer and fasting." In other words, "Don't rely too heavily on your charismatic gifts—surely not at the expense of personal asceticism!" The final episode of Chapter 17 reveals yet another score on which the Jewish leaders were setting traps for Jesus: the payment of taxes for the support of divine worship.

The Children of the Kingdom
(Fourth Discourse: Matthew 18)

This chapter corresponds roughly to I Corinthians 13, as it expresses the Christian ideal in terms of charity in its various manifestations. The "greatest in the kingdom of heaven" is he who has recaptured the simplicity of his childhood.[6] This parable-in-action leads Christ into a solemn warning against the capital crime of giving scandal, especially to children. The seriousness of this sin against charity (and often prudence as well) is indicated by the severity of the "woe" attached. Occasions of sin must also be avoided under pain of guilt— though verses 8–9 are not to be taken literally.[7] The hyperbole used shows that Christ knew how easily human beings become over-optimistic in this regard. The parable of the Lost Sheep inserted here is a mercy parable. That one can sin by omission as well as commission is shown in the teaching on fraternal correction. Here it is not the correction of subjects by superiors which Christ has in mind, but rather the admonition of an equal. When we see one of the brethren sinning or about to sin against us, instead of retaliating or denouncing him we should try to reclaim him gently by 1) a private admonition; 2) the calling of witnesses to confront him with evidence in the event that he denies the crime; 3) referral to the authorities if there is no response; and 4) expulsion from the community if he remains obdurate. This procedure presupposes a hierarchy in the "Church" (the term is Matthew's contribution to the Gospel). Note in verse 18 that jurisdiction in the Church is also given to the other apostles as well as to Peter. This jurisdiction has been passed on to their successors in the college of bishops, but not their personal infallibility

---

[6] The keynote is a clear recognition of one's complete dependence on God—especially characteristic of the sick, the poor, women, and repentant sinners. Recall St. Paul: "charity . . . is not pretentious, is not puffed up, is not ambitious, is not self-seeking, is not provoked; thinks no evil . . ." (Cf. Caryll Houselander, *The Passion of the Infant Christ* [New York: Sheed and Ward, 1953], Chap. 6, for the virtues of childhood).

[7] The early Christian writer Origen was refused ordination by his bishop, Demetrius, for having mutilated himself in the cause of chastity; he was never canonized.

(which was a charismatic gift). Many Protestant churches reject this notion of the transfer of apostolic jurisdiction over local churches viewing such a transfer as detrimental to the whole Church.[8] The second mercy parable at the end of the chapter is probably not in its real-life situation since its main thought is not the *repeated* forgiveness clearly envisaged in the 70 x 7 of v. 22.

The Imminence of the Kingdom and Response to the Challenge
(Matthew 19–22; 25)

The pronouncement on divorce as a messianic development has been discussed on page 99 in connection with Matthew 5:32. Jesus here extends His remarks in counseling voluntary celibacy to "those to whom it has been given. . . . for the sake of the kingdom of heaven" (19:11–12). After a brief digression on the connaturality of children for the Kingdom of Heaven (supporting the propriety of infant baptim: "and do not hinder them"—v. 14), the appearance of a rich lad who is too attached to his wealth to pursue an apparent vocation to the apostolate turns the conversation to the topic of voluntary poverty. In the same breath in which He sets forth poverty as a counsel of perfection, Christ adds a statement which those in the religious life quote as the scriptural basis of the counsel of obedience, "and come, follow me" (v. 21). What follows is a diametric reversal of the pat Deuteronomic formula with which Job had struggled in the dark. The light finally dawns: "And everyone who has left house, or brothers, or sisters . . . for my name's sake, shall receive a hundredfold, and shall possess life everlasting" (v. 29). The Anawim have come into their own!

The theme changes in Chapter 20. The parable of the Laborers in the Vineyard is to be classed as a mercy parable featuring an employer who was willing to pay a full day's wages even to those who had worked only one hour. Like the parable of the Prodigal Son, this one too contains a rebuke for the critics. It is not *explicitly* "a call to God's Vineyard" (as its liturgical use on Septuagesima Sunday would indicate). And since the whole of verse 16 is apparently misplaced, its message as spoken by Jesus is neither *a)* that in the world to come there will be a reversal of fortunes, nor *b)* that the Gentiles will have priority over the Jews: both interpretations represent later inspired allegorizations.[9] Matthew inserts the third prediction of the passion at this point. In the dialogue which follows, John and James, driven

---

[8] In their view Christ sporadically becomes incarnate at particular times and places in the ranks zealous groups of men, who respond to His call through faith (cf. Journet, *Op. cit.,* Chap. 6).

[9] Cf. Jeremias, *Op. cit.,* pp. 23–27 and 108–111. But the application may well have been *implicit* in Jesus' words.

by their mother's consuming ambition, insist that they are prepared to drink of His "cup" (of suffering) in exchange for the first places in the Kingdom. The indignation of "the ten" over this episode gives Jesus an opportunity to reassert His role as Servant of Yahweh (20:28).

The messianic use of the title, "Son of David" in 20:29–34 together with the main historical events in the next two chapters have already been considered on pages 29 ff. All that remains is to treat of what is proper to St. Matthew—mostly his parables. The Cursed Fig Tree, the Evil Vine-dressers, and (in Chap. 25) the parables of the Ten Virgins and the Talents (since the hour of trading is past) are "crisis" lessons pertaining to category 6. The warnings beginning in 24:32 are in a similar vein. The parable of the Marriage Feast proper in 22:1–10, like that of the Two Sons in 21:28–32, is a mercy parable. Both have been allegorized—perhaps by Christ Himself—to apply to the replacement of the Jews by the Gentiles in the Kingdom. We have a "renunciation" parable (category 2: Cost of the Kingdom) in the Wedding Garment episode appended to the Marriage Feast (22:11–14). While these reconstructions add a certain freshness to the study of the parables, they by no means invalidate the traditional applications of them to later problems by the Church.

Denunciation of the Pharisees and Fifth Discourse: Destruction of Jerusalem
(Matthew 23, 24)

St. Matthew gives us a consolidated portrait of various excoriations leveled by Christ against the "Scribes and the Pharisees." Verses 4, 5 and 23 express the crux of the criticism and suggest that these religious leaders (whose authority Jesus nevertheless upholds—vv. 2–3) have formed false consciences. The prohibition against the use of such titles as "Rabbi," "father," and "master" must be taken in context—as the general custom of employing them widely in religious and academic circles would otherwise be reprehensible. It is little wonder that those to whom these denunciations were addressed were out to ruin Christ!

The reader has been already warned against applying the apocalyptic discourse of Jesus literally to the end of world. This whole chapter, and especially verses 30–31, should be compared with Zacharia 12:10–13:9. As Fr. Stanley affirms, the sign of the Son of Man "which causes the conversion of all nations . . . is the proclamation in the apostolic kerygma of Christ's redemptive death and resurrection by the Church."[10] He suggests that the assembled "elect" are none other than the Christian people. There is no doubt but that the destruction

---

[10] Stanley, *Op. cit.*, pp. 102–103.

of Jerusalem is a prototype of the Parousia. Nevertheless, the primary concern of St. Matthew according to his Gospel plan is to stress the emergence of Christianity from Judaism with the end of the Temple. In Chapter 25, however, there is a passage which *does* refer to the end of the world: the separation of the "sheep" from the "goats" at the general judgment (evidenced by the use of the term "king" in v. 34, usually reserved for the Father). In this parable of "realized discipleship" we perhaps can find the rudiments of the Pauline concept of the Body of Christ.

A Further Word on Form Criticism and the Development of the Gospel Traditions

In the light of what has been said regarding the application of the parables by the Christian community, the student is now in a better position to re-evaluate the work of form criticism as illustrated in the chart on the following two pages.[11] The chart is not intended as an exhaustive scientific analysis, but is rather an attempt to illustrate the rapid development of dogma which took place within the framework of the first century of Christianity. More than any other factor this development helps to explain the "discrepancies" in the books of the New Testament. Form criticism has enabled scholars to unravel for us the different "layers" which underlie the gospel tradition—much in the same way that other scholars have elaborated the four Mosaic traditions of the Old Testament (J, E, P, D).

The reader will note that four different "levels" of development are exemplified in the first, second, fourth and sixth columns of the chart. In general, an attempt has been made to carry a given "authentic" statement (or a parallel statement) across the page from left to right by using the same enumeration throughout. For a concrete example of how to use the chart, the reader should study the analysis of Matthew 16:16–19 on page .., then follow statement 14 in the chart across the page.

The following points should be kept in mind also:

1) Under the column "Johannine Tradition" are included quotations from the Apocalypse, Hebrews, and the Pastoral Epistles because these five books manifest an advanced theological tradition. There is no implication that John composed them all.

---

[11] The following books have been very helpful in the compilation of the chart.
Frank W. Beare, *The Earliest Records of Jesus: A Companion to the Synopsis of The First Three Gospels by Albert Huck* (Nashville, Tenn.: Abingdon Press, 1962), 254 pp.

Rudolf Bultmann and Karl Kundsin, *Form Criticism: Two Essays on New Testament Research* (New York: Harper Torchbook, 1962), 161 pp.

Milo C. Connick, *Jesus, the Man, the Mission and the Message* (Englewood Cliffs, N. J.: Prentice-Hall, 1963), 462 pp.

HYPOTHETICAL CONSTRUCT OF VARIOUS STAGES OF GOSPEL

I. HISTORICAL LEVEL:	II. LEVEL OF TRADITION:	
"AUTHENTIC" WORDS OF JESUS —c. 30 A.D.	APOSTOLIC PREACH- ING—C. 40 A.D.	OUTLINE OF CATECHESIS

A. DAWN OF THE MESSIANIC ERA:
1) Fulfilled in Christ, Son of David, as foretold by all of the prophets.

1. "The time is fulfilled, and the kingdom of God is at hand. Repent and believe in the gospel." (Mark 1:15)

Acts 2:16–17: But this is what was spoken through the prophet Joel: "I will pour forth my Spirit upon all flesh." (cf. 10:43; and 2:25–36: Christ vs. David)

B. THE PRECURSOR:
2) John the Baptist anointed and proclaimed Him to be the Messia.

2. "Go and report to John what you have heard and seen: the blind see, the lame walk . . . the poor have the gospel preached to them. And blessed is he who is not scandalized in me." (Matt. 11:4–6)

Acts 2:38: But Peter said to them, "Repent and be baptized . . . in the name of Jesus Christ for the forgiveness of your sins; and you will receive the gift of the Holy Spirit."

C. MINISTRY IN GALILEE:
3) Christ continued the ministry of John, preaching repentance,

3. "For even as Jonas was a sign to the Ninevites, so will also the Son of Man be to this generation . . . The men of Nineve repented at the preaching of Jonas." (Luke 11:30–32)

4. "And other seed fell among thorns; and the thorns grew up and choked it . . ." (Mark 5:7)

Acts 10:37–39: You know what took place throughout Judea; for he began in Galilee after the baptism preached by John: how God anointed Jesus of Nazareth with the Holy Spirit and with power, and he went about doing good and healing all who were in the

4) especially through parables, demanding

5. "If anyone wishes to come after me, let him deny himself, and take up his cross . . . he who would save his life will lose it . . ." (Mark 8:34–5)

5) complete detachment of His followers, with a special appeal

6. "Blessed are you poor, for yours is the kingdom of God . . . Blessed are you who hunger now . . ." (Luke 6:20–1)

6) to the Anawim. In support of His mission,

7. "And this woman . . . whom Satan has bound, lo, for 18 years, ought not she to be loosed from this bond on the Sabbath?" (Luke 13:16; cf. Mark 3:4f)

power of the devil; for God was with him. And we are witnesses of all that he did in the country of the Jews and in Jerusalem.

7) He worked miracles, curing the sick and casting out devils,

8. "But if I cast out devils by the finger of God, then the kingdom of God has come upon you." (Luke 11:20)

9. ". . . some . . . will not taste death, till they have seen the kingdom of God coming in power." (Mark 8:39)

(Luke 6:12: . . . He went out to the mountain to pray . . . and when day broke, he summoned his disciples; and from these he chose twelve [whom he also named apos-

8) illustrating by His deeds that the kingdom of God was being inaugurated on earth. Although present, 9) it was not yet established in full power.

10. "For whoever is ashamed of me . . . of him will the Son of Man also be ashamed when he comes . . ." (Mark 8:38)

11. "There is nothing outside a man that, entering into him, can defile him . . ." (Mark 7:15; cf. also 10:11)

tles] . . . and coming down with them, he took his stand on a level stretch, with a . . . great multitude

. . . Acts 10:34: But Peter began . . . "Now I really understand that God is not a respector of persons . . .")

10) It demands a total commitment from His followers.

11) His pronouncements on the Mosaic Law

12) alienated the religious leaders.

12. ". . . blasphemy against the Spirit will not be forgiven." (Matt. 12:31)

D. SELECTION OF APOSTLES:
13) He concentrated on training a group of followers who would preach first to Jews; Peter's faith won

13. "Do not go in the directions of the Gentiles . . . but . . . to the lost sheep of the house of Israel." (Matt. 10:5; cf. also 15:24)

Acts 10:39–41 (cont'd): . . . And yet they killed him, hanging him on a tree. But God raised him on the third day and caused him to be plainly seen . . . by witnesses . . . that is, by us . . .

14. "Who do men say that I am? . . . who do you say that I am?" (Peter: "Thou are the Christ." [Mark 8:27–30])

14) a promise of primacy.

E. DEATH AND RESURRECTION:
15) Faithful to His Servant-role, He nevertheless claimed messiaship in terms also suggesting divinity.

15. "I am. And you shall see the Son of Man sitting at the right hand of the Power." (Mark 14:62)

Acts 2:36: But God has made both Lord and Christ, this Jesus whom you crucified.

16. "But of that day or hour no one knows . . . nor the Son, but the Father only." (Mark 13:32; cf. 5:30, 6:5)

Acts 10:42: . . . he it is who has been appointed by God to be judge of the living and of the dead.

16) He had predicted the fall of Jerusalem, but His apocalyptic terminology

17. "And then he will send forth his angels, and will gather his elect from the four winds . . ." (Mark 13:27)

17) resulted in a confusion between the Kingdom's proclamation and its consummation.

TRADITION USING THE PRINCIPLES OF FORM CRITICISM

III. LEVEL OF THE WRITTEN GOSPELS:

THE SYNOPTIC GOSPELS— 56–80 A.D.	COMMENTARY	JOHANNINE TRADITION—C. 95 A.D.
1-2. ["The beginning of the Gospel of Jesus Christ, the Son of God. As it is written in Isaias the prophet, 'Behold, I send my messenger before thee, who shall prepare thy way, the voice of one crying in the desert, make ready the way of the Lord ...' "] (Mark 1:1; Ex. 23:20; Mal. 3:1; Isa. 40:3)	Note the shift in emphasis from the coming of the kingdom to the person of Jesus. The precursor becomes identified with specific prophecies: "Word," "Son of God" and "Lamb of God" all suggest a post-pentecostal awareness. Matthew's interpreta-	**1.** "In the beginning was the Word . . . and the Word was God." (John 1:1-2; cf. Apoc. 19:13) **2.** "And I have seen and borne witness that this is the Son of God . . . behold the Lamb of God." (John 1:34, 36)
3. "For even as Jonas was in the belly of the fish 3 days and 3 nights, so will the Son of Man be ..." (Matt. 12:40)	tion of this phrase foreshadows the Resurrection; John's rendering resembles Paul's "Body of Christ."	**3.** "Destroy this temple, and in 3 days I will raise it up." (John 2:19; Mark 14:58)
4. ". . . are they who listen to the word; but the cares of the world, and the deceitfulness of riches, and . . . desires about other things . . ." (Mark 4:18–19)	This detailed application seems to be a later catechesis aimed at fallen-away Christians. Hebrews is even more specific.	**4.** ". . . once enlightened and then fallen away"; "who has trodden under foot the Son of God . . ." (Heb. 6:4, 6; 10:29)
5. ". . . and you will be brought before governors and kings for my sake . . ." (Matt. 10:18)	The doctrine of the cross is extended to cover later persecution actually faced in the Church's apostolate. St. John manifests an advanced mysticism. Luke has in mind the actually poor while Matthew speaks of detachment. John looks to the eschatological fulfillment.	**5.** "Every branch that bears fruit he will cleanse, . . ." (John 15:2)
6. "Blessed are the poor in spirit . . . ; . . . they who hunger and thirst for justice . . ." (Matt. 5: 3,6)		**6.** "Now this is everlasting life, that they may know thee . . . and him whom thou hast sent . . ." (John 17:3)
7. "Do you think that these Galileans were worse sinners than all other Galileans . . .? I tell you, no." (Luke 13:2–3)	The distinction between disease and demons, misfortune and guilt, came gradually: Jesus' main conquest is of Satan!	**7.** "Neither has this man sinned, nor his parents . . ." (John 9:3)
8. "I was watching Satan fall as lightening . . ." (Luke 10:18)		**8.** ". . . because the prince of this world has already been judged." (John 16:11)
9. "And if he refuse to hear them, appeal to the Church . . ." (Matt. 18:17)	Matthew sees God's reign realized in the Church; the pastoral epistles betray an advanced ecclesiology.	**9.** ". . . I left thee in Crete (to) appoint presbyters in every city . . ." (Titus 1:5)
10. ". . . and no one knows the Son except the Father; nor does anyone know the Father . . ." (Matt. 11:27)	Matthew (in a rare synoptic passage) reflects a favorite Johannine theme.	**10.** "No one has . . . seen God. The only begotten Son . . . has revealed him." (John 1:18)
11. "Thus he declared all foods clean." (Mark 7:19) ". . . and if the wife puts away her husband, and marries another, she commits adultery." (10:12)	St. Mark gives two interpolations of the Master's principles for specific audiences. When St. John wrote, the controversy had come to an end.	**11.** "For the Law was given through Moses; grace and truth came through Jesus Christ." (John 1:17)
12. " . . . but whoever blasphemes against the Holy Spirit . . ." (Mark 3:29)	Some form critics maintain that "Holy Spirit" is of Hellenistic origin. John uses "Advocate."	**12.** "But the Advocate, the Holy Spirit, whom the Father will send in my name, he will teach . . ."(John 14:26)
13. ". . . make disciples of all nations, baptizing them in the name of the Father . . . Son . . . and Holy Spirit." (Matt. 28:19)	Matthew has attained universalism and given us a Trinitarian formula. John's Gospel had this perspective from the start.	**13.** "But to as many as received him, he gave the power of becoming sons of God." (John 1:12–13; 10:16)
14. "Thou art the Christ, the Son of the living God." (Matt. 16:16)	Matthew includes Peter's post-Resurrectional faith,	**14.** "Feed my sheep." (21: 17)
15. "The Son of Man has . . . come . . . to serve . . ." (Mark 10:45)	Mark stresses the "servant" theme. John explicitly teaches Jesus' pre-existence;	**15.** "Glorify me with thyself, with the glory that I had with thee before the world existed." (John 17:5)
16. ". . . no one knows, not even the angels of heaven, but the Father only." (Matt. 24:36)	Matthew omits "nor the Son"; John dampens the notion of a quick Parousia which the fall of Jerusalem put into clearer perspective, pointing to the new universe.	**16.** "But Jesus had not said, 'He is not to die.' " (John 21:23)
17. "Then the king will say to those on his right hand, 'Come, blessed of my Father, . . . for I was hungry . . .' " (Matt. 25: 34–35)		**17.** "And I saw a new heaven and a new earth." (Apoc. 21:1; cf. 21:22)

2) In designating certain statements of Christ as "authentic" we do not mean to imply by contrast that other sayings attributed to Him by the Evangelists are "unauthentic" in the sense that they are not reliable testimonies to His life and doctrine. Nor are the pericopae given in the chart by any means a complete enumeration of authentic statements; in fact, many sayings branded by the form critics as not coming from the lips of Christ may well have been said by Him.

3) It must always be kept in mind that it is the New Testament which is inspired, not the reportedly "authentic" statements distilled by the critics. If Jesus has permitted the sayings attributed to Him to be "edited" by the sacred authors—and He surely did do so— then we must recognize this edited version as the official message which He wishes to convey to us.

Psalm 116: The Call of the Gentiles

(Cf. Psalm 86)

This shortest psalm in the Psalter extends the invitation to praise Yahweh to the Gentiles! St. Paul interprets this in a universalist sense, viz., that salvation is for all men, Gentile as well as Jew (Rom. 15:11).

Suggested Readings

Journet, *The Primacy of Peter.*
Key and Young, *Understanding the New Testament,* p. 310.
Stanley, *The Gospel of St. Matthew,* pp. 80–106.
Stock, Augustine, O.S.B., *Kingdom of Heaven* (New York: Herder and Herder, 1964) traces the three gospel layers.

Suggestions for Further Discussion

1. Is there any Old Testament precedent for the symbol of the keys?
2. Where is Matthew 16:18 fulfilled?
3. By what logic does Christ mention Abel and Zacharias in the same breath in 23:35?

Chapter XV

Matthew (V) and Philippians: The Role of Judas and the Jews in Christ's Passion: Exaltation through Humiliation

READINGS: *Matthew 26–28; Philippians 1–4; Psalm 68; Anne Fremantle, ed., "Letter of St. Ignatius to the Romans," A Treasury of Early Christianity, pp. 38–40. (Note: Matthew 26: 28, 64; 27: 25; 28:18–20; Philippians 2:5–13; 3:10-11, 20–21.)*

St. Matthew's account of the Passion closely parallels that of St. Mark, already discussed on pp. 37ff. Our procedure shall be to isolate the texts proper to Matthew in the light of his over-all purpose of showing Christ as the New Moses who not only fulfills but transforms Jewish messianism. Matthew names Caiphas as the leader of the plotters against Christ; they are quite willing to resort to stealth to rid themselves of His embarrassing influence (26:4–5). Judas plays a central role in this Gospel, which links the betrayal decision to the waste of perfume at the Bethany anointing (vv. 7–15). Apparently his initial enthusiasm in the cause of Christ had been geared to a popular, political kingship; one by one the Master has dashed all of his hopes.[1] Matthew alone mentions the price of his treason: thirty pieces of silver. Mark and Matthew both report the terrible condemnation of the deed by its victim: "The Son of Man indeed goes his way, as it is written of him; but woe to that man by whom the Son of Man is betrayed! It were better for that man if he had not been born" (v. 24). Judas, unwittingly, is helping the Servant of Yahweh to fulfill his role (Matt. 20:28=Mark 10:45). All Evangelists except Luke mention the identification of the betrayer through the dipping of the bread. Matthew adds Jesus' direct acknowledgment to Judas: "Thou hast said it" (v. 25).

---

[1] In her intriguing play, "Royal Progress" in *The Man Born To Be King* (New York: Harper and Brothers, 1943), p. 195, Dorothy Sayers portrays Judas as conniving with the crafty high priest to make an eschatological Messia (i.e., martyr) out of Jesus.

Institution of the Eucharist
(Matthew 26:26–29; cf. Mark 14:22–25; Luke 22:19–20; I Corinthians 11)

Suddenly the whole tone of the Passover meal shifts as Jesus introduces an innovation: the consecration of the bread and wine. The formula used in the Mass may actually represent a prototype from which the texts listed above have been drawn. It most closely approximates the Matthaean account, which is the only one to record the words "unto the forgiveness of sins" (v. 28). This phrase relates Christ's death to Jeremia 31:34 where the remission of sins is included in the inauguration of the New Covenant. When will this take place? Verse 29 gives us the clue: "in the kingdom of my Father" (which usually designates the world to come, though Mark and Luke use the term "Kingdom of God"). Hence, Matthew emphatically connects the Last Supper with the eschatological period which it is ushering in; in other words, the Kingdom of God has come through this liturgical rite and the death it symbolizes. Moreover, it is clear that the separate consecration of the bread and wine have special symbolic significance: this meal becomes a prophecy-in-act of the bloody business of Calvary (see p. 37). Christ is symbolically shedding His own blood; He will have to fulfill this symbolism on the morrow or be guilty of a heinous sacrilege. What is often overlooked in the institution rite is the use of the imperative: "Take and eat"; that this is not merely an introduction, but the main clause, is better seen in the liturgical formula where the words of consecration constitute a subordinate clause: "FOR this is my body." Communion is the acceptance of the sacrifice by the communicant, his sharing in the victimhood of Christ. As Fr. Durrwell puts it,

> The communion of his disciples is the final end of our Saviour's offering; "Take and eat, this is my body (Matt., Mark) given for you" (Luke, I Cor.). The sacrificial offering of his body has been delivered up for them, let them take and eat it. . . . All this combines to identify the inauguration of the messianic banquet with the resurrection of our Lord, and to define his glory as a paschal meal, a communion of the Cross. . . . Having so wholly communicated himself, Christ is communicated by God to those who unite themselves with his sacrifice. . . . In all the writings of the various Apostles, the Redemption always appears as a divinization of man in Christ, by way of the death of all in man that is not yet God.[2]

That the apostles were not ready to exercise their roles as victims soon becomes evident. Christ's warning in the form of a quotation from Zacharia is taken lightly by them: Peter glibly seals his alle-

---

[2] Durrwell, *The Resurrection*, pp. 75–76.

giance with an oath in the face of Jesus' prediction of the three denials. They are even able to sleep during the agony in the garden, though Christ is "sad, even unto death" (v. 38)—for this is the "hour of the Son of Man" (v. 45). As Fr. Stanley points out, "Jesus' prayer is essentially the Pater which He had taught His disciples."[3] The latter are quite willing to take the sword (v. 51), but this is not the manner in which the Scriptures are to be fulfilled; otherwise Christ would have summoned His angels to crush the mob.

The End of Judas and the Rejection of Jesus
(Matthew 27)

The trial procedure in Matthew corresponds closely with that of Mark; each mentions a night session before Caiphas and a day session before the Sanhedrin. The words which sign the Victim's death warrant seem to go beyond messianism and to claim divinity: "Thou has said it. Nevertheless, I say to you, hereafter you shall see the Son of Man sitting at the right hand of the Power and coming upon the clouds of heaven" (v. 64). The condemnation finally pricks the conscience of Judas—but too late. Not even the return of the money can salve it sufficiently; like Achitophel, David's treacherous counselor who defected to the side of Absalom and committed suicide when his advice was rejected, Judas goes out and hangs himself (cf. II Kings 17:23). St. Matthew gives us what is probably the actual happenings; Luke in Acts 1 (strangely) allegorizes the story, making Judas the purchaser of the field and describing in conjunction with the hanging a weird bursting in the middle (hence *Haceldama*, "field of blood").

St. Matthew has Jesus admit His kingship before Pilate with the qualified phrase, "*Thou* sayest it" (27:11). Unique in this Gospel is the dream of Pilate's wife, which creates a fear in her husband's mind less in intensity than that inspired by the Jewish rabble. The official condemnation is accompanied and abetted by those awful, prophetic words: "His blood be upon us and upon our children" (v. 25). Judas and the handful of Jews present at the trial can hardly have represented the majority opinion of their contemporaries. Yet, as so often is the case in political affairs, a determined minority can make their voice prevail. Only Matthew records those words which spell the definitive rejection of the Gospel by the synagogue; his account has reached its crescendo. Sacred Scripture is amply fulfilled: there are quotations from Psalm 21 in verses 35 and 46, and allusions to Psalm 68 in verses 34 and 48. To emphasize the parting of the Church and the synagogue, he appends to the rending of the curtain of the Temple (representing "the new, free access to God's forgiveness in Christ")

---

[3] Stanley, *Op. cit.*, p. 111.

two apocalyptic details: the earthquake and the rising of the bodies of the saints (verses 51–52—"the inauguration of the glorious resurrection of the just"; cf. Heb. 10:19–22).[4] The posting of the guards who later have to be bribed to say that the missing body was stolen in 28:15 (details proper to Matthew) is the climactic resistance to the very truth which could have brought salvation: the Resurrection.

The Resurrection: Emmanuel Is Forever
(Matthew 28)

Another earthquake and an angel announce the joyful (though unexpected) event on the following Sunday. The rendezvous with the eleven apostles is in Galilee (Mount of Beatitudes?) in keeping with Matthaean lines. The final instruction reflects Greek Matthew's universalist theme and ends with a baptismal formula combining all three Persons of the Trinity. The apostles are the prophets of the new age, extending the work of Emmanuel in time and space "unto the consummation of the world."

The Epistle to the Philippians: Exaltation Through Humiliation
(Cf. Philippians 2:5–11)

This is St. Paul's "Epistle of Joy," containing no controversies and only mild pleadings for unity (1:27) and against false teachers (3: 2–3). These latter are the "Judaizers" ("dogs") who desire to "mutilate" (circumcise) Gentile converts to Christianity. This warning, together with the mention of bishops and deacons in the very first verse of the epistle show that it is one of his later letters. We have already suggested that it may have been written not during his Roman captivity, but from Ephesus about the year 56 A.D.[5] The recipients were his beloved converts at Philippi to whom he is writing to thank them for money they had sent him (2:25). St. Paul has few complaints against these Christians; they are "obedient . . . not in my presence only, but now much more in my absence; work out your salvation with fear and trembling. For it is God who of his good pleasure works in you both the will and the performance" (2:12–13). Here is a corollary of Paul's teaching on predestination.

We find a strange mixture of joy and seriousness, with the Pauline concept of life-through-death reaching its most intense expression. The famous liturgical hymn to Christ in 2:6–11 was reproduced in

---

[4] Stanley, *Ibid.*, p. 117.

[5] See Sullivan, *St. Paul's Epistle to the Philippians*, p. 9.

Chapter II, extolling Christ's glorification as a result of His ungodly humiliation and death. The saint shows in almost every other paragraph that this cycle must take place also in Christ's members:

> . . . not only to believe in him but also to suffer for him, while engaged in the same struggle in which you have seen me and now have heard of me (1:29–30). . . . For his sake I have suffered the loss of all things, and I count them as dung that I may gain Christ (3:8). . . . so that I may know him and the power of his resurrection and the fellowship of his sufferings: become like him in death, in the hope that somehow I may attain to the resurrection from the dead (3:10–11).

Urging his readers to "rejoice in the Lord always; again I say, rejoice" (4:4), the saint concludes the short letter on a note of unconquerable confidence: "I can do all things in him who strengthens me" (4:14). Paul has attained to the vicarious existence which he constantly preaches to others; we shall resume this theme in the next chapter.

Psalm 68: A Messianic Psalm of Lament

Few psalms are quoted so often by the Evangelists during the Passion story as this cry of anguish which includes also petition, imprecation, and confidence in God. Verse 5 is quoted in John 15:25; verse 10 in John 2:17; as we have just seen, verse 22 is alluded to in Matthew 27:34 and 48; verse 26 is applied to Judas in Acts 1:20. As in Psalm 21, the sufferer is probably the Psalmist himself who serves as a type of Jesus.

Suggested Readings

Adam, Karl, "Reason and the Resurrection" (in Heaney, *Faith, Reason, and the Gospels,* Chap. 8.)
Durrwell, *The Resurrection,* pp. 61–77.
Monro, *Enjoying the New Testament,* pp. 186–187 (lists texts proper to Matthew) and 127–130 (Philippians).
Stanley, *The Gospel of St. Matthew,* pp. 106–124.
Sullivan, *St. Paul's Epistles to the Philippians,* pp. 7–26.

For Further Study

Read the excerpt from St. Ignatius' "Letter to the Romans" in Fremantle, *A Treasury of Early Christianity* (New York: New American Library, MT285, 1960), for a well-known exemplification of "dying with Christ."

Chapter XVI

Colossians and Ephesians: The Vicarious Existence of the Members of Christ's Body

READINGS: *Colossians 1–4; Ephesians 1–5; II Corinthians 13; Psalms 3–4. Fremantle, A Treasury of Early Christianity, pp. 163–169 and 192–194. (Note: Colossians 1:13–29; 2:18–19; 3:1–4, 14; Ephesians 2:1–10, 22; 4:3–6; 5:14, 25–26.)*

In these two letters of St. Paul we see the flowering of the saint's theology of the Mystical Body, the product of his maturity. The ten brief chapters of these epistles are literally packed with profound insights into the heart of the Christian life, and are obviously the fruit of an advanced mysticism. Their common theme is best summarized by the oft-repeated Pauline phrase, "Life in Christ." Both letters must have been written during the latter part of St. Paul's Roman imprisonment, i.e., about 63 A.D.

Modern biblical scholarship sees in Colossians a polemic against a pre-Gnostic sect in Asia Minor which worshipped the angels, both good and bad. The devotees of this cult which was popular in certain Jewish circles were attempting to induce Gentile converts to Christianity to join them in their homage ("self-abasement") designed to placate those spirits and "the elements of this world," i.e., the cosmic forces of nature, particularly the heavenly bodies.[1] The saint's refutation is that all of these beings are under the headship of Christ, hence He should be the object of our worship rather than they. This line of thought leads him into a summary of the doctrine of the Church as the Body of Christ.

The Epistle to the Ephesians contains a parallel exposition, though without polemics; it rather stresses the unity of Christ's Body through charity. The more common opinion of scholars is that this epistle was

---

[1] In referring to this cult, St. Paul in Colossians 2:8 pejoratively calls it *phillosophy,* the only appearance of this term in the Bible. Watch Confraternity footnotes here.

actually a circular letter intended not for the Ephesians (who were well-known to Paul), but for some of the neighboring churches—including Laodicea and Hierapolis. It may even represent a redaction of Colossians by a disciple of St. Paul.[2] The similarity between the two letters is so close that we shall simply use Ephesians to corroborate Colossians.

The Headships of Christ

The Epistle to the Colossians contains two important Christological passages: 1:15–20 and 2:9–15. After noting that Christ "has rescued us from the power of darkness and transferred us into the kingdom of his beloved Son," St. Paul begins the first of these passages with a remarkable statement of the Son's eternal generation from the Father, calling Him the "image of the invisible God" (cf. Wisd. 7:26 and John 1:3). Then follows a declaration of His headship over *all* things, including the angels: Thrones, Dominations, Principalities and Powers—in obvious opposition to the Gnostics.

At this point the saint returns to his favorite topic, the Church: "Again, he is the head of his Body, the Church. . . ." (v. 18). The emphatic connective used here indicates that Paul sees the Church as an entity distinct from the angelic bands, a separate "organization," if you will, so that while Christ is head of both angels and the Church, He heads them through different relationships. The passage ends with a sublime summation of the continuity of all creation, picturing Christ as predestined to "reconcile to himself all things, whether on the earth or in the heavens, making peace through the blood of his cross." This notion of the corporate existence of the Church in Christ is reiterated in verses 22–23 where the saint notes that it is possible to "withdraw" from the unity of the Body through heresy (in this case, the false philosophy referred to above). In 2:19 he goes so far as to declare: "Such a one (heretic) is not united to the head." The criterion of orthodoxy for this universal gospel ("preached to every creature under heaven"—1:23) is the ministry of the hierarchical representative; in this case, "Paul, an apostle of Jesus Christ by the will of God. . . ." (1:1)

Ephesians clarifies the conditions of Christian fellowship. After stating even more explicitly the corporateness of Christians in the flesh of Christ (2:1–10), this epistle spells out the prerequisites of unity: "You are built upon the foundation of the apostles and

---

[2] Cf. Wikenhauser, *New Testament Introduction*, p. 426; also comparative chart showing matching passages in Sullivan, *St. Paul's Epistle to the Philippians, Ephesians, Colossians, Philemon*, p. 49.

prophets with Jesus Christ himself as the chief cornerstone" (2:20). Later in the epistle he states further,

> . . . one body and one Spirit, even as you were called in one hope of your calling; one Lord, one faith, one Baptism; one God and Father of all who is above all, and throughout all, and in us all.[3]

The Kingdom of God, the Church, and the People of God

Although in following St. Matthew's lead we have tended to interchange the terms "Kingdom of God" and "Church," we must beware of seeing a perfect identity between the two realities they represent. The word "kingdom" does not do justice to the Greek term from which it is translated, viz., *basileia.* "Gods rule" is a much better rendering of its true sense, and His reign will prevail over the earth only at the Parousia. Hence, the *kingdom* is, strictly speaking, an eschatological reality. Just as the newly baptized Christian does not at once wholly conquer the flesh and live exclusively in the Spirit, neither does the earthly community of Jesus perfectly mirror the will of His Father. To borrow the words of a recent publication,

> The main significance of the community of Jesus consists in its orientation towards the future kingdom; it is one day to become God's community of the perfect basileia but only after the test and discrimination of Judgment. The Ecclesia is the community of those who look for the kingdom of God, the 'threshold of the basileia, because its members have the promise that, if they persevere to the end (Matt. 13:18) they will have a share in God's reign.' The forces of God's reign are active in Jesus' community.[4]

Pointing out that the great work of the community is to "fight against the powers of evil," the author goes on to say,

> "Membership in this eschatological community . . . does not in itself guarantee acceptance into the future kingdom. Its members must persevere in loyal observance of God's will . . . The

---

[3] This text was cited by Pope Pius XII in his Encyclical *Mystici Corporis* in pointing out the traditional "Triple Bond" of membership: *1)* Baptism (of water); *2)* profession of the true faith; and *3)* submission to the authority of the Church. However, these three conditions are ordered to the possession of charity "which is the bond of perfection" (Col. 3:14), so that *active* membership is had only by those in the state of sanctifying grace. Today, in the wake of both biblical and ecumenical revivals, scholars are stressing the role of charity more and more in discussions of Church membership. The magnificent encyclical of Pius XII just alluded to must be complemented by further investigations, particularly scriptural. Fr. Gregory Baum summarized the leading positions in this theological area in *The Ecumenist*, I:4 (April-May 1963), 49–50. I am personally indebted to Fr. Charles Davis' book, *Theology for Today* (New York: Sheed and Ward, 1963), Chapter 5, for helping me to re-think the position I took in expressing my views in *The Thomist*, XXII:1 (Jan. 1959), pp. 1–24.

[4] Schnackenburg, *God's Rule and Kingdom*, pp. 230–231.

Ecclesia is the assembly ground of the elect who still have to endure their earthly combats . . . she was called into being to receive the elect and to conduct them to the kingdom of glory."[5]

True members of the *basileia*, then, have not only the personal obligation of living up to its moral code, but also the ecclesiastical obligation of working for extension of God's rule. To put it another way, to attain salvation, they must share not only passively but actively as well in Christ's redeeming work: in addition to being saved, they must also be savers.

The Christian Mystery: God's Plan of Salvation for Mankind

Recalling St. Paul's teaching on the Christian solution to the nature of true wisdom in I Corinthians, the reader should note a return to this concept under the title of "mystery":

> For I am to preach the word of God fully—the mystery which has been hidden for ages and generations, but now is clearly shown to his saints. To them God willed to make known how rich in glory is this mystery among the Gentiles—Christ in you, your hope of glory! Him we preach, admonishing every man in all wisdom, that we may present every man perfect in Christ Jesus. (Col. 1:26–28; cf. also Eph. 1:9–10 and 3:9–11; Rom. 16:25–26)

The two salient phrases are "mystery" and "Christ in you." We defined mystery on page 63 as "God's plan of salvation revealed in Christ." Christ revealed this plan in His Passion-death-Resurrection cycle. The phrase "Christ in you"—repeated over and over again in St. Pauls epistles—declares that somehow the life of Christ must permeate His members, the Church: here lies *the* mystery.

A Benedictine monk, Dom Odo Casel (1886–1948) has made a substantial contribution to the understanding of this problem by his theory of mystery-presence in the liturgy. Though the source of much controversy during his life and after his death, his central conclusion continues to have a remarkable impact on contemporary sacramental theology. He makes a comparison between the Greco-Roman mystery rites and the Christian sacrifice, to which he relates the former as "types" in a broad sense.[6]

---

[5] Schnackenburg, *Op. Cit.* pp. 231–234.

[6] Fr. R. E. Brown's Old Testament studies, especially in conjunction with the Qumran Scrolls, have convinced him "that the similarity in word and idea between the New Testament use of *mysterion* and the Semitic background we have presented is far more valid than any of the far-fetched parallels to the Greek mystery religions hitherto presented." ("The Pre-Christian Semitic Concept of 'Mystery'" in the *Catholic Biblical Quarterly*, XX:4 [Oct. 1958], 443). We agree with this conclusion insofar as "parallels" would imply any *dependence* of the New Testament notion on the Greek mysteries. Fr. Jungmann rejects the thought of

131

The Kyrios of a mystery is a God who has entered into human misery and struggle, has made his appearance on earth (epiphany) and fought here, suffered, even been defeated; the whole sorrow of mankind in pain is brought together in a mourning for the god who must die. But then in some way comes a return to life through which the God's companions, indeed the whole of nature, revives and lives on. This was the way of pious faith and sacred teaching, of society in the earliest mythical age. But the world, society, is always in need of life; so the epiphany goes on and on in worship; the saving, healing act of God is performed over and over. Worship is the means of making it real once more, and thus of breaking through to the spring of salvation. The members of the cult present again in a ritual, symbolic fashion, that primeval act; in holy words and rites of priest and faithful the reality is there once more. The celebrant community is united in the deepest fashion with the Lord they worship; there is no deeper oneness than suffering and action shared. Thereby they win a share in the new life of God; they enter his chorus, they become gods. The mysteries' way is, therefore, the way of ritual action as a sharing in the gods' acts; its aim is *union with godhead, share in his life.* We can, then, give a brief definition:

The mystery is a sacred ritual action in which a saving deed is made present through the rite; the congregation, by performing the rite, takes part in the saving act, and thereby win salvation.[7]

In response to Fr. Casel's contention that Christianity is a reproduction (by way of analogy with, *but not of dependence on,* the pagan mysteries) of the actions of Christ in His members, the objection has been raised, "How can a past action become present in any real, historical sense?" As Fr. Charles Davis[8] points out the answer is contained in the *Summa Theologica* of St. Thomas, who shows how God as principal cause is not limited to time or place in His actions—although the historical event which He uses as an instrument may *by itself* be so limited:

Christ's saving act becoming actually present, in favor of Gottlieb Söhngen's explanation of Casel: ". . . the Redemption becomes present in so far as an image of the Redemption is created in those participating in the sacraments or in the Mass . . . the symbol produced in the participant, is not the redemptive act itself but its effect, namely, grace; but here grace is viewed as an effect not only in the line of efficient causality but also in the line of exemplary causality." (Josef Jungmann, *The Early Liturgy,* [Notre Dame, Ind.: University of Notre Dame Press, 1959], p. 162. Louis Bouyer gives a fine analysis in *Liturgical Piety* [Notre Dame, Ind.: University of Notre Dame Press, 1954], Chap. 7–8.)

[7] Dom Odo Casel, *The Mystery of Christian Worship* (Westminster, Md.: Newman Press, 1962), pp. 53–54. See also the article by Burkhard Neunheuser, "Mystery Presence," *Worship,* XXXIV:3 (Feb. 1960), 120–127.

[8] Charles Davis, *Liturgy and Doctrine* (New York: Sheed and Ward, 1960) pp. 86–88.

Now the principal efficient cause of man's salvation is God. But since Christ's humanity is the instrument of the Godhead, as stated above (Q. 43, a. 2), therefore all Christ's actions and sufferings operate instrumentally in virtue of His Godhead for the salvation of men. Consequently, then, Christ's *Passion* accomplishes man's salvation *efficiently* (IIIa, Q. 48, a. 6) . . . Christ's *Resurrection* is the efficient cause of ours, through the Divine power whose office it is to quicken the dead; and this power by its presence is in touch with all places and times; and such virtual contact suffices for its efficiency (IIIa, Q. 56, a. 1 ad 1).

St. Paul seems to be saying the same thing in many texts; for example,

Therefore, if you have risen with Christ, seek the things that are above, where Christ is seated at the right hand of God . . . For you have died and your life is hidden with Christ in God. When Christ, your life, shall appear, then you too will appear with him in glory. (Col. 3:1–4; cf. Eph. 2:4–6)

What we must remember in all of this is the fact that the sacraments have their own unique mode of operation which, while making use of the historical events of Christ's life in their full reality, transcends their limitations of time, place, quantity, etc. As St. Leo the Great put it, "What was visible in our Redeemer passed over into the sacraments." Simply stated, the Pauline concept of the Christian mystery is that of the vicarious existence of the Christ-life in each of the members of His Body, the Church—"the kingdom of the Son." Born into this life-stream through Baptism, fed by the vital blood-transfusion of the Eucharist, the individual members of this Body are further integrated with each other by the animating power of the Holy Spirit, the Soul of the Body. St. Paul can say without the slightest allegorization, "what is lacking of the sufferings of Christ I fill up in *my* flesh for His Body, which is the Church" (Col. 1:24). In a mysterious but real manner, Christians are destined to be other Christs so genuinely that their sufferings are imputable to their Head.[9]

Corollary: Your Lives Must Conform to the Mystery

Both Colossians and Ephesians end with moral exhortations which correspond rather closely: *1)* a catalogue of vices to be renounced; *2)* special emphasis on charity ("Be angry and do not sin"—Eph. 4:26, from Ps. 4:5); *3)* an outline of domestic virtues to be cultivated by husband and wife: Ephesians 5:23ff. contains the Pauline analogy of marriage with the union between Christ and His Church, "a great mystery," whose destiny is to "be holy and without blemish"; and

---

[9] Cf. *Mediator Dei* of Pius XII (1947), paragraphs 29 and 102.

4) an exhortation to slaves to obey their masters, and to slave owners to be considerate to their charges. Slavery is taken for granted, though its eventual demise is hinted at in Ephesians 6:9. This chapter and theme will be treated later. The liturgical hymn in Ephesians 5:14 will be discussed in the next chapter.

Psalms 3 and 4: Morning and Evening Prayers of Confidence

According to Jewish tradition these two psalms were composed by David after he had fled from Absalom. The rebellion reached such a pitch that a messenger reported to the King, "All Israel with their whole heart followeth Absalom" (II Kgs. 15:13). Yet even in the face of calamity David's unwavering trust in Yahweh rises above the pessimism of his associates; he is able to sleep in confidence and awaken refreshed (Ps. 3:6). Psalm 5 is another morning prayer; it is a Psalm of Lament (as are also Pss. 6–7).

Psalm 4 is also a Psalm of Confidence, similar in structure to Psalm 3. Whereas the latter is a morning prayer, this poem is an evening prayer expressing the Psalmist's trust in Yahweh as he lies down to sleep (v. 9). The Confraternity Version footnote on the phrase, "Tremble, and sin not" would suggest that St. Paul is using an accommodated sense in Ephesians 4:26.

Suggested Readings

Davis, *Theology for Today,* Chap. 5.
————, *Liturgy and Doctrine,* Chap. 5.
Journet, Charles, "Who Are Members of the Church?" *Theology Digest,* X:4 (Autumn 1962), 179–183. Fr. Journet holds for degrees of membership.
Jungmann, *The Early Liturgy,* Chap. 12.
Klein, Laurentius, O.S.B., "Who Does Belong to the Church?" *Worship* (Mar. 1963), 210.
Monro, *Enjoying the New Testament,* pp. 121–126 (Colossians) and 131–136 (Ephesians).
Sullivan, *St. Paul's Epistles to the Philippians, Ephesians, Colossians, Philemon* (New Testament Reading Guide, No. 9), pp. 31–74.

For Further Study

1. To what extent was the concept of vicarious existence captured by the early martyrs? Read first the assignment in Fremantle on St. Polycarp, pp. 163–169, for an objective, well-balanced picture; then read from the middle of p. 192 to the birth of St. Felicity's child on p. 194 for an imaginative account with visions, in the martyr-legend genre described by Fr. H. Musurillo, S.J., in *Symbolism and the Christian Imagination* (Baltimore, Md.: Helicon Press, 1962), Chap. 4.
2. To supplement the mystery-presence theory as a penetrating insight into the essence of Christianity, read: Louis Bouyer, *The Paschal Mystery* (Chicago, Ill.: Henry Regnery Co., 1950), Introduction; and Houselander, *The Passion of the Infant Christ* (New York: Sheed and Ward, 1953), pp. 10–16; 91–98; 120; 127–128.

Chapter XVII

The Pastoral Epistles: The Hierarchy, Visible Bond of Unity

READINGS: *I–II Timothy; Titus; II Corinthians 7–9; Hymns: I Timothy 3:16, II Timothy 2:11–13, Ephesians 5:14, I Peter 3:18, 19, 22. Fremantle, A Treasury of Early Christianity, pp. 27–37. (Note: I Timothy 1:20; 2:4; 3 (all); 4:3–4, 14; II Timothy 3:16–17; 4:1–3; Titus 1:5).*

The Pastoral Epistles

This eighteenth-century term adequately describes the contents of these three epistles of St. Paul's last years on earth. They are largely concerned with the duties of a bishop and his household, and provide precious insights into the development of the hierarchy. Timothy was a native of Lystra and was converted to Christianity from Judaism: hence St. Paul circumcised him before taking him on his second missionary journey (Acts 16:1–3). After accompanying Paul on practically all of his travels, Timothy ended his days as Bishop of Ephesus. I Timothy was written c. 64–65 A.D.; II Timothy was perhaps the last letter from the hand of Paul, about 66–67 (cf. II Tim. 4:6–8). Titus, a Gentile convert of St. Paul, was not circumcised (Gal. 2:3). After undertaking a number of missions under the direction of his master, Titus governed the church at Crete until his death. The Epistle addressed to him was written c. 65 A.D.[1]

Besides containing instruction on the duties of the hierarchy, the Pastorals are quite outspoken in rebuking false teachers. The careful reader will note the *great emphasis on sound doctrine* in these letters. The occasion was the "gnosticizing Judaizers" of Asia Minor—converts to Christianity who were infected with a dualism characteristic of later Manichaeism (I Tim. 4:3) which taught that matter and all that is connected with it are evil. Their tenets included mythological

---

[1] However there is a strong and growing current of Catholic scholarship which holds these letters as "deutero-Pauline," i.e., as documents written after the saint's death by his disciple(s) but expressing his mind.

explanations of the Old Testament genealogies, etc. (I Tim. 1:3–4).[2] Our main interest in the epistles is the picture it furnishes of the visible aspects of the Church.

The Visible Structure of the Body of Christ

In the previous chapter we delineated the Christian Mystery in terms of sharing in the life of Christ. To say this another way, charity is the soul of the Church. But a soul demands a body—otherwise we would call it a spirit; and the Church is no exception. Its body or visible aspect includes, in addition to its members, dogmas to be believed and a teaching authority to impart them. The introduction to the Epistle to Titus expresses these two elements quite clearly (cf. also I Cor. 8:5–7 and 15:1–4). Failure to accept the body of proposed truths destroys the unity of the Church and provides grounds for excommunication (I Tim. 1:20; "delivered up to Satan" is Paul's equivalent). Adherence to a moral code is likewise necessary for good standing in the community (I Tim. 6:11–21).

One of the few passages testifying to the inspiration of Scripture is found in II Timothy 3:16–17.[3] But note well that St. Paul does not rest the authority of the Church's teaching on Scripture; the verses immediately following (4:1–5) relate sound doctrine to the episcopal preaching and ministry. Thus, St. Paul had admonished Timothy "to stir up the grace of God which is in thee by the laying on of my hands" (1:6–7)—the episcopal consecration. To insure the success of his ministry, the apostle lays down an ethical code for bishops in I Timothy 3:1–7, and for deacons in the following verses. Clerical celibacy became a law in the West only much later; nevertheless, a man who has been twice married (even legitimately after the death of his first wife) is not to be considered an episcopal candidate. The requirements for deacons (and deaconesses?) are almost as rigid. This office probably had not developed much beyond the role of almoner and catechist at this early date.

In Titus 1:5 we read, "appoint presbyters in every city," followed by the mention of "bishop" in verse 7. The exact relationship between these two offices has been the subject of much conjecture among Church historians. Philip Hughes gives quite a plausible explanation:

> . . . the *presbyteros* was a man to whom was given a title of honor for special service, a distinction which of itself carried with it no power or authority. From among the *presbyteroi* the *episcopoi*—whose duty it was, under the Apostle, to rule, to teach—

---

[2] See Wikenhauser, *New Testament Introduction*, pp. 451–452; also Key and Young, *Understanding the New Testament*, p. 114.

[3] This would not include all of the seventy-three books of the Bible, but only those New Testament books which had been composed at the time of his letter, plus the Old Testament.

were naturally elected. Whence the fact that not all *presbyteroi* were also *episcopoi*. Later the *presbyteroi* who are not also *episcopoi* disappear. The name, however, survives and is henceforward used for the subordinate officials of the new system, successors in part of the old episcopoi, but successors with very restricted powers and with no authority independent of the bishop —as we may now call him.[4]

The apostles themselves possessed both the fullness of *orders* (episcopacy) and *universal jurisdiction* (power to govern the faithful everywhere). During the first century, the apostles and their immediate successors tended to exercise an *itinerant* ministry; St. James in Jerusalem was the exception. But after the death of St. John, *resident* bishops with a vaguely delineated territory became the rule. The "priest" is still an undeveloped notion; the "parish priest" did not emerge until the eleventh century! With the aid of Fr. A. M. Henry, O. P., we offer the following summary.[5]

Differentiation of the Hierarchy

In the beginning, the all-important office was that of *bishop*, possessed by each of the apostles: he WAS the Church as representative of Christ. The main efforts at evangelization were in the cities; only in the fourth century did missionary labors extend into the country districts. The bishop surrounded himself with a group of "presbyters" (elders); these were usually ordained ministers whose duties consisted of praying with the bishop, helping him in conducting public worship—especially by concelebration of the Mass; preparing converts for Baptism, and aiding in the reconciliation of penitents. They did not preach or celebrate Mass alone; they listened to the bishop's sermons along with the faithful. The deacons seem to have been more important than these "priests": they were sent out to minister to the poor, and from their ranks the popes were chosen.

In the East the institution of *chorepiscopi* grew up: they were episcopal envoys who manned outlying churches in the name of the bishop; they had been consecrated. With the Roman persecutions in the West, it became necessary to send out priests to celebrate Mass and thus to bring the Eucharist to those in prison. However, the celebrating priest always carried with him a consecrated particle[6] from the Host of the bishop's Mass which he put in his own chalice—a beautiful testimony to the recognition of the Eucharist as the bond of

---

[4] *A History of the Church,* Vol. I (New York: Sheed and Ward, 1949), p. 51. Cf. I Timothy, 5:17–25.

[5] Abbé Michonneau, *My Father's Business* (New York: Herder and Herder, 1959), Chap. 2.

[6] Known as the "fermentum."

unity. As priests more and more were called upon to minister to the *pagani*, i.e., people of the rural areas, they would form themselves into quasi-monastic groups in imitation of the Benedictine monks. The choral recitation of the divine office became a regular feature of their life. Still, the bishop continued to be recognized as THE pastor of souls, with the priests serving only as his delegates. Gradually the latter became known as "priests of the second rank," while the bishop was a priest of the first rank. In Africa, before this differentiation, bishops were multiplied on a colossal scale: some 500 in the fourth century—(including Donatists). "He was a parish priest among parish priests, and not a senior ecclesiastic in charge of, and remote from, all the parishes and priests."[7] The parochial system, as we know it, was finally "canonized" by the legislation of the Council of Trent, 1545–1563.

The Universal Salvific Will of God
(I Timothy 2:4; Titus 2:11; II Corinthians 5:15)

In commenting on Romans 2:6–7 in Chapter X, we pointed out that the ultimate norm of righteousness is the individual conscience, permitting even infidels to be saved. Now we are confronted with the problem of reconciling this internal forum of conscience with membership (or non-membership) in the external, visible organization we have been describing. But first a more basic question must be asked, "Just what is *salvation?*" For the Old Testament patriarchs, salvation consisted fundamentally in the survival of the line of Abraham-Isaac-Jacob and its corporate destiny. Let us not be too quick to conclude that this social dimension of salvation—howsoever incomplete it seems—has been entirely supplanted by a later concept of individual responsibility and other-worldly retribution. "My first duty is to save my own soul" can be not only unbiblical but very selfish. Peguy was much more scriptural when he wrote, "We must reach God in a body, together. We must come before him together. It will not do for some of us to find God without the others."[8]

At the same time, a true concept of salvation lends no support to the obsession many good people experience regarding the urgency of the Church's reaching out and evangelizing every last pigmy and aborigine in the remotest corners of the earth before they "perish." Although the "salvation of souls" is important and very urgent, we must

---

[7] Michonneau, *Op. cit.*, p. 30.

[8] Yves Congar, O.P. *The Wide World My Parish* (Baltimore, Md.: Helicon Press, 1961), p. 35. I am indebted to Chapters 2 and 3 of this book for many of the ideas expressed in this section.

recognize that it is not the primary purpose of the universe—otherwise God would surely see to it that every soul was saved. God "wishes all men to be saved and to come to the knowledge of the truth"; indeed, "Jesus Christ came into the world to save sinners" (I Tim. 2:4 and 1:15). Yet these texts do not express the over-all goal of creation as adequately as the following:

> To the King of the ages, who is immortal, invisible, the one only God, be honor and glory forever and ever. Amen. (I Tim. 1:17) . . . Christ died for all, in order that they who are alive may live no longer for themselves, but for him who died for them and rose again. (II Cor. 5:14)

The problem of salvation, then, cannot be approached on any quantitative or statistical basis. If we would learn from Scripture, we must recognize that the Bible speaks to us in terms of symbols rather than of numbers. It it not *how many* items there are in a given category, but rather what these items *represent*. Adam was just one man, yet he recapitulated in his loins the whole human race (as Christ was to do later). Noe is treated in Scripture as a second Adam, although the sacred author knew that this was not strictly true (cf. the presumed survival of the Cainites in Gen. 4:22). The Jews were never more than a small minority (Deut. 7:7); still, they constituted the vehicle of universal salvation before Christ. This ability of the part to represent the whole was generally acknowledged by the ancients. For example, the firstborn son represented the continuance of the family; first-fruits and tithes represented the whole of one's produce or income, etc.

As the Old Testament came to an end we find the concept of the *remnant* occupying greater and greater importance, though it is found as early as III Kings 19:18. This term is used to designate *religious action by a minority* who represent the People of God.[9] Even the tiny Jewish state was too large for God's eternal purpose, so He selected only the survivors of the various pagan captivities! And from these He further selected only the pious (and usually poor) faithful fragment who were prepared to do His will—the Anawim. As we have seen, the narrowing process terminated in Christ, the only just "servant" found worthy to mediate redemption for the universe. The process continues in the New Testament as the New Israel replaces the Old, as Church replaces Synagogue. Only in view of the principle of the part representing the whole could St. Paul declare that the gospel "has reached you, even as it is in the whole world," and, "it (the gospel) has been

---

[9] See Albert Gelin, *Key Concepts of the Old Testament* (New York: Sheed and Ward, 1955), pp. xiii–xiv; 91–94.

preached to every creature under heaven" (Col. 1:6, 23). Today the ratio of Catholics to the total population is lower than in the Middle Ages and this ratio is decreasing.

In our democratic society we find it hard to understand how the whole can be represented by a minority; it seems to us that only a majority can perform this function. God's plans are inscrutable; yet a little reflection will cast some light on the problem. During the Israelite Tribal Confederacy a leader named Gedeon was ordered by Yahweh to meet the combined armies of the Madianites, Amalecites, and Cedemites with only 300 soldiers—yet he conquered them (Judges 7). The purpose of the divine strategy is declared in verse 2: ". . . lest Israel vaunt itself against me and say, 'My own power brought me the victory.'" When the minority overcomes the majority, it is easier to see the hand of God in the affair.

Returning to the question of the salvation of the individual, we must insist that it can be answered only in reference to the goal of the universe, which is God's glory, which in turn calls for a "new creation" as affirmed by the prophets (e.g., Isa. 48, esp. v. 11). For man himself the climax will consist in *attaining to the Resurrection* (cf. II Cor. 4:14). But man cannot attain this goal by himself or for himself alone; he can attain it only by being incorporated into Christ and thus vicariously share in HIS Resurrection. The Church serves as the medium of this incorporation, for it represents and it is the visible extension of the Master in the contemporary world. The question of individual salvation, then, narrows down to this: to what extent does one have to be identified with the Church, which is the Body of Christ, in order to reap its leavening effect in the world to come? The topic is not clear as we would like to have it; yet this much can be said:

1) The Church is not only the prescribed or "official" means of attaining to the Resurrection; it is the *only* means thereto; *2)* a *deliberate* sinful rejection of membership in the Church will surely disqualify an individual from salvation, as will also the perseverance of the will in some serious sin; *3)* those baptized Christians who are inculpably not aware of the authentic community of the faithful by defect of belief or church-unity but who remain in charity retain a salvific relationship among God's People; *4)* among the unevangelized, those who heed the ultimate tribunal of conscience are, as Pius XII declared, "unsuspectingly related to the Mystical Body in desire and resolution" and hence have the possibility of salvation.[10] And we can be sure that

---

[10] *Mystici Corporis,* par. 100. In this sense the phrase, "Outside the Church there is no salvation and no remission of sins" (Clarkson, *The Church Teaches,* #153; also, #165) is vindicated: there is no salvation *apart* from the Church, the unique medium.

there will be a number of such "unlikely candidates" who will appear in the ranks of the Blessed on "that day," bearing witness to the fact that God's mercy is His greatest glory and that its peculiar vindication lies in the salvation of "sinners."

The Function of Almsgiving in the Church
(II Corinthians 7–9)

These chapters are assigned at this point because of their many references to Titus and his association with St. Paul. After helping Paul on a number of missions, Titus became Bishop of Crete. But even more important in this section is the light which it throws on the subject of a *financial commitment to the Church*. Indeed, St. Paul lays down almsgiving as the hallmark of virtue. Referring to members of the Church at Macedonia, he states:

> . . . their overflowing joy and their very deep poverty have resulted in rich generosity. For according to their means—I bear them witness—yes, beyond their means, they gave, earnestly begging of us the favor of sharing in the ministry that is in behalf of the saints. And beyond our expectation they gave themselves, *first to the Lord, and then by the will of God to us.* (II Cor. 8:2–5)

We learn from the portion in italics what a close connection the Saint makes between the love of God (always first in order) and love of neighbor (second, but vitally important). The charity of these Macedonian Christians impelled them to give "beyond their means" to the famine-strickened faithful in Jerusalem. Done out of love of God and zeal for the ministry, their act was not mere humanitarianism!

Liturgical Interlude: Ancient Christian Hymns in the Epistles of St. Paul

The magnificent Pauline hymn to the exalted Servant has been quoted in Chapter II. It should be noted that Colossians 1:15–20, considered in the previous chapter, existed before the epistle in which it appears. There, it has been used to illustrate the New Adam theme. Other hymns are found in Ephesians and I and II Timothy. Following the suggestion of Fr. Stanley,[11] who puts together the fragments from Ephesians and I Timothy, and including an addition furnished by St. Clement of Alexandria, we may combine these correlations in a composite poem and compare it with a passage from I Peter:

---

[11] The reader is again referred to Fr. Stanley's article, "Carmenque Christo Quasi Deo Dicere" in *The Catholic Biblical Quarterly*, XX:2 (April 1958), 173–191.

Eph. 5:14	"Awake, sleeper, and arise from among the dead, And Christ will enlighten thee."		First part of a baptismal hymn continued in I Tim.	
St. Clement	"He, the Sun of immortality, Who was born before the dawn, and who By his rays has given life to us,"		From Protrepticos IX, 84, 1, 2.	
I Tim. 3:16	". . . was manifested in the flesh, Was justified in the spirit, Appeared to angels, Was preached to Gentiles, Believed in the world, Taken up in glory."	"Put to death indeed in the flesh, He was brought to life in the spirit, In which also he went and preached to those spirits that were in prison. For he went to heaven, Angels, Powers and Virtues being made subject to him."		I Pet. 3:18 3:19 3:22

Suggested Readings

Bible de Jerusalem, pp. 1488–1489.

Congar, *The Wide World My Parish,* Chap. 2 and 3.

Davis, *Theology for Today,* Chap. 6.

Hughes, Philip, *A History of the Church,* Vol. I, Chap. 2.

Key-Young, *Understanding the New Testament,* pp. 340–342. This Protestant text repeats the claim of second century Gnostic influence on the Pastoral Epistles—a theory which Wikenhauser states has long been abandoned by most critics.

Michonneau, *My Father's Business,* Chap. 2.

Monro, *Enjoying the New Testament,* pp. 137–143.

Pius XII, *Mystici Corporis* (N.C.W.C. edition, 1943).

Siebeneck, *The Pastoral Epistles: I Timothy, Titus, II Timothy* (New Testament Reading Guide, No. 10).

Wikenhauser, *New Testament Introduction,* pp. 438–452.

For Further Study

1. What is the precise role of the bishop? The priest?
2. Is the power of Orders sufficient to enable any priest in good standing to hear your Confession licitly? Validly?
3. What was St. Clement of Rome's position in the Church? What was the occasion of his letter? What remedy did he propose to the offenders? (See Fremantle, *Op. cit.,* p. 35). To which Pauline Epistle is St. Clement's letter related?
4. What doctrine does II Timothy 1:9 suggest?
5. Does the quality of inspiration guarantee that Jamnes and Mambres (II Tim. 3:8) were Egyptian magicians?
6. Does II Timothy 3:16–17 provide adequate evidence for the inspiration of the Bible?
7. Where are the following passages found in the Mass liturgy: II Timothy 4:1–8? Titus 2:11–15? 3:4–7?

Chapter XVIII

Hebrews (I): From Mosaic Covenant to the New Testament

READINGS: *Hebrews 1–5, 7, 9; Psalm 101; Fremantle,* A Treasury of Early Christianity, *pp. 284–287: First Apology of St. Justin Martyr. (Note: Hebrews 1:1–4, 10–12; 2:9, 14, 15; 7:11–17.)*

The deuterocanonical epistle, Hebrews, is still one of the most controversial books of the New Testament. Its authorship, date and place of composition, destination, and occasion continue to be debated. It seems unlikely that St. Paul wrote this letter himself, since a probable date for its origin is c. 90 A.D. Likely candidates for authorship are Apollos or Barnabas (both close to Paul during his lifetime). As for the occasion and audience, we can only guess: perhaps it was intended for the Jewish Christians of Rome; it may even have been intended for Gentile Christians.[1] At any rate, Hebrews is the *first complete Christian sermon* which we possess. It was prepared by a preacher but probably never delivered—so the author wrote it out and sent his message by letter to the intended audience.

This epistle represents the best Greek in the New Testament; perhaps it is a translation from Hebrew, i.e., Aramaic. Carefully planned and composed (unlike genuine Pauline epistles), the letter is an apology for Christianity based on the incompleteness of the Old Law, especially in its sacrificial system. The Christians to whom it was written seem to have been in danger of apostasy and perhaps of relapsing into Judaism. We may suppose it was sent to Jewish Christians sometime after the destruction of the Temple, who may well have been nostalgically yearning for "the old days" and tempted to return to the faith of their ancestors in the face of charges of unpatriotism from their former Jewish associates in the synagogue. As the author points out in 6:1, Hebrews is not elementary teaching.

---

[1] Cf. Wikenhauser, *New Testament Introduction,* p. 465. Fr. Sebastian Bullough's introduction in *St. Paul and Apostolic Writings* (Westminster, Md.: Newman Press, 1950), pp. 200–216, is also very helpful. Note Heb. 10:32–34; 13:24.

Christ, Son of God and a Milestone in Divine-Human Communication
(Hebrews 1-2)

In true Pauline-Wisdom style we are presented with a sublime statement of Christ's identity as "the brightness of his [God the Father's] glory and the image of his substance" (1:3); however, the customary inscription is lacking. The person of Christ is portrayed as the final link in the history of divine communication, for God has now sent His Son into the world in person. Quotations from the Old Testament abound, including a passage from Psalm 101 (cf. end of this chapter). In stressing Christ's superiority over the angels, the author seems to be inveighing against the same Platonic doctrine of angelic intermediaries that was refuted in Colossians. The typical exaltation-through-humiliation theme is forcefully stated in Chapter 2, the final verse of which gives us a touching picture of Jesus' humanity: "For in that he himself has suffered and has been tempted, he is able to help those who are tempted."

Temple and Synagogue Replaced by Christ's Sacrifice
(Hebrews 3ff.)

It is doubtful that the average Catholic appreciates the striking similarity between his form of worship and that of the synagogue, and it would be futile for him to deny the dependence of the former on the latter. It is the purpose of the author of Hebrews to emphasize the differences: yet even this brings out many of the likenesses between the two systems. The chart below notes—very possibly at the expense of over-simplification—the principal arguments of the saint for the superiority of the New Testament over the Old. (Unassigned portions will be treated at length in Ch. XIX.)

Relationship Between the Fore-Mass and the Jewish Synagogue Service

For a better understanding of the Mass, it will be helpful at this juncture to make a comparison between the prayer service as carried out in the synagogue and the early Mass of the Catechumens. From the New Testament we learn that the Jewish Sabbath observance continued, after the opening prayer, with readings from the Pentateuch and then from the Prophets (Acts 13:15). The singing of a psalm would be interspersed with the readings (cf. Col. 3:16). Then one of the more distinguished men present at the service would give a sermon on one of the texts read, as we learn from Jesus' own experience

OLD TESTAMENT INSTITUTION	LIMITATION	NEW TESTAMENT TRANSFORMATION
1. Mediatorship of Moses (Chap. 3)	Was the servant of God, a human being. Minister of a covenant.	Christ, the new Mediator, is the Son of God. Minister of a will (unilateral).
2. The Promised Land (Chap. 4; cf. Ps.94)	The "Rest" of Chanaan, attained by a few.	The "Rest" of eternal life, open to the many.
3. Promise to Abraham (Chap. 6:13–20)	A true will, but of something in the future.	Christ's last will and testament, realized in His death.
4. Priesthood of Levi– Aaron	Inferior to the "Order of Melchisedec" to which it yielded (7:9–12).	Christian priesthood (of the Order of Melchisedec) is eternal and backed by oath (7:16–25).
5. Sacrifices (Chap. 10)	Animals offered daily.	Christ offered Himself in a unique, unrepeatable immolation.
6. Mosaic Law (Chap. 8)	Type, shadow, figure of what was to come: may reflect Platonic forms. Tabernacle made by hand.	Antitype, "reality" of the Old Law, fulfilling Jeremia 31:31–34 theme of intimacy. Tabernacle not made by hand.
7. Moral implications (Chap. 6, 10)	Apostasy from Judaism a crime meriting death.	Apostasy from Christianity is equal to trodding on Christ: "unforgivable."
8. Faith (Chap. 11)	The (true) link with a Christ Who has not come.	Perfected by the coming of Christ.
9. Sinai, Sion (Chap. 12)	Yahweh unapproachable on Mt. Sinai: transcendence.	God now approachable through His Son in the company of the angels.
10. Tabernacle (Chap. 13)	Servers of the tabernacle and of the dietary laws "found no profit."	Worshippers at the altar of Christ, nourished by His body in charity.

at Nazareth (Luke 4:16–22). The setting for the Mass is provided by the *Didache,* probably the most ancient liturgical manual we possess:[2]

> And on the Lord's Day, after you have come together, break bread and offer the Eucharist, having first confessed your offenses, so that your sacrifice may be pure. But let no one who has a quarrel with his neighbor join you until he is reconciled, lest your sacrifice be defiled. For it was said by the Lord: 'In every place and time let there be offered to me a clean sacrifice, because I am the great king'; and also, 'and my name is great among the Gentiles.' (Mal. 1:11, 14)

For the details of the comparison, we shall turn to *The First Apology* of St. Justin Martyr, who wrote about 155 A.D. It is addressed to a pagan audience.[3]

SYNAGOGUE SERVICE	MASS OF THE CATECHUMENS
1. Opening prayers (standing) . . .	"And on the day which is called Sunday, there is an assembly in the same place of all who live in cities, or in (the) country."
2. First reading: the Pentateuch . .	". . . the writings of the prophets are read as long as we have time."
3. First psalm chanted	(Gradual)
4. Second reading: Prophet	". . . and the records of the Apostles . . ."
5. Second psalm chanted	(Alleluia)
6. Sermon by invitation	"Then the reader concludes: and the president verbally instructs, and exhorts us . . . ."
7. "Great intercession" for the needs of the community	"then we altogether rise and offer up our prayers . . . for ourselves . . . and all others."
8. Priestly blessing, prayer for peace, kiss	"We salute one another with a kiss when we have concluded the prayers."
9. Almsgiving, money, gift in kind	"Such as are in prosperous circumstances, and wish to do so, give what they will, each according to his choice . . . (to) assist the orphans, and widows . . . " (See p. 184 for Mass of the Faithful).
10. Dismissal	

---

[2] Chapter 14. Some authorities date this work as early as 90 A.D., others c. 135. Cf. F. Cayre, *Manual of Patrology,* Vol. I (Paris: Desclee & Co., 1936) pp. 43–51.

[3] Gerald Ellard, *Christian Life and Worship* (Milwaukee, Wis.: Bruce Pub. Co., 1956), pp. 84–85; 154–155.

146

Psalm 101: A Psalm of Lament Petitioning for a Longer Life

This is the fifth of the seven Penitential Psalms. It describes the sad plight of the Psalmist in some crisis, probably the Babylonian Exile. We can actually detect three poems here: verses 2–12 are a personal lament, to which a national lament (vv. 13–23) for the restoration of Sion has been added, while the last six verses (24–29) return to a personal note as the poet begs for a longer life, reminding God of His own eternity. It is this portion (vv. 26–28) that is applied to Christ in Hebrews 1:10–12 by way of bearing witness to His divinity.

Suggested Readings

Bullough, *St. Paul and Apostolic Writings*, pp. 200–216.
Davis, *Theology for Today*, Chap. 17.
Dix, Gregory (ed.), *The Treatise on the Apostolic Tradition of St. Hippolytus of Rome*, pp. 6–11, 40–43. Contains primitive Mass formulary.
Durrwell, *The Resurrection*, pp. 358–359. Eschatological dimensions of *Hebrews*.
Ellard, *Christian Life and Worship*, Chap. 7 and 12.
McConnell, *The Epistle to the Hebrews* (New Testament Reading Guide, No. 11).
Monro, *Enjoying the New Testament*, pp. 104–110.
Wikenhauser, *New Testament Introduction*, pp. 454–470.

For Further Study

1. Does our meager knowledge of the authorship of Hebrews impinge on its historicity?
2. In which ways does this epistle resemble St. Paul's other writings?
3. Is the *priesthood* a personal grace or a charism? (Find definition in Hebrews.)
4. Is the use of Melchisedec in Hebrews a true typical sense?
5. Interpret Hebrews 1:5.

Chapter XIX

Hebrews (II) and St. Jude: Apostasy and the Remission of Sins in the Church

READINGS: *Hebrews 6, 8, 10–13; Jude; II Corinthians 1–2; Psalm 39; Fremantle, A Treasury of Early Christianity, pp. 42–46: The Shepherd of Hermas. (Note: Hebrews 6:4–6; 8:6–13; 10:26–31; 11:1, 6; Jude 4, 6, 23–24; Psalm 39:7–8.)*

Christ, The "Liturgist" of the "New Covenant"
(Hebrews 6, 8, 10)

Twice the author of Hebrews quotes at length from the key messianic passages found in Jeremia 31:31–34: Hebrews 8:8–12 and 10: 16–17. It is from the first of these passages that we get the term "New Testament" (8:13). The apostle suggests the reason for the change from "Covenant" to "Testament": both here and in Galatians 3:15–18 he notes that the latter is more in the nature of a *will* (implying unilateral benefits from Christ's death) whereas the former (Mosaic) Covenant made heavy demands (hence bilateral) on the Jews without conferring equivalent helps.[1] As the official minister (the Greek word is "liturgist") of this New Covenant, Christ serves as its High Priest. Through Him Christians gain a *much closer approach to God than did the followers of the Old Testament; the New Testament accomplishes the intimacy predicted by Jeremia* which the Jews never attained. The price of this intimacy was the blood of Christ (10:5–10). In surrendering His life-blood, this High Priest has made the only offering satisfactory to God: that of His will. Here the author sees the fulfillment of Psalm 39:7–8; we are reminded of Amos and of Psalm 49.

The Remission of Sins and the Salvation of Apostates
(Hebrews 6:4–6 and 10:26–31)

What is the characteristic ritual feature of the New Covenant? In each of the two references to Jeremia cited above, the author makes a point of mentioning the *forgiveness of sins as an essential element* (cf. Jer. 31:34). However, both texts contain a fearful warning: those

---

[1] Cf. Monro, *Enjoying the New Testament,* pp. 108–109.

who have accepted baptism and then fallen into apostasy cannot expect to be saved. Fr. McConnell offers a penetrating explanation:

> It is important to notice that the epistle nowhere envisages the case of a repentant sinner seeking re-admission to communion with the Church. The point of view is quite different. The Christians addressed have not fallen away. The preacher is trying to keep them away from the brink by making it clear that no man has a right to count on being given a second chance. The Hebrews were converted as adults; in their case "falling away" will mean deliberately closing their eyes to the light.
>
> The prospect is of ultimate apostasy, but the preacher's immediate concern is rather with the deliberate infidelities which pave the way for apostasy, with the secret, interior "falling away" from Christ without which formal apostasy is unintelligible. The Christian vocation commits the Hebrews for all time; if they break their pledge, they must expect the most fearful consequences. The enlightenment here (and in 10:32) may very well be a technical term for baptism, although it is more generally understood as the Christian grace. The tasting of the heavenly gift may allude to the Eucharist, and the becoming partakers of the Holy Spirit to the laying on of hands (v. 2). . . .
>
> The man who has had this taste of heaven and turned his back on it cannot be renewed again to repentance. The impossibility does not derive from any lack of effectiveness in God's working, either directly or through the Church, but from the interior state of such a person, who has turned off the light and made a complete break with "our" high priest. His actions manifest his deliberate intention of aligning himself with those who crucified and mocked Christ.[2]

These texts illustrate the Church's consciousness of her power of remitting sin in behalf of penitents who are properly disposed. St. Thomas reduces the efficacy of the seven sacraments to two categories: the perfection of man in worship and the provision of a remedy for sin.[3] We have already noted in the excerpt from the *Didache* quoted in the previous chapter that confession of one's sins (either publicly or privately) was a prerequisite to the Eucharistic banquet. Moreover, public penance for more grievous sins was adopted very early in the Church. Tertullian has captured the nature of penance as a new baptism, a new death through our humiliation; but unlike the first baptism, this cleansing demands satisfaction:

> . . . confessing our sins to the Lord, not indeed as if He were ignorant of them, but because thereby a satisfaction is made for them; repentance, too, is born of confession, and by repentance God is appeased. And so confession becomes a disciplinary act

---

[2] The *Epistle to the Hebrews* (New Testament Reading Guide Series, No. 11 [Collegeville, Minn.: Liturgical Press, 1960]), pp. 30–31. Cf. above, p. 109.

[3] *Summa Theologica*, IIIa, Q. 65, Art. 1.

of great humiliation and prostration to the penitent; it regulates the dress, the food; it enjoins sackcloth, and subdues the spirit with anguish; it bids a man alter his life, and weep over his past sins; it restricts meat and drink to the greatest simplicity possible; it nourishes prayer by fasting . . .[4]

Four classes of penitents were distinguished: *mourners* (forbidden entrance to the church); *hearers* (forbidden to join in the fore-Mass prayers); *kneelers* (who could say the prayers, but had to depart with the catechumens); *bystanders* (permitted to remain for the Mass of the Faithful,, but not to offer gifts or receive Communion). Larger and larger numbers of penitents resulted in the gradual abandonment of public penance: absolution was granted immediately on the assignment of a "penance." Also, public confession and absolution of lesser sins fell into disuse. For a time the strictness of the discipline led certain individuals (e.g., Montanists) to interpret the two texts cited in Hebrews as barring certain sins from the power of the keys (apostasy, murder, adultery). Although these sins were reserved to higher ecclesiastical superiors at one time, the Church never taught that they are unforgivable. It seems that *The Shepherd* of Hermas was a reaction *against* this rigorism—even though Hermas himself was inclined to look upon Christians as a society of the perfect. The aged, white-haired woman in the assigned excerpt represents the Church oppressed and weakened by the sins of her erring children. In two subsequent visions, she becomes rejuvenated and her wrinkles removed as these sins are forgiven.[5]

The Nature and Importance of Faith in the Christian Life (Hebrews 11)

As we have seen in conjunction with Chapter IX of *God's Kingdom in the Old Testament,* St. Paul is the great herald of the theological virtues—especially faith. An echo of this emphasis appears in Chapter 11 of Hebrews which begins with a classic definition of this virtue: it is the acceptance of the *unseen* based on (divine) internal *conviction* ("substance," "evidence") of God's authority. A series of Old Testament vignettes follows after the fashion of Sirach and Wisdom to illustrate the indispensability of the virtue even before Christ. Another classic text, this chapter in Hebrews sets down the bare, minimum requirements of belief for salvation: *1)* the existence of (one) God, and 2) that He is a "Remunerator" (11:6). To these St. Thomas

---

[4] *On Penance,* Chap. 9 (quoted in Ellard, *Christian Life and Worship,* pp. 299–300).

[5] See Cayre, *Manual of Patrology,* Vol. 1, pp. 83ff.

adds belief in the Trinity and the Redemption where access to a preacher is had.[6]

Hebrews 12 tackles the second theological virtue, hope, based on the example of Christ "who for the joy set before him, endured a cross, despising the shame" (v. 2). Hebrews insists also on self-discipline, alleging its lack as the cause of Esau's failure to obtain the birthright (vv. 16–17). Chapter 13 returns to a favorite Pauline theme, charity. If the reader has come to the conclusion that the Pauline tradition is opposed to matrimony, he should carefully note 13:4. The epistle concludes with a solemn injunction that "here we have no permanent city, but we seek for the city that is to come" (v. 14).

The Epistle of Jude and the Nature of Hell
(Jude and II Corinthians 1–2)

This is the second of the "Catholic Epistles" which we are considering—written not to a specific church, but constituting rather a moral homily sent out as a kind of pastoral encyclical. We are not sure who the author was, though it is probable that it was written by Jude, the brother of James and relative of Jesus (cf. Matt. 13:55). As noted in connection with the chart of the Apostolic College in Chapter XIII, this Jude seems to be distinct from the Jude (Thaddeus?) who was one of the Twelve. Although internal evidence would seem to date the letter c. 70–80 A.D., it is impossible to be very definite in this matter. The author apparently has in mind the same false teachers (Jewish gnostics) as did St. Paul in the Pastoral Epistles, but he also condemns the "antinomians," i.e., those insincere Christians who opposed all forms of law and discipline (v. 4). The fact that "Jude" cites apocryphal literature (e.g., vv. 9, 14) causes this epistle to be ranked among the deuterocanonicals.

In verse 6 we find a reference to the fallen angels, who are described as "kept in everlasting chains under darkness for the judgment of the great day." To this II Peter adds the detail that they were "dragged . . . down by infernal ropes to Tartarus and delivered . . . to be tortured and kept in custody" (2:4). Meditating on these texts as well as on the Lord's own words ("everlasting fire" in Matt. 25:41; cf. also Mark 9:43) leads one to conclude that there has to be more than fire or any other physical punishment involved, since neither the angels nor the damned souls have bodies at present. These descriptions of hell seem to be in the same literary genre as the destruction of Jerusalem (Matt. 24) and the apocalyptic phenomena which accompanied Christ's death (Matt. 27:51–53). Thus, the term

---

[6] *Summa Theologica,* IIa IIae, Q. 2, Art. 5, 7, 8.

"hell" may very well include a great variety of punishments.[7] Although theologians assure us that hell-fire is not a pure metaphor, they insist that the principal "pain" is that of the loss of God,[8] followed by that of remorse in the wake of eternal, irremovable guilt and frustration. In a real sense each one will make his own hell; as Origen says,

> Each sinner kindles for himself the flame of his own fire. . . . The fuel of this fire is our sins, which feed it. It seems to me that, just as too much food or its bad quality produces fevers in the body . . . so the soul heaps up sins and misdeeds, and in due course this accumulation of wickedness catches fires in retribution and flares up in punishment.[9]

In his second Epistle to the Corinthians, St. Paul has left us a slight testimony regarding the future. In the first two chapters he returns to the theme of the Christ-life within the faithful, e.g., 1:5. He suggests that the call to Christianity is a sign of predestination in 1:21–22, then testifies that there are some who are not so fortunate and who do not make the grade: there actually are some souls in hell!

> For we are the fragrance of Christ for God, alike as regards those who are saved and those who are lost; to these an odor that leads to death, but to those an odor that leads to life. (2: 15–16)

As to the number of the damned, we can only guess: God wills this delicate information to remain hidden from human eyes. From Matt. 7:14 and 22:14 we do not obtain too much light on the subject as these texts refer to the number accepting His invitation to follow His teaching, not the number of the predestined. Some years ago Cardinal Louis Billot proposed an interesting possibility: a great many souls may never reach the full use of reason necessary to make the critical choice between heaven and hell, and thus end up in a state of natural happiness ("limbo"). The safest way to conclude this consideration is with a question: Is salvation, taken in the sense of the attainment of God through a blessed resurrection, for the many or for the few? Does God's primary aim in creation—His own glory— demand that the remnant which enters heaven be any larger proportionately than the remnant which entered the Promised Land or the remnant which accepted Him as the Messia?

---

[7] The Second Council of Lyons decreed in 1274: "The souls of those who die in mortal sin or with only original sin soon go down into hell, but there receive different punishments." Tradition designates the "punishment" of the latter by the term "limbo." (See I Pet. 3:19 and 4:6.)

[8] Cf. *Summa Theologica*, Supplement, Q. 70, Art. 3; the effect of the "fire" is basically that of confinement.

[9] From Congar, *The Wide World My Parish*, p. 90.

Psalm 39: A Mixed Psalm of Thanksgiving (Vv. 1–11) and Lament (Vv. 12–18)

This poem could well serve as the answer to the blind trust found in Psalm 38: the author of Psalm 39 now knows through a specific instance (rescue from death) that the Lord IS man's only true guide. He also learns how to thank God: not by ritual sacrifice (alone) but by submission of his will (applied in Heb. 10:5–7 to Christ). The petition of the Lament portion begins in verse 10; verses 14–18 closely resemble Psalm 69.

Suggested Readings

Congar, *The Wide World My Parish*, Chap. 8–9.
——————, Liturgy and Doctrine, Chap. 6.
Davis, *Theology for Today*, Chap. 8.
Ellard, *Christian Life and Worship*, Chap. 20.
Maly, *The Epistles of Saints James, Jude, Peter* (New Testament Reading Guide, No. 12), pp. 25–33.
Winklhofer, *The Coming of His Kingdom*, pp. 91–98; 139–144.

For Further Study

1. Do modern Jews still look upon God as "unapproachable"? How does this affect their attitude toward Christianity?
2. Is the absolution of a penitent in the confessional a public act?
3. Would there be any advantage in the restoration of a modified form of public penance? (Cf. *Worship*, XXXVII:2 [Jan. 1963], pp. 106–110.)

Chapter XX

I Peter and Philemon: A Baptismal Liturgy and the Christian's Adjustment to the World

READINGS: *I Peter 1–5; Ephesians 6; Philemon; Psalm 33. St. Cyril of Jerusalem,* Mystagogical Catecheses I and II (*see Appendix, pp. 215–220*). (*Note: I Peter 2:9; 3:18–22; 5:8–9; Ephesians 6:12.*)

In the previous chapter attention was focused on the Sacrament of Penance. In introducing the First Epistle of St. Peter in this chapter, we bring into focus the Sacrament of Baptism. No definite evidence has yet been produced to exclude this protocanonical work from Petrine authorship, though it seems, from 5:12 and from its excellent Greek style, that the apostle used Silvanus as his "secretary" in its composition. A disciple of St. Paul (cf. II Cor. 1:19), the latter is probably the presbyter Silas mentioned in Acts 15:22. Some unknown trial suffered by the "sojourners of the Dispersion" (here, not the Jews, but the Christians of Asia Minor) occasioned this encouraging letter. Assuming Petrine authorship, we must fix its composition shortly before the apostle's martyrdom. The logical date would be c. 64 A.D., and the place of origin, "Babylon" (code name for Rome in 5:13; cf. Apoc. 14:8, etc.).

Many of the phrases used in I Peter bear a striking resemblance to the Pauline epistles, especially Romans and Ephesians, but without the same level of meaning. The term "in Christ" occurs in 3:16, 5:10, 14. Other similarities are: 1:14 to Romans 12:2; 2:13–17 to Romans 13:1–8; 2:18 to Ephesians 6:5; 3:9 to Romans 12:14, 17; 5:8–9 to Ephesians 6:11–13; the baptismal creed in 3:18, 19, 22 to I Timothy 3:16 (noted on p. 142). Did St. Peter—as a number of critics claim— borrow his theology of salvation from St. Paul's epistles (with which he was probably familiar; cf. II Pet. 3:15–16); or did both apostles obtain their material from a common catechetical source in the early Church?

Solution: A Baptismal Liturgy

Many modern exegetes argue quite convincingly that St. Peter took a great deal of this letter from a primitive baptismal liturgy from which St. Paul also drew. This "liturgy" comprised hymns, a creed, and a moral exhortation or homily to which the author of I Peter has added an epistolary greeting and farewell.[1] There are frequent references to Baptism throughout the epistle: "begotten again" in 1:3; "redeemed" in 1:18; "purified" in 1:22 and "reborn" in 1:23; "newborn babies" who "have tasted that the Lord is sweet" in 2:2–3; "living stones" in 2:5; "chosen race . . . royal priesthood . . . holy nation . . . purchased people . . . called out of darkness into his marvelous light . . . who . . . now have obtained mercy" in 2:9–10; "having died to sin" in 2:24, "co-heir of the grace of life" in 3:7; "baptism" and "heirs of eternal life" in 3:21–22. The charisms are referred to in 4:10: "according to the gift that each has received." The liturgical character of the epistle becomes further evident through an analysis of its structure:

1) A baptismal *hymn:* 1:3–5.
2) Pre-baptismal homily: 1:13–21. (The sacrament would be conferred as this point.)
3) Post-baptismal homily on the newly acquired dignity of the baptized: 1:22—2:10.
4) Moral exhortation concerning the duties of one's state in life: 2:11—3:17.
5) Baptismal creed similar to I Timothy 3:16: 3:18ff.
6) Exhortation to perseverance (4:1–11), especially in the present crisis: 4:12—5:4.
7) Another baptismal *hymn:* 5:6–11.

In describing the new dignity of Christians, St. Peter applies two phrases from Exodus 19:6, "kingdom of priests" and "holy nation." Only by synecdoche could the Jews be termed a "royal priesthood," since only a fraction of their numbers exercised this office. But every member of the Christian community shares in Christ's priesthood through his baptism, according to St. Peter. This New Testament priesthood of the laity includes the obligation of bearing witness to Christ, according to the charter of Christian apologetics given in 3:15: "Be ready always with an answer to everyone who asks a reason for

---

[1] See Claude Peifer, O.S.B., "Primitive Liturgy in the Formation of the Gospels" in *The Bible Today*, I:1 (Oct. 1962), 19–20; also Key and Young, *Understanding the New Testament*, pp. 432–444; and Wright and Fuller, *The Book of the Acts of God*, pp. 369–372.

the hope that is in you." The ritual of Baptism included, from the very earliest times, the recitation of a creed. I Peter 3:18–22 is a primitive model, reminding us of the Israelite's credo in Deuteronomy 26:3–10. This New Testament creed shows Baptism to be an antitype of Noe's ark. The Apostles' Creed and most of the other creeds used by both Catholics and Protestants originated as *baptismal professions of faith.*[2]

The Christian's Adjustment to the World

It cannot be insisted upon too often that the New Testament is not a series of biographies of Christ, but rather testimonials of the faith of the Christian communities which produced them. This is particularly true of the epistles. We have previously noted the development of dogma, e.g., the theology of the Resurrection; in I Peter we see the Church formulating her moral theology. The delay in the Parousia and the impossibility of continuing the common life on any large scale compelled the apostles to lay down some norms of behavior for their flocks living in a secularized environment. While very little moral adjustment would have to be made by Jewish Christians because of their strict Mosaic code, converts from paganism would have to do an about-face and St. Peter's audience is composed largely of the latter. After advising a spirit of detachment and giving a general exhortation on the apostolate of good example, he gets down to particular topics:

1. CIVIL OBEDIENCE. It seems somewhat incongruous to find an injunction to obey the civil powers on the eve of Nero's violent persecution.[3] A reason is suggested in 2:16; "not using your freedom as a cloak for malice": some Christians may have gotten the idea that baptism had emancipated them from their allegiance to the state.
2. SLAVERY. The term "servants" no doubt includes slaves in 2:18; we are surprised to find the Head of the Church not only *not* condemning this heinous institution, but actually demanding that slaves obey their masters, even the severe. Here we see St. Peter prudently working within the scope of existing institutions. When we consider that slaves outnumbered freemen in the Empire, we can more readily understand why it would have been foolhardy to preach emancipation. The motive offered for their obedience is the example of Christ, "Who when he was reviled, did not revile, when he suffered, did not threaten, but yielded himself to him who judged

---

[2] Four early creeds are given in Fremantle, *A Treasury of Early Christianity,* pp. 275–279; they are followed by a list of the first seven ecumenical councils.

[3] While many Protestant critics are inclined to see in 4:12ff. a reference to the persecution of either Domitian or Trajan, this position is not demanded by the text. Cf. *La Sainte Bible,* p. 1592.

him unjustly" (2:22–23). A similar injunction had already been issued by St. Paul in Ephesians 6:5–8. Both apostles see salvation possible even in a servile environment, especially since they envisioned the Parousia as rather imminent.

3. MARRIAGE. Christian wives have not been emancipated from the dominion of their husbands, St. Peter insists. Yet, if they practice the apostolate of example, they may win the conversion of their spouse "without word," e.g., without argumentation. Without suggesting any radical changes in matrimonial customs, the epistle reflects the Christian concept in the words, "co-heir of the grace of life" (3:7).

St. Paul's Epistle to Philemon: An Example of Christian Adjustment

We would hardly expect to find the intrepid St. Paul sending a converted slave back to his master; yet, this is the message conveyed through his shortest epistle. Onesimus, the slave in question, had apparently robbed his master, Philemon (v. 18), and fled to Rome. Here he met St. Paul during the latter's first imprisonment and was converted by him. (Thus, we are permitted to date the epistle c. 61–63 A.D.) In writing to Philemon—also, it seems, St. Paul's convert: "thou owest me thy very self," verse 19—the apostle makes bold to ask him "to receive him (Onesimus) forever, no longer as a slave, but instead of a slave as a brother most dear . . . in the Lord" (v. 16).

In line with what was said in the previous section on adjustment to the world, we see St. Paul also working within the existing institution of slavery. Although it is the Church's prerogative to change human institutions, slavery was too much a part of the Empire's existence to be abolished overnight: this victory over inhumanity would require centuries. The first step in emancipation—noticeable in this epistle—was insistence on the dignity of slaves as true persons. They were considered apt subjects for Baptism, implying the right of freedom of worship. The next step was to note "that with [the Lord] there is no respect of persons" (Eph. 6:9; cf. also Col. 3:11); this text clearly suggests a basic equality among men. Hence we find St. Paul boldly asking Philemon to receive Onesimus back as a brother in the context of the Body of Christ. The saint even agrees to make good the damages which Onesimus committed against his master.

The Didache: An Ancient Christian Moral and Liturgical Source

In 1873 a Greek Orthodox scholar and later Archbishop of Nicomedia re-discovered a precious document which had apparently been used by the Church Fathers: the *Didache*,[4] or *Doctrine of the Twelve*

---

[4] See this text p. 146.

Apostles. After describing the life of the baptized as the "Way of Life" in contrast to that of the unbaptized or "Way of Death," this document, written by an unknown author, outlines the administration of Baptism and the Eucharist. We shall give only the former here to illustrate the next stage of the development of that sacrament.

Chapter 7

Regarding baptism, baptize thus. After giving the foregoing instructions, 'Baptize in the name of the Father, and of the Son, and of the Holy Spirit' in running water.[5] But if you have no running water, baptize in any other; and if you cannot in cold water, then in warm. But, if the one is lacking, pour the other three times on the head 'in the name of the Father, and Son, and Holy Spirit.' But, before the baptism, let the one to be baptized fast, and any others who are able to do so. And you shall require the person being baptized to fast for one or two days.

Chapter 8

But do not let your fasts be with the hypocrites; for they (Jews) fast on Monday and Thursday; but you shall fast on Wednesday and Friday. And do not pray as the hypocrites, but as the Lord directed in His Gospel, 'Thus shall you pray: "Our Father in heaven, hallowed be Thy Name, Thy Kingdom come, Thy will be done on earth as in heaven; give us this day our bread from above, and forgive us our debt as we also forgive our debtors, and lead us not into temptation, but deliver us from evil,"' for Thine is the power and glory forever. Three times in the day pray thus.[6]

St. Cyril of Jerusalem's Mystagogical Catecheses I–II: The Rite of Baptism

It will be revealing to skip two centuries to observe the baptismal rite of the fourth century through the writings of St. Cyril, Bishop of Jerusalem, who died in 386 A.D. It was the custom at that time for the bishop personally to prepare the catechumens for baptism through a series of daily homilies delivered during Lent. St. Cyril has left us twenty-four such sermons, probably preached about 350 A.D. Nineteen of them were pre-baptismal homilies given during Lent; the remaining five were delivered after Easter to the newly baptized, and hence known as "mystagogical catecheses" because they deal with those aspects of the sacraments which were not revealed to the unbaptized. This secrecy was known as the *disciplina arcani* (discipline of the secret).

---

[5] "Running water" refers to spring water, probably preferred because of its purity.

[6] Although the *Didache* does not expressly link the Lord's Prayer with the baptismal rite, it was taught to the catechumens from earliest times. Cf. Ludwig Schopp (ed.), *The Apostolic Fathers* (*The Fathers of the Church*, Vol. I [New York: Cima Publishing Co., 1947]), pp. 177–178.

The first of these catecheses assigned gives an explanation of the preliminary rites of the Sacrament of Baptism, which was conferred by a series of distinct steps staggered throughout Lent.[7] Beginning in the third week, the catechumens were exorcised seven times. On each of these occasions they were examined or "scrutinized" to see if they were rightly disposed. Realizing the genuine power of Satan, the early Christian Church took no chances! The words of I Peter 5:8 (used in the hour of compline and chosen by St. Cyril as the text for his discourse) were taken seriously: "Be sober, be watchful! For your adversary the devil, as a roaring lion, goes about seeking someone to devour. Resist him, steadfast in the faith . . ." St. Paul likewise bears testimony that our greatest enemy is those cosmic powers of evil, the fallen angels: "For our wrestling is not against flesh and blood, but against the Principalities and the Powers, against the world-rulers of this darkness, against the spiritual forces of wickedness on high" (Eph. 6:12).[8]

The second catechesis, a commentary on Romans 6:3–14, explains the symbolism behind the actual ceremonies. Here we have a source of the first magnitude on the signification of the sacramental signs. The student should carefully list the steps of the rite, noting the meaning of each detail or antitype, especially: "crossing the Red Sea"; facing first West, then East; Lot's wife; the undressing ceremony; *the threefold immersion;* the mountain, the wild olive tree, the good (olive) tree. The Christian liturgy owes much to the formative work of St. Cyril, both on the Mass and the Divine Office. In the West, St. Ambrose has left us a similar series of mystagogical catecheses entitled "On the Sacraments" and "On the Mysteries" (see Suggested Readings below).

Psalm 33: A "Baptismal" Hymn Par Excellence

This Psalm of Thanksgiving, written in the wisdom vein, almost seems to have anticipated the institution of the Sacrament of Baptism. The Christian tradition behind I Peter thought it appropriate, quoting from it twice. I Peter 2:3 is from verse 9 of the psalm: "Taste and see how good the Lord is"; the word *taste* carries the force of "know by experience," applied to the newly baptized. They are now among those around whom the angel of the Lord sets his camp (v. 8). The exhortatory portion of the epistle quotes in 3:10–12 the advice of

---

[7] By a decree of April 16, 1962, the Congregation of Rites restored the ancient rite to a notable degree; cf. "The Restored Liturgical Catechumenate" in *Worship,* XXXVI:8 (Aug.–Sept. 1962), 536–549, by Fr. F. R. McManus.

[8] See Conrad Pepler, O.P., *Lent* (St. Louis, Mo.: B. Herder Book Co., 1944) pp. 131–139. A specific instance of diabolic possession is cited.

the psalmist to him who "desires life"; he must "refrain his tongue from evil."

Suggested Readings

Ellard, *Christian Life and Worship*, Chap. 17. Contains rite with commentary.
La Sainte Bible, pp. 1592–1593.
Maly, *The Epistles of Saints James, Jude, Peter* (New Testament Reading Guide, No. 12), pp. 34–52.
St. Ambrose, *On the Sacraments and on the Mysteries* (London: S.P.C.K., 1950), 157 pp.
Sullivan, *St. Paul's Epistles to the Philippians, Ephesians, Colossians, Philemon* (New Testament Reading Guide, No. 9), pp. 27–30.
Wikenhauser, *New Testament Introduction*, pp. 493–509.

For Further Study

1. What effects of baptism are stressed in I Peter? When was it conferred?
2. What points, if any, does St. Peter add to Christian theology? Summarize his Christology. Who are the "spirits" referred to in I Peter 3:19 and 4:6?
3. How could the Church tolerate slave-holding by its members for one instant?
4. How does St. Peter use Psalm 33?

Chapter XXI

The Johannine Literature (I): The Word of Life and the Anointing from the Holy One

READINGS: *I John 1–5; John 1–2. St. Cyril of Jerusalem*, Mystagogical Catechesis III *(see Appendix, p. 221). Fremantle,* A Treasury of Early Christianity; *pp. 281–284. (Note: I John 2:20; 3:9; John 1:1–18; 1:33; 2:4, 19.)*

From earliest times questions have been raised regarding the unity of authorship of the books attributed to St. John the Evangelist, Son of Zebedee: the Fourth Gospel, the three Johannine Epistles, and the Apocalypse. Without entering deeply into the controversy, we merely wish to point out that today within Catholic circles the tendency is to accept the traditional attribution, while admitting the possibility of translation and of some editing by another (disciple's) hand. Protestant scholars still debate the issue, although they are inclined to agree that the Fourth Gospel and I John are from the same hand. These two works are very similar in style and content. The Epistle seems to represent a transitional stage in the development of St. John's thought, which finds its mature expression in the Gospel. In both works the author declares himself an eyewitness of the events described.

St. John is traditionally associated with the See of Ephesus where he may have taken the Blessed Virgin Mary, although evidence is lacking. When the persecution decreed by Domitian raged in Asia Minor, the Evangelist was exiled to the Island of Patmos shortly after 90 A.D. There he wrote the Apocalypse; the First Epistle and his Gospel probably followed upon his return to Ephesus c. 96 A.D. His death seems to have taken place about 100 A.D. St. Irenaeus informs us that the Gnostic, Cerinthus, was active during the lifetime of St. John; critics are inclined to see in his heresy the occasion for the First Epistle and perhaps for the Gospel also. According to Cerinthus, the divine, "spiritual" Christ descended upon a human being named Jesus at his Baptism and "inhabited" this creature until just *before* he died

161

(hence, "Christ" didn't suffer, nor are we redeemed, for it was only the human *Jesus* who underwent death).[1]

In entering the world of St. John one is aware of an atmosphere quite different from that of the Synoptic Gospels. The Fourth Evangelist penetrates to a deeper layer of theology, his approach being analogous to that of the Chronicler in relation to the Deuteronomist. Symbols and allegories have replaced the Synoptic parables in the Gospel of St. John, who delights in antithetical thought-patterns: light–darknes, truth–lie, life–death, God–devil. However, these diversities must not be pushed too far. Both John and the Synoptics stem from the same historical situation and represent, basically, the same primitive kerygma: John the Baptist's witness to Jesus as the Messia confirmed by the intervention of the Holy Spirit; His preaching of the arrival of the Kingdom of God verified by "signs" (miracles); the formation of a corps of witnesses (the Apostles); His glorification-via-Resurrection; the continuation of His mission by the Holy Spirit. Like the wise man, St. John views creation from above, the Synoptics from below, as illustrated by an analysis of two key concepts:

GOSPEL	THE PERSON OF JESUS	THE USE OF MIRACLES BY EVANGELIST
St. Matthew	A greater Moses	Christ's first assault against Satan
St. Mark	A true son and servant of God	Manifestations of power
St. Luke	A new Adam	Tender illustrations of Jesus' humanity
ST. JOHN	THE SON OF GOD	THEOPHANIES: PRESENCE OF DIVINITY

Until recently it was taught that St. John's theology of the *Logos* (Word) was borrowed from Greek philosophy. However, there is no evidence to substantiate this claim. If the reader will re-examine such Wisdom texts as Proverbs 8, Sirach 24, and Wisdom 7, in the light of Apocalypse 19:13, he will be struck by the fact that St. John's treatment of the Word represents the flowering of the Old Testament Wisdom literature. Jewish monotheism prohibited anything short of an identification between God and wisdom; in the Fourth Gospel,

---

[1] See Wikenhauser, *New Testament Introduction*, especially pp. 523–526. The author links up the false teachers and Antichrists of I John with the Gnosticism of Cerinthus rather than with Docetism. This latter system taught that Christ always had a body, but that it was not real, only apparent. The selection assigned in Fremantle is also pertinent here, especially p. 283. Note apostolic succession on p. 282.

wisdom emerges as a divine Person distinct from the Father: the *Logos*. This dogmatic development paves the way for the evolution of the Holy Spirit as *Agape* or *Love*. It is with the concept of Logos that I John begins, thus introducing us to the heart of Johannine thinking. The epistle can perhaps be best analyzed by a consideration of its key phrases.

I John: A Johannine Glossary

Vv. 1:1 *Word of Life.* Divinity has been manifested in Christ, Whom "we have seen with our eyes . . . and have handled" in opposition to the spurious body claimed by the Gnostics. Christ is called "Life Eternal" in verse 2, distinguished clearly from the Father, for He was "*with* the Father, and has appeared to us." In St. John's Gospel Life Eternal stands as the equivalent of the Synoptics' "Kingdom of God."

1:3 *Fellowship.* Here is a term not found in the Gospels, but proper to St. Paul. In I John it parallels the Pauline doctrine of the Body of Christ; indeed, it goes beyond Christ and introduces us into the lifestream of the Trinity.

1:5 *Light vs. darkness.* A synonym for divine revelation, "Light" signifies the practical acknowledgment of God by "*practising the truth*" (of the Commandments). Darkness is more than mere ignorance; it implies malice on the part of the will. The Old Testament fool was one who lived in darkness.

1:8 *Acknowledge our sins.* This text may be used as an argument for the Sacrament of Penance.[2] Perhaps with an eye to Gnostics (who taught that their esoteric theology emancipated them from sin), St. John declares the universality of sin on mankind. Without a very special grace such as the Mother of God enjoyed, it is impossible even with sanctifying grace to go through life without committing at least venial sins.[3]

2:1 *Advocate.* Here a heavenly Intercessor is meant; in St. John's Gospel, this term will designate a divine Teacher.

2:3 *Keep His Commandments.* This is the test of our love of God. Special emphasis is placed on the "old" commandment of Leviticus 19:18 re-interpreted and renewed by Christ. For the Evangelists, St. Paul, and St. James, the best index of of love of God is the love we have for our neighbor (cf. 2:10–11). Fellowship with God demands fellowship with our neighbor.

---

[2] See *The Church Teaches,* No. 793.
[3] *Ibid.,* No. 597. See also the *Summa Theologica,* Ia IIae, Q. 109, Art. 8.

2:13 *Because you have conquered the evil one.* St. John has the most highly developed eschatology of any of the Evangelists; Satan has been overcome, life eternal is a present reality in the risen Christ (cf. also 4:4–6).

2:16 *Lust of the flesh, lust of the eyes, pride of life.* Concupiscence, avarice, and pride epitomize the spirit of the world for St. John (cf. John 17:9ff.). Notice the realized eschatology in the phrase, "the world with its lust is passing away."

2:18 *Antichrist.* Here and in verse 22 this term seems to designate the false teachers (Gnostics) mentioned above (cf. also 4:1–3). However, it is unwarranted to rule out the possibility of the appearance of an individual Antichrist before the end of the world who will challenge Christ at His return. We shall consider this notion again in connection with II–III John and II Peter.

2:20 *An anointing from the Holy One.* It is difficult to determine whether St. John has in mind Baptism or Confirmation (or both) in this passage, since the Holy Spirit is given in each of these sacraments. If we skip to verse 27, however, and compare it with John 14:17, 26, the passage would seem to suggest primarily Confirmation. This is the interpretation given by St. Cyril of Jerusalem in his *Mystagogical Catechesis III* assigned with this chapter. In commenting on this text, St. Cyril seems almost to admit of a kind of transubstantiation of the Sacred Chrism.[4] The phrase, "and you have no need that anyone teach you" in I John 2:27 sees the anointing from the Holy Spirit as the fulfillment of Jeremia 31:45 describing the new covenant.

3:2 *We shall see him just as he is.* It is not certain whether "as he is" refers to Christ's humanity at the Parousia, or to the Beatific Vision. The latter interpretation is plausible as it parallels I Corinthians 13:12; cf. I John 4:12 also.

3:9 *Whoever is born of God does not commit sin.* Not a contradiction of 1:8, but rather a statement that sin and grace are incompatible (cf. 2:29).

4:9 *God is love.* Matching this verse with 4:16 and 3:24, we can surely make a case for the activities of the Holy Spirit, Third Person of the Trinity. Note that 4:18 does not exclude a holy or reverential fear of God, but only servile fear.

---

[4] St. Cyril, *Mystagogical Catechesis III*, par. 3. Three different oils are used in the Church: *Oil of the Infirm* (used in Last Anointing); *Oil of the Catechumens* (used in Baptism, etc.); and *Sacred Chrism* (used in Baptism, Confirmation, Holy Orders, and certain consecrations).

5:6 *In the water and in the blood.* The Holy Spirit bore witness to Christ at His Baptism in the Jordan (the water?), but His death on the cross (the blood?) was also required as the first step in His glorification. The water may well also symbolize the Sacrament of Baptism, and the blood, the Eucharist. Both together flowing from the side of Christ symbolize the birth of the Church.[5] The bracketted phrase in verse 7 is probably spurious.

5:16 *Sin unto death.* A certain kind of sin known to the people of Asia Minor to whom St. John was apparently writing; apostasy is a likely candidate.

The Prologue of St. John's Gospel: The Theology of the Logos
(John 1:1–18)

We are now ready to approach the Fourth Gospel. Although St. John did not write (as has frequently been supposed) to fill in details omitted by the Synoptics, he often does supply additional information. On the other hand, scholars have been able in many instances to correlate disparate items in St. John with passages in the Synoptics (e.g., the agony in the garden is suggested in John 12:23, 27–30; 14:30–31; 18:11).[6] John often uses the term "Jews" where the Synoptics would use" Pharisees" to denote the hostility of the authorities—a characteristic of the whole Fourth Gospel. We find the same literary characteristics: duplication, inclusion, realized eschatology. In addition, St. John has his own special techniques; ironic double meanings and play on words; a systematic typology to illustrate the replacement of Old Testament institutions by Christ—similar to the Epistle to the Hebrews; and theological insights in the form of monologues in the mouth of Jesus.[7] More than any of the Synoptics, St. John's is the world of symbolism.

The first eighteen verses are known as the "Prologue"; they also summarize John's theology of the Word of God, Who has come down to earth to share divine life with men. The very first line takes us back to the beginning of creation, for the Incarnation represents a New Creation.

---

[5] Pius XII, *Mystici Corporis,* par. 26.

[6] See Raymond Brown, S.S., "Incidents That Are Units in the Synoptic Gospels but Dispersed in St. John," *Catholic Biblical Quarterly,* XXIII:2 (April 1961), 143–160.

[7] The Johannine features are catalogued conveniently in Brown, *The Gospel of St. John and the Johannine Epistles* (New Testament Reading Guide, No. 13), pp. 11–14. His purpose in writing his Gospel is clearly stated in John 20:31.

TEXT	EXPLANATION
1. In the beginning was the Word, and the Word was with God; and the Word was God. 2. He was in the beginning with God.	The "Word" is not merely an attribute of God, but a divine Person, "the image of his substance" (Heb. 1:3). The Old Testament Wisdom literature has attained its fulfillment.
3. All things were made through Him, and without Him was made nothing. That (which) has been made 4. In him (found) life; and the life was the light of men. 5. And the light shines in the darkness; and the darkness grasped it not ("grasped" has the force of "overcame").	(Note variant reading given vv. 3–4; a period has been added after the word nothing). The Word served as the divine blueprint of creation; indeed, the Father sent Him into the world as its light (revelation: work of the First Day of creation) and life. The darkness (man's sinfulness) resisted the light but did not overcome it (cf. Gen. 3:15).
6. There was a man, one sent from God, whose name was John. 7. This man came as a witness, to bear witness concerning the light, that all might believe through him. 8. He was not himself the light, but was to bear witness to the light.	This parenthetical section (probably after v. 18 originally) introduces the one who is to announce God's plan for a visible mission of His Word into the universe through the Incarnation. The "witness" was John the Baptist, the Precursor.
9. It was the true light that enlightens every man who comes into the world. 10. He was in the world, and the world was made through him, and the world knew him not. 11. He came unto his own, and his own received him not.	And so the divine Word became man under the name of Jesus Christ, a descendant of Abraham and Juda according to the flesh. He manifested himself first to His own race, the Jews, who as a people rejected Him. The forces of darkness are still at work in the world.
12. But to as many as received him he gave the power of becoming sons of God, to those who believe in his name: 13. Who were born not of blood, nor of the will of the flesh, nor of the will of man, but of God.	Christ then turned to the Gentiles, since salvation is for all men; those who accepted His message were reborn to divine life and made members of His kingdom. Thus came the "New Covenant" promised by the prophets, especially Jeremia.
14. And the Word was made flesh, and dwelt among us. And we saw his glory—glory as of the only-begotten of the Father—full of grace and truth . . . . 17. For the Law was given through Moses; grace and truth came through Jesus Christ.	And so God "pitched His tent" among us as the "Shekinah" once again made its appearance (cf. Ex. 40:34–38). God had told Moses what He is ("Yahweh"); He now tells us Who He is. This is one of His greatest graces, the revelation of His personality and intimate life. The Son's mission is to reveal the Father.

The Seven Days of the New Creation
(John 1:19—2:12)

The Evangelist continues his literary scheme of the New Creation by seemingly spelling it out in seven episodes:[8]

1. John the Baptist's witness to the Pharisees (1:19–28).
2. His witness to the disciples after Christ's baptism (1:29–34).

[8] Cf. Brown, *The Gospel of St. John and the Johannine Epistles*, pp. 18–24.

3. The first call of the disciples: from the Baptist to Jesus (1:35–40).
4. The call of Simon, renamed Peter (1:41–42; 1:42 = Matt. 16:16).
5. The call of Philip and Nathanael (1:43–51).
6. } The wedding feast at Cana: Christ plays the role of the New
7. } Adam opposite Mary, the New Eve. He anticipates His "hour" to
    perform a corporal work of mercy, not a stunt; "the woman"
    emerges as a helpmate, not a temptress: "Do whatever HE tells
    you" (2:5). The wine of the Eucharist will replace Jewish puri-
    fication rites. "And his disciples believe in him" (2:11).[9]

It seems strange to link up the marriage feast at Cana with the
Eucharist and to say not a word about matrimony. Can we not see
here in the interplay between Jesus and Mary the restoration of the
husband–wife relationship which Adam and Eve had deranged? It
hardly seems possible that the occasion of the miracle (a wedding
feast) should be purely accidental. The first Adam sinned because
he "listened to his wife"; the New Adam refuses the ready-made decision of Mary, the New Eve, and decides for Himself what is right.
Such an interpretation does not demand that Cana represent the institution of sacramental marriage; however, the episode would surely
appear to be the first step in the process.[10]

Jesus Replaces the Temple
(John 2:13–25)

Jesus took an even bolder step in the cleansing-of-the-Temple affair,
interrupting what seems to have been legitimate traffic. Yet, Jeremia
had warned the Jews that the Temple would lose its meaning; indeed,
the Ark of the Covenant was no longer present in the Holy of Holies.
Christ's cryptic statement in 2:19 is more of a prophecy than a command. After His death, the assembly of the People of God will be in
His own Body, not in the Temple.[11]

Suggested Readings

Boismard, *St. John's Prologue.*
Bouyer, *The Meaning of Sacred Scripture,* Chap. 21.
Brown, *The Gospel of St. John and the Johannine Epistles,* (New Testament
    Reading Guide, No. 13), pp. 1–26; 101–118.

---

[9] Cf. also the analysis of the Epiphany cycle in Parsch, *The Church's Year of
Grace,* Vol. I, pp. 264–266.

[10] Fr. Brown admits only of a "remotely possible" connection between Cana
and the Sacrament of Matrimony in his article, "The Johannine Sacramentary
Reconsidered," *Theological Studies,* XXIII:2 (June 1962), 205.

[11] Herod the Great, in one of his grandiose attempts to assuage the outraged
sensibilities of the Jews, had begun rebuilding the Temple (of Zorobabel) in
20–19 B.C. Tearing down the old building bit by bit, he constructed the edifice
on a grander scale. This helps us to date Jesus' public life c. 27 A.D. The quotation in 2:17 is from Psalm 68:10 (cf. Chap. XV). The reference to Jeremia is 7:4.

————, "The Problem of Historicity in St. John," *The Catholic Biblical Quarterly*, XXIV:1 (Jan. 1962), 1–14.

La Sainte Bible, pp. 1393–1396.

Monro, *Enjoying the New Testament*, pp. 154–159.

Rahner, Karl, et al., *The Word* (New York: P. J. Kenedy and Sons, 1964). Studies on the meaning of the Word of God.

Wikenhauser, *New Testament Introduction*, pp. 520–533; 279–320.

For Further Study

1. What light do the Epistles of St. Ignatius of Antioch "To the Trallians" (Fremantle, *Op. cit.*, p. 37) and "To the Smyrnans" (pp. 40–41) cast on the purpose of I John?
2. Why is oil used in some sacraments?
3. What is St. John's concept of the Word of God? Of the Body of Christ?
4. Is Cana a fitting climax to St. John's New Creation? Does this explanation show clearly that Jesus was not being disrespectful to His mother?
5. What knowledge of Christ is expressed in John 1:34? In 1:49?

Chapter XXII

The Johannine Literature (II): Water, Spirit, Baptism; the Bread of Truth and the Bread of Life

READINGS: *John 3–12; Psalm 79. St. Cyril of Jerusalem*, Mystagogical Catechesis IV, *(see Appendix, p. 223). (Note: John 3:14–21; 4:14, 22, 26; 5:25; 6 [all]; 7:37–39; 8:32, 58; 9:39; 10:16–17; 11:25–26; 12:31–32.)*

The Gospel of St. John divides rather neatly into a Prologue (1:1–1:18); The Book of Signs (1:19—12:50); and The Book of Glory (13:1—20:31). The last chapter (21, post-Resurrection appearance of Christ) was added by another hand but is included with the best Greek manuscripts; we may term it The Epilogue. Although sacramental symbolism is highly developed (this Gospel has been termed the "Johannine Sacramentary"), we must beware of concluding that we are dealing with a tradition less primitive and less reliable than the Synoptic tradition. St. John's account is that of an eyewitness, and the many intimate details of his kerygma standing side by side with his carefully worked-out didache should convince us of the utter reliability of the Fourth Gospel. The reader will note that, though there is a definite development of thought throughout, the individual chapters are more able to stand on their own than in the case of the Synoptics. Hence our plan is to give a brief synopsis of each one, trying to catch the key concept.

The Book of Signs (Continued)
(John 3:12)

CHAPTER 3: ENCOUNTER WITH NICODEMUS. A member of the Sanhedrin, Nicodemus, is vacillating between belief in Christ and his official position: hence the nocturnal visit. St. John uses his gross misunderstanding of Christ's words to evoke a notion of the supernatural character of the new birth about which He is speaking (St. Peter uses the term "reborn" in I Pet. 1:23). In John 3:5 the Greek may also be translated "begotten from above" as well as "again." Baptism is not mentioned in the whole chapter; however, the mentioning of *water* and *Spirit* together is an unmistakable clue—especially as this new

169

birth is laid down as a condition of entering the Kingdom of God. St. John is careful to remain faithful to the primitive kerygma even when he inserts later theological insights.

In verses 14–21 we have a summary of the Johannine theology as the dialogue with Nicodemus turns into a monologue—typical of St. John's style: Jesus must die in order to accomplish His goal, the salvation of the world, for His mission is one of mercy; however, His death will also serve as a judgment of the children of darkness because it will inaugurate the eschatological period. Everlasting life is a *contemporary* reality for those who believe in Him: being a son of Abraham is not the criterion, but rather the new birth referred to earlier. Finally, there is a subtle suggestion that virtuous action is as much an avenue to wisdom as the latter is an avenue to moral virtue (v. 21).

We must interpret 3:22 in the light of 4:2. The disciples of Jesus were simply carrying on John the Baptist's rite; in all probability, Christian Baptism had not yet been instituted. John's Baptism was more of a *sign* of spiritual regeneration than a *cause* of this grace. Whereas the Christian sacrament can produce regeneration through the faith of the Church, the Baptist's rite could do so only through the faith of the recipient. The "water" versus the "Holy Spirit" in 1:33 hint at this distinction; Matthew 3:11 and Luke 3:16 add the note of "fire."[1] St. Thomas summarizes the opinions of the Fathers of the Church regarding the significance of the Baptism of Christ:[2]

1. Christ bore witness to the authenticity of John's rite by undergoing it; and John, in turn bore witness to Christ's messiaship on the occasion of His Baptism (1:31–34; however, Matt. 11:2–6 indicates that his knowledge of Christ at this time was definitely limited).
2. Christ was "anointed" for His public life; under this aspect, we might compare the rite with Christian confirmation.
3. Christ "consecrated" water to make it a fit instrument of sacramental Baptism. However, John 7:39 indicates that the last step in its institution took place only at Pentecost.[3]

In his profound humility, John the Baptist is content to play the role of best man to the bridegroom: "He must increase, but I must

---

[1] At the same time we must agree with Raymond Brown, S.S., that the primary reference here is to general outpouring of the Spirit in the messianic era; cf. "The Eucharist and Baptism in St. John," *Proceedings of the Eighth Annual Meeting of the Society of Catholic College Teachers of Sacred Doctrine* (1962), pp. 30–32.

[2] *Summa Theologica*, IIIa, Q. 39.

[3] *Ibid.*, Q. 66, Art. 2.

decrease" (3:30). This turned out to be his last witness to Christ, for shortly afterward he was imprisoned. Verses 31–36 seem to duplicate verses 11–18; this practice is characteristic of the Fourth Gospel.

CHAPTER 4: THE LIVING WATER; MANIFESTATION OF MESSIASHIP. Perhaps Our Lord's conversation with a member of the hated Samaritan race was meant to serve as a hint of the future conversion of the Gentiles. The water symbolism is further developed, with Nicodemus-like misunderstanding on the part of the woman. The "living water" promised by Christ represents spring water (as opposed to stagnant cistern water; cf. Jer. 2:13 and Isa. 55:1). In I Corinthians St. Paul equates water with Christ (10:4—"spiritual drink"), and also with the *Spirit* (12:13). As the community's theology gradually evolved through succeeding centuries, the term "sanctifying grace" was employed to designate this notion; it is the source or "seed" of life everlasting (John 4:14), which has already begun in the baptized. After opting for the worship of the Jews over the schismatic religion of the Samaritans, Jesus proclaims the advent of a new era of worship "in spirit and in truth." He openly identifies Himself as the Messia to the woman (v. 26). We do not find the same reticence about revealing His true nature in this Fourth Gospel as we noted in the Synoptics; the messianic secrecy has yielded to monstrous blindness ("darkness") on the part of the Jews in the face of Jesus' cryptic statements about not only His messiaship but also His divinity. The "harvest" in verse 36 is another indication of realized eschatology; Christ is reaping the fruits of the labors of the prophets, including John the Baptist. The "royal official" may be the centurion in Matthew 8:5ff. and Luke 7:1ff. This incident illustrates the subtle development in St. John's Gospel: Jesus reveals the need of *rebirth* to Nicodemus; its source, *living water*, to the Samaritan woman; and offers a *prophecy-in-act* presaging the resurrection to eternal life in the chapter's finale.[4]

CHAPTER 5: THE RESURRECTION OF LIFE. Seven of the first twelve chapters of this Gospel refer directly to Jewish feasts. These references relate to St. *John's theme of the replacement of the feasts by Christianity at the coming of Jesus.* On the occasion of this unspecified feast (5:1), Jesus replaces the Jewish Sabbath. What merely natural water "unstirred" by divine intervention—though this passage may be spurious) failed to accomplish on the paralytic, Jesus accomplishes simply by His word—on the Sabbath when one was not supposed to practice medicine. He and His Father are Lord of the Sabbath. They are also Lord of life, and will confer everlasting life on the just through the resurrection (of the body). Note the use of the present

---

[4] See Fr. Stanley's article, "Samaritan Interlude" in *Worship*, XXXIV:3 (Feb. 1960), 137–144.

tense in verse 24; also, the transition from "Son of Man" in verse 27 to "Son of God" in verse 28, followed by verse 30: "Of myself I can do nothing." The divine-human nature of Christ is delicately insinuated. Four witnesses to His mission are cited: John the Baptist, His works, His Father, and the Scriptures. All of these the Jews reject; their crime is not lack of knowledge, but lack of love. In this life, charity enjoys the primacy over knowledge!

CHAPTER 6: BREAD, DOCTRINE, AND THE EUCHARIST. Here is one of the richest, most complex chapters in the whole Gospel. Although it is definitely Eucharistic, authorities disagree as to the actual breakdown of the material. Our analysis follows that of Fr. Brown; we distinguish three levels of teaching in the chapter:[5]

Vv. 1–13   Christ replaces the Passover as He provides physical nourishment, *food,* for His listeners in the multiplication of the loaves. (Verse 15 seems to be the equivalent of Christ's third temptation as described in Matt. 4:8–9; his crossing of the Sea of Tiberias resembles the Jews' crossing of the Red Sea; their asking a sign of Him harks back to His first temptation in Matt. 4:3–4, and thus to the Jews' demand for food in the desert which was satisfied by the manna.)

26–50   The basic meaning of the "bread of life" in this section seems to be *divine revelation,* possessed only by means of *faith;* note verses 45–47. This divine wisdom will lead to life everlasting. There are definite Eucharistic overtones here; the implication is that one must graduate to the third level for his faith to produce its fruit. The sapiential level ends with verse 50.

51–59   Here begins the "Eucharistic" or sacramental level. In the Greek, a new word for "eat" is introduced, *trogo,* which carries the notion of "masticate" and can hardly be verified of mere doctrine. The suggestion has been made that perhaps St. John *has combined the institution of the Eucharist at the Last Supper with the multiplication of the loaves in this Chapter 6 of his Gospel.*[6] This would explain why he has no account of the institution in that context. Note the phrases "giving thanks," "distributed," and "fragments" ("hosts"?) in verses 11–12; "the bread that I will *give* is my flesh . . ." where "give" has the connotation of *deliver up.*

---

[5] Brown, *The Gospel of St. John and the Johannine Epistles,* pp. 37–42.
[6] Fr. Lagrange makes this division in *The Gospel of Jesus Christ,* Vol. I (Westminster, Md.: Newman Press, 1938), p. 228.

60–70 These words seem to be part of Christ's original discourse, i.e., He seems to revert back to the sapiential theme. Verse 69 may be the Johannine parallel of Peter's confession at Caesarea Philippi; verse 71 sounds like the Last Supper exposé of Judas.

CHAPTER 7: THE REPLACEMENT OF TABERNACLES. His brethren's urging, "manifest thyself to the world" is suspiciously like the second temptation, "throw thyself down" (Matt. 4:6). Jesus refuses to go into Jerusalem publicly for the celebration of Tabernacles, but does go up privately. This was a joyous feast in which the Exodus was commemorated by the building of tents or booths recalling the trek through the wilderness (hence the feast was also called "Booths"). On each day of the octave, a solemn libation of water was made in the Temple to petition God for the necessary fall rain following the fruit harvest. As the water was being carried from the pool of Siloe, Jesus cries out, "If anyone thirst, let him come to me; and let him drink who believes in me" (vv. 37–38; this is the better reading). His exodus to the Father will replace the Exodus from Egypt as the center of worship and will release the true water from heaven, the Holy Spirit. But verse 39 notes that the outpouring of the Spirit will be deferred until Jesus' "glorification" (death on the cross, at which water and blood came from His side) followed by Pentecost. Note the irony in verses 35 and 42.

CHAPTER 8: CHRIST AND YAHWEH. The adulteress episode was apparently inserted at this point by a later editor, as it is out of place here. It proves how much the mercy of God transcends human justice. This whole chapter centers about the notion of the word. As the "light of the world," Christ is the Father's witness to the truth; those with whom He shares His word "shall know the truth, and the truth shall make you free" (v. 32). The freedom Christ has in mind is not the ability to do as one pleases, but the freedom to act as sons of God. Christ's witness is true because HE IS (YAHWEH).

CHAPTER 9: CHRIST "ENLIGHTENS" THE BLIND MAN. Blind from birth (a suggestion of original sin?), the man's sight is restored by the anointing of Christ and the washing in the pool of Siloe. There seems to be a definite reference to Baptism here; the early Church called it the "sacrament of enlightenment." The plucky responses of the cured blind man immediately appeal to the reader and serve to set up the punch line of the chapter, "For judgment have I come into this world, that they who do not see may see, and they who see may become blind" (v. 39). Here is a genuine Anawim manifesto. The blind man is contrasted with the conceited Pharisees.

CHAPTER 10: THE GOOD SHEPHERD. The campaign against the Pharisees is carried on in this chapter as they are branded as hirelings. The symbol of the Good Shepherd was a favorite theme in primitive Christianity; the modern parallel is devotion to the Sacred Heart. The Christology of verses 16–17 is the Johannine counterpart of St. Paul's notion of the Body of Christ. The word "fold" in verse 16 should be read "flock." This verse suggests the commingling of Jew and Gentile in the Church, rather than a prophecy that the whole world will be converted. The cycle of feasts is rounded out by the introduction of the *Dedication* (of the Temple in 164 B.C. after its profanation by Antiochus Epiphanes). That institution is being replaced by "him whom the Father has made holy and sent into the world" (v. 36). Note the dialectical argument used here to throw the Jews off the scent after Jesus' statement, "I and the Father are one" in verse 30.

CHAPTER 11: CHRIST IS LIFE. The dramatic dimensions of Christ's public life come into full bloom with the resurrection of Lazarus. The Master allows Lazarus to die that He may raise him from the dead and demonstrate that *He* is man's life and resurrection.[7] Yet, the Jews "will not believe even if someone rises from the dead" (Luke 16:31, from the story of the only other Lazarus in the Gospels). The *real* death is not the death of the body, for Christ will have to pay the price of resurrection with His own death; it is rather the death of the spirit, which those who believe in Jesus will never have to undergo (v. 26). This event sealed the earthly fate of Christ (cf. vv. 47–53). The chapter cannot end without a reference to a feast (Passover, v. 55).

CHAPTER 12: THE HOUR OF JESUS. "There is no solid basis for identifying Mary of Bethany with the Galilean sinner or Mary of Magdalene."[8] This (messianic ?) anointing exposes the avarice of Judas, and may have constituted the last straw in his rift with Jesus. He is now completely disillusioned with regard to the possibility of any political dimension being attached to the Master's messiaship; there is no future in HIS cause. Indeed, the Jews are even plotting to kill some of the evidence (Lazarus)! In the theophany that follows, Jesus insists

---

[7] An example of how this symbolism is used in the liturgy is contained in the excellent development of this theme and related events by Conrad Pepler, O.P., *Lent*, pp. 222–243.

[8] Brown, *Op. cit.*, p. 62. This is also Fr. Lagrange's opinion, *Op. cit.*, pp. 168–172.

on identifying Himself with Zacharia's meek king (9:9–10) rather than with Daniel's glorious "Son of Man." Verses 20–23 represent a final manifestation to the Gentile world, verses 24–26 smack of the Synoptics. *The "hour of Jesus" is His death, the royal road to glorification.*[9] His hearers easily understood the idiom, "lifted up" in verse 32. The same evaluation which Jesus attached to His parables in the Synoptics (cf. Matt. 13:11–15) is now attached to His "signs" (John 12: 37–41): they have not succeeded in generating faith, "for they (the leaders) loved the glory of men more than the glory of God" (v. 43). The remaining verses summarize John's theology and bring to a close the Book of Signs.

St. Cyril of Jerusalem and the Real Presence
Mystagogical Catechesis IV

Quoting I Corinthians 11:23, St. Cyril offers an explicit statement of the doctrine of the real presence of Christ under the Eucharistic species (par. 1, 6, 9). He gives the changing of the water into wine at Cana a Eucharistic orientation (par. 2), and urges an ontological change in the recipients of the Sacrament (par. 3), whom he refers to as "Christophers"; he cites II Peter 1:4 ("partakers of the divine nature") in support of this thesis. A common Protestant opinion reckons St. Cyril as "the first theologian to interpret the Lord's presence in conversionist language."[10] St. Cyril allegorizes Psalm 22 into a Eucharistic context in par. 7; even the Book of Ecclesiastes is made to bear witness to Baptism, Confirmation and the Eucharist (par. 8).

Psalm 79: The Shepherd Hymn

A reasonable conjecture might well place this Lament on the lips of a Judean poet after the sack of the Northern Kingdom (Ephraim, Benjamin, and Manasse were all in the Kingdom of Israel). The touching metaphor making Yahweh the "Shepherd of Israel" has been immortalized in Ezechiel 34 and Psalm 22. In John 10:16 Christ implicitly claims to be fulfilling Ezechiel 34:23–24 and 37:22–24. In Psalm 79:9ff. Israel passes from the status of Yahweh's *flock* to that of His *vineyard*. This metaphor was suggested by Osee 10:1; Isaia 5 made it a standard symbol. Note the refrain in verses 4, 8, 20.

---

[9] This lends force to the alternate translation of Genesis 3:15, "and he (Satan) will *bruise* your heel."

[10] St. Cyril of Jerusalem's *Lectures on the Christian Sacraments* (London: S.P.C.K., 1951) p. xxxii. For a scriptural argument in favor of the real presence, see Jacques Dupont's "This Is My Body"—"This Is My Blood" in *Theology Digest,* IX:1 (Winter 1961), 49–51. He argues quite convincingly on the grounds that the Last Supper was a prophecy-in-act.

God's Kingdom in the New Testament

Suggested Readings

Bouyer, *The Meaning of Sacred Scripture,* Chap. 20.

Brown, "The Eucharist and Baptism in St. John," *Proceedings of the Eighth Annual Meeting of the Society of Catholic College Teachers of Sacred Doctrine,* (1962), pp. 14–33.

——————. *The Gospel of St. John and the Johannine Epistles* (New Testament Reading Guide, No. 13), pp. 26–66.

——————, "The Johannine Sacramentary Reconsidered," *Theological Studies,* XXIII:2 (June 1962), 183–206; the analysis on the last two pages is especially helpful.

——————, "Incidents that are Units in the Synoptic Gospels but Dispersed in St. John," *Catholic Biblical Quarterly,* XXIII:2 (April 1961), 143–160.

Lagrange, *The Gospel of Jesus Christ,* Vol. 1.

Hoskyns, E. C., *The Fourth Gospel* (London: Faber and Faber, 1947.) One of the best commentaries on St. John by a Protestant authority.

For Further Study

1. According to St. John's Gospel, what is the relationship between Baptism and the Eucharist?
2. How does Jesus' revelation of His messiaship and divinity compare with this revelation in the Synoptics?
3. What is probably the unnamed feast in Chapter 5? (Which major feast otherwise has been left unmentioned?)
4. During the latter part of Lent, which of the four Evangelists is best represented in the Gospel selections?
5. Be sure you can distinguish the *physical, sapiential,* and *Eucharistic* phases of the material in Chapter 6 of St. John's Gospel.

Chapter XXIII

The Johannine Literature (III): The Divine Indwelling and the Church

READINGS: *John 13–21; Psalm 40. St. Cyril of Jerusalem,* Mystagogical *Catechesis V (See Appendix, p. 225). (Note: John 13:34; 14:6; 15:2; 16:7; 17:22–23; 18:36–37; 19:34; 20:17, 23, 31; 21:17; Zacharia 14:9.)*

As the "Book of Glory" opens we find Jesus preparing for His exodus from this world. It is only this event (His death) which—though an apparent defeat—will effect His glorification. St. John continues to give us the deep layer of meaning behind the words and deeds of the Master; his Gospel is the fruit of decades of meditation. More than any other Evangelist, the Beloved Disciple gives us an incarnational orientation: Christ's birth is an invasion of Satan's domain, and His death is its conquest. We must not feel cheated because the Fourth Gospel lacks an infancy narrative! Chapter 13 begins the account of the Last Supper with scarcely any introduction. The actual date of this event is one of the most elusive problems in the New Testament. We cannot enter into the controversy here except to point out the two leading solutions: *1)* The Last Supper was observed on Thursday night, as St. John indicates, and was not a Passover meal, but simply an imitation of it which Christ replaced with His sacrifice;[1] *2)* Christ and the apostles celebrated the Passover on Tuesday night, according to the ancient priestly calendar, whereas the Jews as a whole observed the feast on the official night, Friday.[2] In this latter case, it seems that Jesus' party would not have been able to eat a Paschal lamb as the priests would probably not have begun their work yet. As a matter of fact, no mention is made in the Gospels of the use of a lamb, although the Synoptics definitely imply that the Last Supper was a Passover celebration.

---

[1] *La Sainte Bible,* p. 1325; this is also Fr. Brown's opinion, *Op. cit.,* p. 67, and in *The Bible Today,* April 1964, p. 127.

[2] Proposed by Anne Jaubert in *La Date de la Cène* (Paris: Gabalda, 1957) and cited by P. W. Skeehan in the *Catholic Biblical Quarterly,* XX:2 (April 1958), pp. 192–199. Fr. Stanley prefers this solution in *Gospel of St. Matthew,* pp. 82–83.

The Washing of the Feet: Baptismal Overtones
(John 13)

This touching episode suggests the passage in Luke 22:24ff. where the apostles are arguing over their respective rank in the Kingdom; Jesus refutes their ambition with His own example: "But I am in your midst as one who serves" (v. 27). Although humility is the main lesson taught, the element of cleansing takes precedence over that of fraternal service; hence, we should see here a symbol of Baptism (or even Penance) rather than that of the Eucharist. The words in verse 10 may even suggest (as it did to the Fathers) the impropriety of re-Baptism in the case of heretics. In line with our suggestion in the last chapter, *it is possible that the institution of the Eucharist took place after the foot-washing: this would put much more logic into verse 17* (cf. Luke 22:19).[3]

Jesus' poignant human emotions manifest themselves in the interlude which follows; the thought of the betrayal already plotted by Judas troubles Him. After quoting Psalm 40:10, he proceeds to single out the betrayer, "And after the morsel, Satan entered into him (Judas)" (13:27). Note that this event is also referred to at the end of the Eucharistic discourse in 6:72, thus lending more evidence to the *anticipation* by the Evangelist of the account of the institution mentioned above. And certainly the "new commandment" (Latin, *mandatum*, giving rise to the designation "Maundy Thursday") of verse 34 fits in with the theme of Agape.

The Last Discourse of Jesus
(John 14, 16)

We might call this section St. John's "Sermon on the Mount"—except that it begins in the Cenacle and ends elsewhere. Most of the Fourth Gospel represents realized eschatology; 14:2 is an apparent exception, where Jesus is referring to the Parousia. He seems to suggest that there is a great variety of rewards in the next life. At any rate, here is a Johannine "divine assurance" for the true follower of Christ. He is the *way* because His incarnation bridges the gap between creature and Creator; as the Divine Teacher, He is *the Truth;* He gives *life* because His person is the Church (14:6). Philip's question next plunges Jesus squarely into the theology of the Trinity, so difficult to grasp in view of their monotheistic background. Chapter 16 (probably a parallel version of 14) has matching passages as indicated below.

---

[3] Again the reader is referred to Fr. Brown's article in the *Proceedings of the Eighth annual Meeting of the Society of Catholic College Teachers of Sacred Doctrine* (1962), p. 25.

John 14	Verses:	Verses:	John 16
1. To those who accept the Son's mission, the Father will give the "Advocate" ("Defender"). The work of Christ is seen as continued in the world by the Holy Spirit (note also v. 26).	15–17 — THE SPIRIT	7–15	Indeed, the Son's departure is a condition of the Spirit's coming; the *invisible* mission of the Spirit will replace the Son's *visible* mission only after He departs. (In v. 8, justice implies vindication.)
2. Christ's death will inaugurate the messianic era of personal intimacy with Him.	18–22 — THE SON	16–22	This intimacy will demand a period of testing through tribulation, followed by perfect joy.
3. The unity of Father and Son demands that where the Son is, there also is the Father.	23–24 — THE FATHER	23–27	Henceforth prayers are to be addressed to the Father in the name of Jesus.

The Vine and the Branches: St. John's Equivalent of the "Body of Christ"

(John 15)

The final words of Chapter 14 suggest the little group left the Cenacle for Gethsemani at this point, continuing the dialogue (which now becomes a monologue) en route. Jesus shows how He recapitulates His followers in His own *Person* through the allegory of the vine and the branches. Two decades later St. Paul will recapitulate the members of the Church in Christ's *body;* yet, this is also a *personalist* concept (e.g., "It is now no longer I that live, but Christ lives in me" —Gal. 2:20). We noted some Old Testament references to Israel as Yahweh's vineyard in the previous chapter; here a few words should be said about the phrase, "and every branch that bears fruit he (the Father) will cleanse, that it may bear more fruit" (v. 2). The Douay-Rheims Version has "purge" for "cleanse"; spiritual writers see here a reference to the purgation which the Christian must undergo in order to attain perfection. This purgation is ordinarily divided into three stages: those penitential exercises, freely undertaken for the love of God, which constitute the *active* purification of the *senses* and lead to separation from mortal sin and willful affection to venial sin; the *passive* purification of the *senses* wherein God sends trials such as sickness and humiliation to complete the process and raise the soul to occasional infused contemplation; finally, God continues to purge the person through the *passive* purification of the *spirit* by means of spiritual dryness and severe trials—a veritable crucifixion known as

179

the "dark night of the soul"—leading to habitual infused contemplation, "heaven begun."

But Christianity is not an individualistic religion; to be the friend of Jesus, one must be social minded, apostolic: "Greater love than this no one has, that one lay down his life for his friends" (v. 13). Those who have been called to the full-time, organized apostolate have a special, God-given "vocation" (v. 16) which will not be lacking in persecution. The last part of the chapter (from v. 18) closely parallels the Apostolic Discourse in Chapter 10 of Matthew's Gospel (e.g., compare John 15:26 with Matt. 10:19–20).

The Emergence of the Church in St. John
(John 17)

If St. Matthew portrays the Church as the summation of the Reign of God, St. John depicts it as the summation of the People of God. The sublime priestly prayer of Christ recapitulates the conclusions of the three previous chapters. Verse 3 suggests the essence of the Beatific Vision: the perfect *knowledge* of God. Jesus sees His work as already accomplished: He sees His Servant-role, which has led Him to glory, now passed on to His apostles who likewise have the seeds of glory within them. It is possible to find in this chapter the biblical foundation of the "four marks" of the Church: *1)* "Even as thou hast sent me into the world, so I also send them into the world" (v. 18: *catholicity*); *2)* "And for them I sanctify myself, that they also may be sanctified" (v. 19: *holiness*); *3)* "Yet not for these only do I pray, but for those also who through their word are to believe in me" (v. 20: *apostolicity*); *4)* "that all may be one, even as thou, Father, in me and I in thee; that they also may be one in us" (v. 21; *unity*). This last phrase is underscored in verses 22–23. Here the Pauline doctrine of the Body of Christ is perfected by being given a Trinitarian orientation: God wills to share with us the very heights of His divinity, His triple personality. The Church is not only Christ, it is the Trinity present in the believers.[4]

Passion and Death of the King of Glory
(John 18–19)

The whole trial and death sequence in St. John is presented in the light of Christ's kingship. Not even Gethsemani is without a theophany (18:6). Jesus Himself, according to information supplied by John, opens the door for their desertion (v. 8). The Evangelist substantiates

---

[4] Cf. André Feuillet, "The Era of the Church in St. John," *Theology Digest* XI:1 (Spring 1963), 3.

St. Luke in mentioning two Jewish interrogations, one before Annas (unofficial); the other before the high priest, Caiphas (official). The death-sentence passed by the latter has to be ratified by Rome in the person of the skeptical procurator, Pontius Pilate. Before He can admit His kingship, Jesus must show Pilate the drastic re-orientation which this concept had undergone in Israel. The admission definitely impresses (and frightens) the procurator, even though his thorough skepticism manifests itself in the rhetorical question of verse 38. Turning now to the Jews, we find them carefully avoiding legal defilement as they wallow in blood-guilt (v. 28).

In Chapter 19 the scene degenerates to mockery. The whole issue is made to center around Christ's kingship. Refusing to declare His origin, the Victim solemnly assures Pilate that His real adversary is on another level (19:11). Recently, philological arguments have been adduced in an attempt to show that verse 13 actually has Pilate seat Christ (ironically) on the judgment-seat instead of himself.[5] This would be in keeping with the Evangelist's suppression of many of the details in the Synoptics which have no reference to Jesus' kingship and emphasis of those details which do refer to it. Even the inscription carries on the irony; only it just so happens that Christ is the King of the Jews!

St. John shows the crucifixion scene as the climax of Cana: now, at the Hour of Jesus, the New Eve (the "woman" here becomes "mother") proves herself definitively as the true helpmate and He, in turn, touchingly fulfills the Fourth Commandment.[6] Jesus dies at the sixth hour as the Paschal lambs are being slaughtered in the Temple. In "giving up His spirit," He bequeaths it to followers in the form of blood and water (the Eucharist and Baptism). As in the case of the Paschal lamb, not a bone was broken. Again St. John quotes one of his favorite prophets, Zacharia 12:10, after first citing a text from our "baptismal hymn," Psalm 33:21. What the Jews were so ardently hoping and praying for through the words of Zacharia 14:9 is now accomplished but it goes tragically unrecognized. Verse 39 encourages us to conclude that the man to whom rebirth in water and the Spirit had first been proclaimed was able to witness its fulfillment with new faith.

---

[5] De la Potterie, Ignace, "Jesus King and Judge in John 19," *Theology Digest* XI:1 (Spring 1963), 3, 21. The evidence is not convincing, however.

[6] Three distinct women besides the Blessed Mother seem to be indicated at the cross: her unnamed sister—probably Salome, St. John's mother, since Mark 16:1 also has her at the empty tomb; Mary, the wife of Cleophas; and Mary Magdalene. If the conjecture regarding Salome is correct, then John and James the Greater were first cousins of Jesus, along with James the Less and Jude.

The Resurrection and Exaltation of Jesus: Peter's Primacy
(John 20–21)

John alone informs us that Mary Magdalene left the empty tomb before the angelic explanation of the Resurrection given in the Synoptic Gospels. Yet, it is to her that the first recorded appearance takes place. The refusal of Jesus to let Mary touch His feet presages the new relationship with Him now open to His followers: their new point of contact transcends the physical order; it is the contact of faith and the Eucharist. The cryptic reference to the Ascension in this same verse (17) together with the failure of St. John and the Synoptic Gospels (with the exception of Mark 16:19) to mention that event urges upon us the conclusion proposed by Fr. Benoit. He distinguishes two "Ascensions": *1)* the *theological* one, i.e., Christ's exaltation at the "right hand" of the Father: this took place simultaneously with the Resurrection and was entirely invisible; *2)* the *historical* Ascension, i.e., the final farewell of Jesus to His followers, postponed according to Acts 1:3 until forty days after the Resurrection to furnish a thematic framework for the various apparitions of Christ.[7] What convinces "the other disciple" (the Evangelist himself) of the reality of the Resurrection is the tidy position of the burial cloths. We have the testimony of the Council of Trent to the effect that John 20:22–23 represents the conferral of the power to remit sins on the apostles (and therefore the Church).[8] Thomas' disbelief enables the Evangelist to build up to a final summation of his whole purpose as expressed in the last verse of the chapter.

Chapter 21 is an added (though inspired) epilogue. Its purpose is to show us: *1)* the commissioning of the apostles on their mission of "catching fish," i.e., converting the world (ancient biology listed a total of 153 species; cf. v. 11, Luke 5:1ff., and Ezech. 47:9–10, of which this episode seems to be a fulfillment); *2)* the conferring of the primacy on Peter by way of a reversal of his triple denial (v. 17), and a prediction of his martyrdom; and *3)* the correction of the mistaken notion that St. John was to remain alive until the Parousia: another disillusionment regarding the expectation of Christ's quick return that was prevalent in the early Church.

The Eucharistic-Centered Spirit of the Early Church
(Didache 9, 10)

Almost continuous in point of time with the Fourth Gospel is the *Didache*, introduced on page 157. The passages quoted below clearly indicate the central position of "the holy vine" (cf. *Didache* 9:2, which

---

[7] "The Ascension of Christ," *Theology Digest*, VIII:2 (Spring 1960), 105–110.
[8] Cf. Clarkson, etc., *The Church Teaches*, No. 802 (Denz. No. 913).

gives a Eucharistic orientation to John 15:1) in first-century Christianity. There is a suggestion of a lingering expectation of the Parousia in the near future in *Didache* 10:6.

Didache 9

1. In regard to the Eucharist, you shall offer the Eucharist thus: 2. First, in connection with the cup, 'We give Thee thanks, Our Father, for *the holy vine* of David Thy son, which Thou hast made known to us through Jesus Thy Son; to Thee be glory forever.' 3. As this broken bread was scattered upon the mountain tops and after being harvested was made one, so let Thy Church be gathered together from the ends of the earth into Thy Kingdom, for Thine is the glory and the power through Jesus Christ forever. 4. But let no one eat or drink of the Eucharist with you except those baptized in the name of the Lord, for it was in reference to this that the Lord said: 'Do not give that which is holy to dogs.'

Didache 10

1. But after it has been completed, give thanks in the following way: 2. 'We thank Thee, Holy Father, for Thy holy name, which Thou hast caused to dwell in our hearts, and for the knowledge and faith and immortality, which Thou hast made known to us through Jesus Thy Son; to Thee be glory forever. 3. Thou, Lord Almighty, has created all things for Thy name's sake and has given food and drink and eternal life through Thy Son. 4. For all things we render Thee thanks, because Thou art mighty; to Thee be glory forever. 5. Remember, O Lord, Thy Church, deliver it from all evil and make it perfect in Thy love, and gather it from the four winds, sanctified for Thy kingdom, which Thou hast prepared for it; for Thine is the power and the glory forever. 6. *Let grace come, and let this world pass away,* 'Hosanna to the God of David.' If anyone is holy, let him come; if anyone is not, let him repent. Maranatha. Amen. 7. But allow 'prophets' to render thanks as they desire.[9]

Mystagogical Catechesis V *and the Mass of the Faithful* (Sequel to Fore-Mass, p. 146)

This document enables us to complete the ceremonies of the Mass at the time of Cyril of Jerusalem (Fourth Century; the creed is missing, as it was added about 800).

1. Washing of the hands by the celebrant, followed by (another ?) kiss of peace.
2. Offering of gifts by the people; laying his hand on them, the priest prays:
3. THE PREFACE, setting the tone of the Eucharist (thanksgiving) for the day.

---

[9] See Schopp, *The Fathers of the Church,* Vol. I, pp. 178–180. (See p. 146 for Chapter 14.)

4. The Sanctus: added since the *Apostolic Tradition* of St. Hippolytus c. 225 A.D.

5. Words of CONSECRATION, followed immediately by EPICLESIS (Prayer to Holy Spirit).

6. The ANAMNESIS or *commemoration* of Passion, Resurrection, Ascension of Christ.[10]

7. Commemoration of the living, then of the dead, followed by the great AMEN.

8. The PATER NOSTER (minutely analyzed by Cyril); then "Holy things to holy men."

9. COMMUNION of *Host* (received in palm of hand) and the *Cup;* (deacons take to absent).

10. Prayer of thanksgiving (followed by collection of alms; cf. Justin's *Apology*).

Psalm 40: A Sick Man's Confidence in the Lord

Requesting aid from on high in his illness, the Psalmist ends with a powerful expression of trust in God; however, verse 13 must not be construed as an expectation of the Beatific Vision! Christ quoted verse 10 concerning Judas' betrayal. The first three verses have been adapted in the Church as a public prayer for the reigning Pope.

Suggested Readings

Bouyer, *The Meaning of Sacred Scripture,* Chap. 19. Helpful also for the Apocalypse.

Brown, *The Gospel of St. John and the Johannine Epistles* (New Testament Reading Guide Series, No. 13), pp. 66–100.

Davis, *Theology for Today,* Chap. 12.

de la Potterie, I., "Jesus King and Judge in John 19," *Theology Digest* XI:1 (Spring 1963), 21.

Durrwell, *The Resurrection,* Chap. 8; especially pp. 330–332. See also Sloyan's analysis in, "The Eucharist as an Eschatological Meal," *Worship* XXXVI:7, 444–451.

Ellard, *Christian Life and Worship,* Chap. 13–14.

Feuillet, "The Era of the Church in St. John," *Theology Digest* XI:1 (Spring 1963), 3.

Lagrange, *The Gospel of Jesus Christ,* Vol. II, pp. 196–198.

Schillebeeckx, "Ascension and Pentecost," *Worship* XXXV:6 (May 1961), 336–363.

For Further Study

1. Is the washing of the apostles' feet more symbolic of Baptism or the Eucharist?
2. Why did Christ have to leave (cf. John 16:7)?
3. Which do you consider a more apt metaphor, the *Body of Christ* or the *Vine and the Branches?*
4. What sort of unity did Christ will for His Church?

---

[10] St. Cyril does not mention an anamnesis, but it is found in St. Hippolytus.

Chapter XXIV

Apocalypse (I): Enthronement of the Lamb of God and the Fall of Jerusalem

READINGS: *Apocalypse 1–11; Psalm 83. Didache, Chap. 15 (Note symbolism in par. A.)*

Although the Greek word from which "Apocalypse" is taken means *revelation,* this title may well deceive the unwary. To look upon the final book of the Bible as simply a series of heavenly visions recorded verbatim by the sacred author does it a notable injustice.[1] It would be more accurate to describe it as an anthology of allusions to the Old Testament. The Book of Daniel is the pivotal source, with Isaia and Ezechiel making substantial contributions. From these allusions an elaborate mosaic has been worked out to convey a message to the Christian community of the late first century. There is some justification in considering the Apocalypse a "problem" book. However, the greatest problem will probably be the reader's unfamiliarity with Old Testament themes and literary genres and the Semitic mentality which gave rise to them.

In true apocalyptic style the author of the Apocalypse offers his contemporaries consolation in the midst of trials and persecution— after the manner of the Book of Daniel—by portraying local evils as a reflection of the protracted conflict between the cosmic forces of good and evil: God versus Satan. Prototypes of this genre are also to be found in Isaia 27 and Ezechiel 37–38. A comparison of the apocalyptic elements employed in this book with those found in the Book of Daniel provides a basis for analysis of its technique on the next page.

We have already introduced the student to the Johannine literature in Chapter XXI; it will suffice to note here that the authorship (and as a consequence the canonicity) of the Apocalypse posed a severe problem in the early Church. The heart of the problem lies in the marked diversity between this book and the Fourth Gospel. The polished Greek phrases of the latter contrast so glaringly with the Hebraisms

---

[1] Fr. Heidt suggests in *The Book of the Apocalypse* (New Testament Reading Guide Series, No. 14 [Collegeville, Minn.: Liturgical Press, 1960]), p. 18, the possibility that the author had no visions at all; i.e., the visions are simply a literary device. Wikenhauser, in *New Testament Introduction,* p. 545, holds the opposite view and has the weight of tradition on his side.

ELEMENTS	IN THE BOOK OF DANIEL	IN THE APOCALYPSE
Use of bizarre symbols:	The composite statue in Chap. 2; the four animals in Chap. 7; the ram and he-goat in Chap. 8.	The seven lampstands; the four living creatures; the woman and the dragon; the beast with horns.
The presence of visions:	Two visions of Nabuchodonosor in Chaps. 2 and 4; Daniel's visions.	The whole book is presented as a vision of the author, "John."
Angelic intermediaries:	Explanations by the angel Gabriel.	Angelic interpretations in 1:1, 17:1ff., 22:8.
Symbolic use of numbers:	The 70 weeks of years and its division into parts: 62, 7, 1, ½.	The ½-week of Daniel in terms of 3½ years, 42 months, 1260 days.
Pre-dating:	The author lived during the Machabean era, pre-dating events from the Babylonian Exile (587 B.C.) until 167 B.C.	The author pre-dates events from the death of Christ until about 95 A.D.
Pseudonymous:	Message is put in the mouth of a legendary wise man, Daniel, by an unknown author.	The identity of the author, one "John, your brother and partner in the tribulation" is debated.
A book of consolation:	Written for Jews being persecuted by Antiochus Epiphanes.	Written for Christians being persecuted by the Roman Empire.
Eschatological perspective:	The author looks forward to the replacement of all earthly kingdoms by messianic kingdom.	The author goes beyond this perspective in his last two chapters and looks to the second coming.

and even barbarous Greek of the Apocalypse that numerous scholars have concluded that both could not have come from the same hand. They are not agreed, however, as to which work is more directly the work of the Apostle and which comes from the hand of a disciple.[2] Although its canonicity was quite generally recognized by 500 A.D., individual churches and exegetes continued to challenge its status well into the Middle Ages. The date of the book is usually placed at about 95 A.D. (i.e., before that of the Fourth Gospel). The unity of the book will be treated along the way.

The interpretation of the Apocalypse likewise poses a problem. The main hurdle, however, has been jumped: it is clear today that the

---

[2] Fr. Brown, *The Gospel of St. John, the Johannine Epistles,* pp. 4–5, and Fr. Heidt, *The Book of the Apocalypse,* p. 14, opt for the Johannine authorship of the Apocalypse over the Fourth Gospel. Not so Fr. Boismard.

book is *not* a cryptogram containing a detailed timetable of future historical events leading up to the end of the world. The bizarre symbols are merely part and parcel of the apocalyptic genre, and the overall work is almost universally recognized as *a polemic against the Roman Empire for its persecution of the Christian Church, together with a prediction of the ultimate triumph of the latter and the punishment of her enemies.* Understandably, the symbols employed usually turn up in groups of seven.[3] Beyond this point, there are almost as many interpretations as there are exponents, except that it seems generally agreed that the seven churches of Asia Minor to whom the letters (comprising the first three chapters of the book) are addressed actually represent the whole Christian body and may at one time have constituted a separate document.

How one divides the remaining nineteen chapters depends upon his theory of interpretation. Fr. Boismard, for example, finds two Apocalypses amalgamated into one book by a later editor.[4] It seems to us, however, that this dismemberment of the work is unwarranted and that the apparent duplications can, for the most part, be explained by seeing that the book consists of two units: *a)* an historical section: the fall of Jerusalem; and *b)* an apocalyptic section: the fall of Rome. This represents a radical departure from the traditional interpretation, which construes the bulk of the Apocalypse as a polemic against the Roman Empire alone.

Now, it is clear that the second half of the work (Chap. 13ff. portraying the fall of "Babylon") is devoted to this theme. But is this also true of the first half? It seems to this author that to make Chapters 4–11 part of this same theme is to ignore the climax reached in Chapter 11 and the transitional character of Chapter 12. The destruction of Rome is nowhere specifically referred to in this portion. Moreover, such an approach undersells the apocalyptic genre by neglecting both the customary historical perspective and the manifest Old Testament oracle-pattern: *a)* oracles against Israel; and *b)* oracles against the Gentiles. In our opinion the sacred author does much more by way of building up confidence in his audience than simply predicting the death of Rome. There is ample evidence, we believe, to show that the burden of these early chapters *is to recall the triumph of Christianity over Jewry* (already accomplished) as the historical "springboard" from which to launch the assurance that Rome, too, will fail to stamp out the infant Church. We trust that our commentary on the text will

---

[3] Fr. Heidt, *Op. cit.,* pp. 10–11, ingeniously finds six sets of septettes. Other commentators offer different divisions.

[4] Outlined in *La Sainte Bible,* p. 1620; also, Heidt, *Op. cit.,* pp. 5–6.

demonstrate the validity of this interpretation; the following points are offered as prima facie evidence.[5]

In Chapters 4 and 5, John not only clinches the divinity of Christ as the Lamb of God Who receives divine worship in the heavenly Temple, but he also depicts in unmistakable symbols the replacement of the Old Covenant by Christianity in language reminiscent of the Epistle to the Hebrews. This first stage of New Testament salvation history is offered as an accomplished fact to the author's contemporaries. The definitive victory of God over the early persecutors of His Church—themselves once the Chosen People—climaxes in the destruction of Jerusalem and is presented as a sign of His ultimate triumph over the New Israel's current enemy, pagan Rome. Besides safeguarding the unity of the Apocalypse, this explanation justifies the pejorative references to the Jews which occur (e.g., "synagogue of Satan" in 2:9 and 3:9; reference to Jerusalem as "Sodom" and "Egypt" in 11:8). A simplified outline of the book follows.

Verses

INTRODUCTION: Title and greeting (Chap. 1); letters to the seven churches 2– 3

HISTORICAL PERSPECTIVE: God's visitation on Israel 4–11

A. Enthronement of the Lamb via the heavenly liturgy . . . . { without Lamb (O.T.) . . . 4
{ with Lamb (N.T.) 5

B. God's *decree* regarding Israel { of punishment, from Synoptic Apoc.: 7 seals 6
{ of predestination: sealing of 12 Tribes 7

C. God's *judgment* on Israel { the 7 trumpets, turning exodus plagues on Jews. 8– 9
{ Israel's doom: destruction of unmeasured court 10–11

APOCALYPTIC VISION: God's impending judgment on Babylon (=Rome) 12–20

A. Setting { Birth of Christianity via Messia's Resurrection–Ascension 12
{ Cosmic enemy of new People of God: the two Satanic beasts 13

B. God's judgment on Rome { Announcement of impending doom by angels; the 144,000 "virgins" 14
{ 7 bowls (plagues turned on Rome) . . . 15–16
{ Description of Rome's fall (model: Babylon) 17–18

C. Transition to the cosmic arena: Satan and his agents are expelled and punished by the King of kings; invitation to wedding feast . . . 19–20

THE HEAVENLY JERUSALEM: A new universe; Paradise regained 21–22

---

[5] Unknown to this author, Fr. André Feuillet had previously reported a similar division of the Apocalypse in his book, *L'Apocalypse: État de la question*, pp. 48–52.

Symbols Used in the Apocalypse

It will help at the outset to have a ready list of commonly used symbols for reference. A supplementary list proper to the second portion of the book will be furnished in the next chapter.

OBJECTS	NUMBERS	COLOR

White hair—eternity
Eyes—knowledge
Wings (also the
  eagle)—mobility
Legs (ox)—strength
Lion—courage
Hands, horns—power
Crown—royalty
Golden girdle—kingship
Long robe—priesthood
Palm branch—victory
 	
Key(s)—jurisdiction
Sword—vengeance
Measuring—protection
	4—the created world
	6—imperfection
	7 perfection, comple-
	    tion (hence, seven
	    eyes = omniscience)
	12—the New Israel
	24—the elect in heaven
	1000—a great multitude
	3½ years ⎱ Time of trial
	42 months ⎰ on earth; per-
	1260 days ⎰ secution
	        (Dan. 7:25)
	5 months—life-span of the
	  locust; brief duration?
		White —joy, innocence,
		     purity, victory
		
		Red —death
		
		Scarlet—sorrow, magnifi-
		    cence (royalty)
		
		Olive —pestilence (the
		    color of decayed
		    flesh—pale
		    green)

The Seven Letters: Warnings to the Universal Church
(Apocalypse 1–3)

Since the founding of the Christian community at Antioch much water has passed under the bridge. The practice of applying the term "church" *(ekklesia)* only to local communities had been expanded into the notion of the corporate unity of all the churches as the one body of Christ by the time St. Paul wrote the Captivity Epistles. Hence, in this context the "seven churches" designate the universal Christian Church. After stating his credentials, "John" proceeds with the customary epistolary greeting in verse 4. Here the "seven spirits" represent the Holy Spirit, giving the work both a Christological and Trinitarian orientation. In the four verses which follow it is evident that John wishes to establish Christ as the fulfillment of the Mosaic Covenant: He is THE WITNESS (the Greek word is *martyros*), His death was redemptive (v. 5), He has made us "a kingdom and priests" (vv. 5–6; compare this phrase and 5:10 with Ex. 19:6), He is the one "pierced" (by the Jews; v. 7), and Who enjoys divine status (v. 8, modelled after Isa. 44:6 and Ex. 3:14). The "son of man" in the midst of the seven lampstands can be seen as a Johannine equivalent of the doctrine of the Mystical Body.[6] Both in 1:18 and 3:7 Christ is por-

---

[6] Cf. Heidt, *Op. cit.*, p. 21. Old Testament references are Daniel 7:9–13; Zacharia 4:2–3.

trayed as possessing keys; in the latter reference, it is the key of David —thus linking up Jesus with the Messia via Isaia 22:22 (cf. Matt. 16:19).

The crimes enumerated in the letters would be typical of the moral condition of the whole Church. They center around two faults: listening to false teachers and lack of fervor. We do not know much about the Nicolaites mentioned in 2:6 and 2:15. However, their implied kinship with Balaam in the latter passage suggests a certain syncretism of Christianity and paganism (or perhaps Judaism?). This temptation might be fruitfully compared to modern secularism (cf. 2:20 also). Only the churches of Smyrna and Philadelphia escape without rebuke. In each instance, the designation for Christ, His words of praise and condemnation, and the reward and punishments meted out are highly symbolic and are ordered to the eschatological era. The over-all lesson is clear: in every age Christ's bride, the Church, must constantly renew herself in preparing for the consummation.

A New Canticle: The Christian Liturgy Replaces that of the Temple (Apocalypse 4–5)

In an interesting study, Lucetta Mowry, a Protestant scholar, sees in these two chapters a liturgical drama combining elements of heaven and earth:[7]

1. THE CALL TO WORSHIP	4:1ff.	(Leader)
2. SINGING OF TRISAGION (Holy, Holy . . .)	4:8	(Congregation)
3. PRAISE TO GOD AS CREATOR	4:11	(Choir)
4. READING FROM SCRIPTURE	5:1ff.	(Leader)
5. PSALM	5:9	(Leader)
6. RESPONSE	5:12	(Congregation)
7. DOXOLOGY TO GOD AND CHRIST	5:13	(Congregation)
8. AMEN	5:14	(Choir)

In line with our own suggested exegesis, this scene has still a deeper layer of meaning: it represents the replacement of the Jewish liturgy (Chap. 4) by the Christian sacrifice (Chap. 5). To depict the Old Testament liturgy, the author harks back to the four creatures of Ezechiel I and the vision of Isaia in the Temple (Isa. 6). The twenty-four elders praise God as Creator; there is no suggestion of the Trinity. Indeed, true to tradition, Yahweh Himself is not portrayed, only His throne.

In Chapter 5 the imagery is abruptly different. Heaven is in a quandary: no one there can be found who is worthy to open the scroll.[8] Suddenly a new figure is revealed in the celestial array: "a

---

[7] Cited in Key and Young, *Understanding the New Testament*, p. 376.

[8] Cf. Ezechiel 2:9–10; Zacharia 5:1–4. The scroll is probably the Old Testament, whose contents take on their full meaning only in the light of Christianity.

Lamb standing as if slain (Christ's role in the Eucharist), having seven horns and seven eyes" (5:6). Obviously the Lamb is Christ, the perfection of the messianic hope, for He is described as "the lion of the tribe of Juda, the root of David (who) has overcome" (i.e., by His death and Resurrection). It is the Lamb alone Who is able to open the seals and read the scroll: is He not the one described therein? After the reading, the Lamb is accorded divine honors as a "new canticle" is sung to Him.[9] Not only the redemptive value of His passion, but also its universalism, is affirmed in 5:9 ("every tribe and tongue and people and nation"—cf. 2:26 and 7:9). And the next verse suggests the transcendent fulfillment of Psalm 109:4, i.e., the union of priest and Messia in Christ.

The Great Day of Wrath and the Fall of Jerusalem
(Apocalypse 6–11)

With the breaking of the first of the seven seals of the scroll by the Lamb, plagues begin to rain down upon the earth. The use of diversely colored horses to symbolize these plagues has a precedent in Zacharia 6:2–3; Fr. Boismard and others see here a reference to the Parthian invasion of the Roman Empire. This is certainly possible; however, the author's main purpose seems to be setting the stage for the dénouement of Jewry in Chapter 11. The apocalyptic section (6:12–17) is reminiscent of the language used in the Gospels to describe the fall of Jerusalem (cf. Mark 13:24–27).[10] In the same vein, the 144,000 "servants of our God" from each of the twelve tribes would seem to represent those Jews who acknowledge Christ (cf. 7:10); this sealing ceremony has its prototypes in Ezechiel 9:4. The tribe of Dan is omitted, perhaps because a Jewish tradition maintained that the Antichrist was to come from it! The universalism of Christianity is underscored in 7:7. Martyrs possess a unique place in the heavenly court; their shepherd in the new (Christian) temple will be the Lamb (vv. 9–17).

A fresh series of disasters is introduced by the trumpet blasts in Chapters 8 and 9. We don't know just what the sacred author had in mind, though it is evident that he has modeled these plagues after the ones Moses inflicted on the Egyptian Pharao. Perhaps the purpose is

---

[9] In 13:8 the Lamb is further described as "slain from the foundation of the world"—indicating His eternal predestination to the work of redemption. Bouyer suggests here a portrait of Christ's members being wafted up into the divine eternity via the Holy Sacrifice (cf. Bouyer, *The Paschal Mystery*, p. 244).

[10] "In Apoc. 4–11, we have a repetition and authentic interpretation of Mark 13 in the double light of the Holy Spirit and of the lived experience of the Church in the years following 70." (Feuillet, *Op. cit.*, p. 50) In both the seals and the trumpets can be found type-examples of recurring historical phenomena.

to portray the preaching and warnings of the apostles toward the Jewish nation that they might accept Christ as their Savior: the five months of 9:5 and 9:11 suggest a brief period for repentance. "And they did not repent of their murders or of their sorceries . . ." (9:21). If the large scroll represents the Old Testament prophets, cannot the small scroll in 10:2 equally represent the prophets of the New Testament—or the rest of the Apocalypse? The prophet's upset stomach would thus result from the dire pronouncements of the latter against the Jews (see Ezech. 3:3). God's final attempt to break through His people's stubbornness consists in measuring the temple via the agency of the prophet—a symbol borrowed from Ezech. 40:3–5. The outer court and the city destined for destruction (therefore not measured) would seem to represent the Jews, whereas the altar "and those who worship therein" (11:1) would thus represent the Christian community, those now worshipping God in spirit and in truth.

The two witnesses in 11:3ff. are mystical descriptions fitting Moses (the Law) and Elias (prophecy) but are ambivalent enough to suggest New Testament counterparts: John the Baptist, Peter and Paul have all been proposed. The initial imagery is based on Zacharia 4: 11–14. Continuing the analogy, the 3½ years (42 months, 1260 days) becomes the period of the two witnesses' preaching. The beast—mentioned in verse 7 for the first time—symbolizes the cosmic powers of evil: Satan and his agents (in this case, the Jews?). "Sodom" and "Egypt" are pejorative epithets for Jerusalem, whose fall—predicted in 11:2—can be seen as accomplished in 11:13. The apostolic preaching of the "Good News" which began in earnest with the Resurrection and reached a certain climax with the destruction of Jerusalem and the Temple, and marked the inauguration of the "kingdom of our Lord and of his Christ . . . (who) has *begun* to reign" (11:15, 17) is a typical Johannine theme. This interpretation is strengthened by the reappearance of the Ark and the Temple in heaven.[11] Hence, salvation-history has not yet reached its final goal; this mid-point in the Apocalypse finds the world at the end of the first "half," so to speak, with Christianity having supplanted Jewry. By contrast, at the end of the final eschatological period (during which Christianity will vindicate herself against paganism—foreshadowed, perhaps in 11:18) the heavenly Jerusalem will have no need of Temple or Ark (cf. 21:

---

[11] According to a Jewish tradition reproduced in *II Mach.* 2:5–8, the Ark— lost at the time of the Babylonian Captivity in a cave—was supposed to reappear in the Messianic era. Cf. *La Sainte Bible, L'Apocalypse* (fascicle edition, 1959), p. 57, footnote a. But we part company with the reference on p. 55, footnote, where it is stated that Apoc. 11:13 means Rome; cf. Wikenhauser, *Op. Cit.*, p. 537, who holds for Jerusalem.

22). This era, inaugurated in Apocalypse 12, will be treated in the next chapter.

Hierarchical Development in the Early Church
(Didache, Chapter 15)

As noted above, the term "church" was, by the time of the publication of the Apocalypse, used to designate the whole Mystical Body—although this book makes it clear that the term could still be employed of local churches as well. Each church seems to have had its own "overseer" or bishop by the end of the first century. According to *Didache* 15:1, the bishop ranked next to prophets and teachers. In fact, to the Christian community the bishop was Christ in their midst, his place being behind the altar in the apse of the church. Each community was seen to constitute a miniature Mystical Body of Christ.

Didache 15

1. Elect therefore for yourselves bishops and deacons worthy of the Lord, humble men and not covetous, and faithful and well tested; for they also serve you in the ministry of the prophets and teachers. 2. Do not, therefore, despise them, for they are the honored men among you along with the prophets and teachers. 3. And correct one another, not in anger but in peace, as you have it in the Gospel. And let no one speak with anyone who has harmed his neighbor, nor let him be heard until he repents. 4. Offer your prayers and alms and do all things according to the Gospel of our Lord.

Psalm 83: The Liturgical Orientation of the People of God

One of the most emotional poems of the Psalter, this one is both a Psalm of Yahweh's Kingship and a Psalm of Sion. It is similar to the Pilgrimage Psalms (119–133); in fact, its nostalgic tones suggest a period of exile. The Psalmist's religious sentiments are so wrapped up in the Temple liturgy that the very thought of it ravishes his "heart and his flesh," i.e., his whole being. He is certain that Yahweh will welcome him just as a mother bird shelters her young (v. 4). Note the colorful hyperbole in verse 7. The "anointed" in verse 10 refers to the king. The reference to God as a "sun" in verse 12 is unique in the Old Testament. The author of the Apocalypse struck a tender note in selecting the liturgy as his medium of exposition.

Suggested Readings

Davis, *Theology for Today*, Chap. 9.
Heidt, *The Book of the Apocalypse* (New Testament Reading Guide, No. 14), pp. 1–83.
La Sainte Bible (Jerusalem), *L'Apocalypse* (fascicle ed., 1957), pp. 1–57.
Monro, *Enjoying the New Testament*, pp. 147–153.
Wikenhauser, *New Testament Introduction*, pp. 535–563.

For Further Study

1. Do you think that St. John the Evangelist wrote the Apocalypse? Did he have visions?
2. Is the Apocalypse in any way Trinitarian, or merely Christocentric?
3. What symbol does John use to indicate the doctrine of the Mystical Body?
4. What characteristics of Christ as He now exists in heaven does the symbolism of the Lamb bring out?
5. Does the Apocalypse aid you in any way in the understanding of such books as Esther and Judith?

Chapter XXV

Apocalypse (II): The New Israel and the Fall of "Babylon"; the Heavenly Jerusalem

READINGS: *Apocalypse 12–22; Psalm 26.* Didache, *Chapter 16 (note symbolism).*

True to its literary genre, the Apocalypse contains the answer to a crisis. The Christian community had just emerged from its encounter with Judaism—bloody, but victorious—as the walls of Jerusalem tottered before the might of Rome. As we have just seen, this victory is exploited by the sacred author: he is using it as a mark of divine assurance that the community will overcome its new and much more formidable crisis. The emergence of the New Israel from the synagogue provides John with an excellent springboard from which he is able not only to see beyond the present emergency, but from which he soars up into the precincts of the heavenly Jerusalem. But what was this new obstacle? Ironically, it was none other than the community's unwitting ally against Jewry: the Roman Empire. Thus, we have a continuation of Acts 28:31, but in quite a different context.

The conflict was a long time in brewing. In the first place, Christianity was not at the beginning recognized as a religion distinct from Judaism; in fact, it was only during the reign of Trajan (98–117 A.D.) that the distinction became recognized throughout the Empire. And it was not simply the fact that the state religion was paganism which precipitated the showdown: it was the opprobrious form which it took; namely, emperor worship. Although alien to Roman tradition, this practice first came into vogue shortly after the death of Julius Caesar. Divine honors had been paid him in the outlying provinces while he was still alive; now Rome itself took up the practice. The first living emperor to receive religious worship (as opposed merely to religious reverence) was Augustus, who had assumed the title "Son of god." We are speaking here of the city of Rome: in the provinces temples had been built to accommodate the worship of emperors for centuries. The first emperor to demand divine homage from his subjects was Domitian (81–96 A.D.). Herein lay the crisis of Christianity. It may well be that the First Epistle of St. Peter was designed to meet, at least in part, this same challenge (cf. 4:12). Be that as it may, the epistle is a masterpiece of mildness in comparison with the vehement imprecations of the Apocalypse.

"A Woman Clothed with the Sun"
(Apocalypse 12)

Before undertaking the exegesis of this chapter, we must furnish a supplementary table of symbols by way of addition to those on page 189.

SYMBOL	MEANING	
I. A WOMAN (12:1)	THE PEOPLE OF GOD (cf. Isa. 26:17; 66:7ff.)	Her child (12:2) = the Messia / Her offspring (12:7) = new People of God, Christians
II. THE DRAGON (12:3)	SATAN (cf. 20:2)	
III. BEAST FROM THE SEA (13:1). . (cf. Isa. 27:1; Dan. 7)	SATAN'S TOOL, EMPEROR WORSHIP	Its heads (13:3) / Hills of Rome } Emperors / Horns = vassal kings / Its names = titles of divinity usurped by beast.
IV. THE SECOND BEAST (13:11). . . (= false prophet of 16:13)	RELIGIOUS PROPAGANDISTS SERVING EMPEROR.	
V. BABYLON (14:8) VI. THE HARLOT (17:1)	CITY OF ROME	
VII. FORNICATION	IDOLATRY, ESPECIALLY EMPEROR WORSHIP.	
VIII. VIRGINS (14:4)	CHRISITANS WHO REFUSED TO FALL INTO IDOLATRY.	

To comprehend the rich symbolism contained in Chapter 12, we must have recourse to a key passage in the Book of Isaia overlooked by most commentators:[1]

> As a woman about to give birth writhes and cries out in her pains, so were we in your presence, O Lord. We conceived and writhed in pain, giving birth to wind; salvation we have not achieved for the earth, the inhabitants of the world cannot bring it forth. But your dead shall live, their corpses shall rise; awake and sing, you who lie in the dust (26:17–19).

From the context it is evident that Isaia is speaking here of Israel, the people of God. But as he prophetically admits, the Old Israel was incapable of bringing forth a savior. The Messia did come from their

---

[1] But see André Feuillet, "The Messia Born of the People of God," *Theology Digest*, XI:1 (Spring 1963), 10–11, where this text is cited in identifying the "woman" primarily with the People of God, but *secondarily with the Virgin Mary.*

ranks, but only according to the flesh.[2] It required a New Israel to produce a Messia according to the Spirit. He redeemed His people only after he had been "caught up to God and to his throne" (12:5, i.e., by His Resurrection and Ascension, which occasioned the release of the Holy Spirit on Pentecost). Though Satan was conquered by these events, he retains considerable power to continue to plague the Church. This he does through various agents, e.g., emperor worship.

The Conflict and the Divine Judgment
(Apocalypse 13–17)

To escape the dragon, the woman flees into the wilderness (that is, the world). Temporarily frustrated in his persecution of her progeny (the Christian community), Satan employs clever agents to subvert those "who keep the commandments of God." Chapter 13 introduces the notion of emperor worship under the guise of a beast "coming up out of the sea, having seven heads and ten horns." Though borrowed from Daniel 7, the remote source of the symbol is no doubt the Canaanite Leviathan myth (cf. Isa. 27:1). Apocalypse 13:3 and 14 suggest the "Nero redivivus" legend, according to which that infamous emperor was expected to return to life at the head of a Parthian army (i.e., on the side of the enemy). The beast is formidable: a world-wide edict to worship Caesar (v. 4, "Who is like to the beast?" is a blasphemous parody of Ex. 15:11). Though Christians will be persecuted and discriminated against because they lack the "mark" of the beast, their lot and their glory is to resist unto death (v. 9). The second beast of 13:11 is identified in 16:13 with the false prophet mentioned later; this title represents the religious charlatan who can work apparent wonders to deceive people. The cryptic number of the beast (extreme imperfection) has evoked the solution "Nero Caesar," since the consonants of the Hebrew equivalent of this phrase add up to 666 when given their numerical values.[3]

Chapter 14 parallels Chapter 7. The sacred author again has recourse to the liturgy as his medium of expression. The 144,000 "virgins" are those faithful members of the Christian Anawim who are marked with the Lamb's name rather than with the mark of the beast, i.e., those who have not capitulated to the imperial idolatry. Though pictured on Mount Sion, they are surrounded with a celestial aura. A note of hope is sounded in verse 8 as the fall of Rome ("Babylon") is predicted,

---

[2] But Israel could not even claim to have given a human father to the Messia, except legally. The Marian implications of this passage are boundless, if not direct.

[3] A confirmation of this was recently discovered in an Aramaic document dating from the time of Caesar. Cf. Delbert Hillers' article in the *Bulletin of the American Schools of Oriental Research*, (April 1963), No. 170, p. 65.

together with the punishment to be meted out to all who get themselves drunk on the wine of that city's immorality. Judgment becomes imminent as the "son of man" (we are still in the Danielic tradition) gets ready to reap the earth.[4] The lesson of the chapter is contained in verses 12–13 (epistle in the Requiem Mass): Christians are called to undergo martyrdom for their faith.

The next two chapters resemble Chapters 8 and 9 in format. Chapter 15 continues in a liturgical vein, using Old Testament rites to convey the message. Note that the altar speaks in 16:7. Although the divine chastisements are prepared (the seven bowls), "they did not repent and give him glory" (16:9: mankind at large). Verse 12 may be another reference to the impending Parthian invasion. Apocalypse 16:16 is one of the most famous verses in the book; widespread opinion would see "Armagedon" as the place of the general judgment. Here it refers to the three unclean spirits—probably Rome and her allies. There Yahweh judged good King Josia according to the words of Necho (II Par. 25:21–24). Again, however, the name is a symbol. Chapter 16 closes with more apocalyptic language. In a brief interlude, divine judgment is delayed by the introduction of a companion symbol to the beast, viz., the great harlot. She is identified as Rome in the last verse of Chapter 17. Reminiscent of Zacharia 5:5–11, this symbol underscores the figurative reference to idolatry as a kind of fornication. A revolt against Rome on the part of her vassal kings is indicated in verses 12 and 16, and the ultimate vindication of the Lamb as "Lord of lords, and King of kings" is assured in verse 14.

The Fall of Babylon and the Harlot: Their Punishment (Apocalypse 18–19)

As the harlot-city falls at last, we hear once again the saving cry issued originally to Abraham (Gen. 12:1): "Go out from her, my people, that you may not share in her sins" (cf. Jer. 50:8). Reading verse 6 we instinctively think of Matthew 22:21: "Render, therefore, to Caesar the things that are Caesar's, and to God the things that are God's." The whole Book of the Apocalypse can be considered a commentary on this one Logium—although here it is applied in reverse. The symbolic dirges over "Babylon" are modeled after Ezechiel 27–28, especially 28:13.

In Chapter 19 we find another liturgical interlude to celebrate the victory of the Lamb. The use of the beautiful imagery of the marriage supper in verse 7 does more than indicate the reward of the Lamb's "spouses"; it contains a profound development of Christology. The Lamb has a new name in heaven, "The Word of God"—i.e., His

---

[4] Be sure to compare verse 20 with Isaia 63:3–6.

divinity is now manifest. He is triumphant, for another name written on His thigh reads: "King of kings and Lord of lords" (v. 16). And yet His garments are sprinkled with blood! (v. 13; recall the phrase, "as if slain" in 5:5, and "I was dead, and behold, I am living forevermore," 1:18). The lesson? Christ exists in heaven in His glorified state. But He still clings to His wounded humanity, which includes those faithful on earth who have espoused His cause and fight His battles. His members, in other words, must bear in their mortal frame a copy of both His glorification and His humiliation in order to reign forever with Him in heaven.[5] The purpose of 19:10 may be an underscoring of the divine prohibition of worshipping any creature. The chapter concludes with the punishment meted out to idolaters; cf. Ezechiel 39.

Johannine Eschatology and the Heavenly Jerusalem
(Apocalypse 20–22)

As the Apocalypse moves into the era of the Parousia we find a formal identification of the dragon as the cosmic force of evil, Satan (20:2). He has been judged in his terrestrial agent, Babylon, and is to remain bound—i.e., restrained to some degree—for a long period of time ("1000 years"). His release mentioned in verse 3 suggests a final, monumental tryst just before the Parousia—another showdown such as John's contemporaries were going through at the time of his writing. The knotty question of the two resurrections can best be explained by a timetable, supplementing that to be given on page 207:

THE TWO DEATHS AND TWO RESURRECTIONS	
1. THE FIRST DEATH: death of the body by all men.	THE FIRST RESURRECTION: the reign of the just with Christ either after death without their bodies, or after baptism in the Body.
2. THE THOUSAND-YEAR PERIOD during which Satan is chained (20:2). The faithful on earth will be tried.	
3. THE SECOND DEATH: a symbol representing the eternal punishment of the wicked in their risen bodies.	THE SECOND RESURRECTION: The rising of the just with their bodies to enjoy everlasting happiness.

Chapter 21 begins a grand synthesis of Isaia, Jeremia, and especially Ezechiel. As we shall document on pages 206–207, the "new heaven and new earth" of Apocalypse 21:1 does have a literal fulfillment. If not actually a "second" creation, it will at least be a renewal of the physical universe—presumably as a habitation for mankind, and by way of overflow from the Beatific Vision. The fabulously large dimen-

---

[5] See Durrwell, *The Resurrection*, pp. 121–124.

sions of the New Jerusalem outdo Ezechiel 40ff. Verse 16 suggests the perfect symmetry of the edifice. This Johannine Utopian model shows the transcendent, transforming character of the new order: eye cannot conceive its magnificence. However, the principal transformation will take place in the moral order of charity rather than in the physical order. No sun is to be found; God Himself will supply all needs; cf. Isaia 60:19.

A more impressive sign of the unity of Sacred Scripture could hardly be found than the return to paradise in the last chapter of this final book of the Bible. The life-giving river harks back to Ezechiel 47:1, 12 (as does also the *Vidi aquam* of paschal time). In Ezechiel, the water flowed from the Temple; here, however, it flows from the throne of God, for the Temple has ceased to exist in eternity (cf. Apoc. 21:22). At this point we are reminded of Hebrews 12:22–24:

> But you have come to Mount Sion, and to the city of the living God, the heavenly Jerusalem, and to the company of many thousands of angels, and to the Church of the firstborn who are enrolled in the heavens, and to God, the judge of all, and to the spirits of the just made perfect, and to Jesus, mediator of a new covenant, and to a sprinkling of blood which speaks better than Abel.

John, like the author of Hebrews, shows himself to be a liturgist par excellence. Both the John of the Fourth Gospel and the John of the Apocalypse demonstrate the continuity of Christian worship with that of the synagogue. (Here is one of the strongest arguments for the identity of the two men.) The Fourth Gospel is primarily interested in the earthly liturgy, which has replaced that of the Temple. Professor Oscar Cullmann goes a step further:

> . . . the Gospel of John regards it as one of its chief concerns to set forth the connection between the contemporary Christian worship and the historical life of Jesus . . . it seeks to point to the full identity of the Lord, present in the early Christian congregation, with the historical Jesus, and to do so in terms of the facts of Jesus' life. It traces the line from the Christ of history to Christ the Lord of the Community, in which the Word continually becomes flesh.[6]

The Apocalypse progresses beyond the confines of the earthly liturgy into that of heaven, demonstrating the further continuity to be found between these two phases. It is no longer the historical Jesus Who occupies the stage but rather the risen, ascended, mystical

---

[6] *Early Christian Worship* (Studies in Biblical Theology, 10 [Chicago, Ill.: Henry Regnery Company, 1953]), pp. 37–38. Cullmann underscores the relationship between Hebrews and the Apocalypse in *The Christology of the New Testament* (Philadelphia: Westminster Press, 1959), p. 105.

Christ. Though invisible, He continues to dominate the earthly scene through His faithful spouse, the Church. Fr. Siegman applies the lesson for us:

> The point that emerges is this: the Apocalypse gives no ready-made formula to solve the problems which the Church faced in the last decade of the first century; much less is it the history of the future written beforehand in cryptograms designed to tease the reader's ingenuity. It is rather an elaborate demonstration that the Church must in all ages solve her problems by reading the Bible in church, i.e., in the liturgy. This means at once that we shall read the Old Testament as promise, the New Testament as fulfillment, both of which are here and now actualized for the participants in the liturgical action.[7]

Early Christian Eschatology: The Didache

Once again we have recourse to this ancient document this time for an illustration of the speculation still prevalent about the turn of the first century regarding the Parousia. Verse 7 below reflects an erroneous view concerning the resurrection—unless the author has in mind the "First Resurrection."

Didache 16

1. 'Be vigilant' over your life; 'let your lamps' not be extinguished, or your loins be ungirded, but be prepared, for you know not the hour in which our Lord will come. 2. Come together frequently, and seek what pertains to your souls; for the whole time of your faith will not profit you, unless in the last hour you shall be found perfect. 3. For, in the last days, false prophets and seducers will increase, and sheep will be turned into wolves, and charity will be changed into hate. 4. For, as lawlessness grows, men will hate one another and persecute one another and betray one another, and then will appear the Deceiver of the world, as though he were the Son of God, and will work signs and wonders; and the world will be delivered into his hands, and he will do horrible things, which have not been done since the beginning of the world. 5. Then shall all created men come to the fire of judgment, and 'many will be scandalized' and perish; but those who persevere in their faith will be saved from the curse itself. 6. And then will appear the signs of the Truth: first, the sign of confusion in the heaven; second, the sign of the sound of the trumpet; and third, the resurrection of the dead— 7. not the resurrection of all men, but, as it was said: 'The Lord will come and all His saints with Him.' 8. Then shall the world see the Lord coming on the clouds of heaven.[8]

---

[7] "Teaching the Liturgy According to the New Testament," *Education and the Liturgy: 18th North American Liturgical Week* (Elsberry, Mo.: The Liturgical Conference, 1958), p. 70.

[8] Schopp, *The Fathers of the Church*, Vol. I, pp. 183–184.

Psalm 26: Confidence in the Lamb Who Has Conquered

This mixed Psalm of Confidence (vv. 1–6) and Lament (vv. 7–14) seems to express the spirit of the Apocalypse extremely well. Though God's "team" is destined to win, it must go through many trials in the process. One readily imagines the early Christians chanting its strophes as they solemnly marched through the catacombs (cf. Cardinal Wiseman's *Fabiola*, Chap. 16)

Suggested Readings

Durrwell, *The Resurrection,* pp. 38, 189–196; 121–124; 46–50.
Heidt, *The Book of the Apocalypse,* pp. 83–124.
Monro, *Enjoying the New Testament,* pp. 147–153.

For Further Study

1. Does the "woman" in Apocalypse 12:1 in any sense refer to the Virgin Mary? What parallel passages can you find for Apocalypse 12:2? What is their context?
2. Are the 144,000 "virgins" of Chapter 14 and the "harlot" of Chapter 17 to be taken literally?
3. What special virtue is required of Saints (cf. Apoc. 14:12)?
4. Find parallels in the Synoptics for Apocalypse 12:11 and 12:17.
5. What is symbolized by the "marriage supper of the Lamb" in Apocalypse 19:9?
6. At what point in the book does the main thread of the Apocalypse pass from earth to heaven?

Chapter XXVI

II-III John, II Peter: The Era of the Church and the Role of the Laity

READINGS: *II–III John; II Peter; I Corinthians 15; Romans 16; Psalm 89. Fremantle*, A Treasury of Early Christianity: *St. Ignatius' Letter to the Philadelphians, p. 40; St. Leo the Great, Letters, pp. 131–135. (Note: II John 9; II Peter 1:4, 20; 2:4; 3:8–13, 15–16.)*

The Second Epistle of St. John: The Bond of Charity and Unity of Doctrine

There is no serious reason to doubt that the Second and Third Epistles of John come from the same hand as the Fourth Gospel and First Epistle of John.[1] The same crisis (Gnosticism) seems to have occasioned II–III John, which were apparently written about the same time (c. 90–100 A.D.). II John 7 contains a reference to these false teachers. Two bonds of unity are set forth in First John: charity and "the doctrine of Christ" (v. 9; this is in line with the cryptic introductory note in v. 3: "in truth and love"). Whether this phrase means doctrine *about* Christ or the doctrine *of* Christ, it is a strong apologetical argument for the need of dogmatic unity in the Church.

Third John and Unity of Authority

Somewhat obliquely we find an argument for authority (of the local bishop, in all probability) as a requirement for Church unity in II John. A certain Diotrophes who has charge of a church (the only Johannine use of this term outside of the Apocalypse) has declared war against John, whom he refuses to receive. St. John threatens this bishop(?) for abusing his authority and thereby rending the unity of the Christian Church.

By the time that St. John wrote these epistles, the episcopacy must have become monarchical in at least some churches (cf. quotation on

---

[1] Both II and III John are addressed *by* "The Presbyter" (John) to "the Elect Lady" (II John; this would be an epithet for church) and "Gaius" (III John).

p. 136). This conclusion is indicated by the Letter of St. Ignatius to the Philadelphians, written just a decade or so later. It states:

> Be careful to observe one Eucharist (for there is one flesh of our Lord Jesus Christ and one cup unto union in His blood; there is one altar, as there is *one bishop,* together with the presbytery and the deacons my fellow-servants) . . .[2]

We have already cited the First Epistle of St. Clement of Rome in support of the primacy of the Bishop of Rome;[3] by the time that Pope St. Leo I (the Great) ascended the papal throne, little doubt remained on this subject. This is clear from the "Letters" assigned in Fremantle, especially those to the bishops of the Province of Vienne and the Synod of Ephesus. St. Leo openly declares that they who reject St. Peter's primacy (continued in the incumbents of the See of Rome) are "far removed from union with this building" (the Church).

Separated Brethren: The Scandal of Disunity[4]

For centuries now since the Protestant Reformation, both Catholics and Protestants have tended to take their disunity for granted, assuming that this condition will continue indefinitely. With the advent of Pope John XXIII to the throne of Peter, however, the whole outlook —at least among Catholics—has changed. More and more is it being realized that this situation is neither normal nor, in fact, healthful. The term "separated brethren" has come to replace "heretic" and "schismatic." The smoke of prejudice has had time to clear, and it is evident that most of the grievances which drove the Reformers out of the Church have dissipated. Whereas the old grievances were largely in the doctrinal and moral order, those of today are more in the political area: Protestants fear the "power" of the Catholic Church. They feel that it is prepared to use the social pressure at its command to force its position on controversial issues upon the rest of men; in a word, they tend to assume that the Catholic Church is "structured against Christ." The "dialogue" initiated by Pope John and pushed in certain European countries—notably Germany—is doing much to offset these fears. Today the emphasis is shifting away from the differences which separate into the area of what is agreed upon. The two most fundamental issues on which hope of reconciliation largely hinges are:

---

[2] Fremantle, *Op. cit.,* p. 40.

[3] Chapter XVII, this text. The quotation from Pope Leo is contained in Fremantle, *Op. cit.,* p. 133. Read also pp. 300–308 for St. Cyprian's testimony.

[4] Review chart on p. 114.

1. *The Word of God.* It is generally recognized that it is most urgent to work out a common text of Sacred Scripture agreeable to both Catholics and Protestants. There is no great difficulty involved, as Protestants customarily include in an appendix the so-called Deuterocanonical books acknowledged as inspired by the Catholic Church. Moreover, Protestants are becoming more acutely aware that private interpretation of Scripture is a risky business; they appreciate more than ever that the living Word of God needs the safeguard of tradition as contained in a teaching Church. As for Catholics, the current biblical revival has renewed interest in Sacred Scripture tremendously.[5]
2. *The Church.* The concept of "the People of God" is receiving fresh emphasis among Protestants. Curiously, their appreciation of the Eucharist as a necessary bond of unity over and above the proclamation of the word is in fact daily increasing. Both Catholics and Protestants alike realize more fully that the scandal of disunity is preventing the full flowering of the Body of Christ unto the *pleroma.* The willingness of the Second Vatican Council to re-think the role of the bishop to establish a clearer definition of his rights and powers in the universal Church adds further stimulus to Protestant hopes for eventual reunion.

II Peter and the Parousia

This is probably the most controversial book in the New Testament, so far as authorship is concerned. Modern scholars feel that the weight of evidence is against Petrine authorship but in favor of someone who belonged to the Saint's circle and wrote some time after 70 A.D.[6] Indeed, the author "lays it on thick" in identifying "Simon Peter" as the source (cf. 1:14, 17; 3:1). However, the fact that he refers to "all" the epistles of St. Paul in 3:16; the obvious borrowing of Chapter 2 from St. Jude's epistle; and the statement in 3:4 that "the fathers fell asleep" gives strong clues in support of a late date. But as we have noted previously, *authorship* and *authenticity* in a biblical work are by no means synonymous: II Peter is recognized as canonical by the Church, hence it is an inspired document. Because Catholics today are prepared to acknowledge pseudepigraphy as an accepted literary form, it is possible for them to consider seriously the *hypothesis* that II Peter was written after his death by one of his disciples.

---

[5] The mysterious unity between Word and sacrament is expertly treated in the collection of essays by Karl Rahner and others, entitled *The Word* (New York: P. J. Kenedy and Sons, 1964).
[6] *La Sainte Bible,* pp. 1593–1594; Maly, *The Epistles of Saints James, Jude, Peter,* p. 54.

Important doctrinal texts are found in this letter. The definition of grace as a *partaking of the divine nature* (1:4) is basic. There are two powerful apologetical texts reprobating private interpretation of Scripture: 1:20 and 3:16, which should be carefully noted; in fact, 1:21 provides the basis of our definition of inspiration, whereby the sacred authors become the instruments of the Holy Spirit. But the reader's attention is especially directed to the teaching on the Parousia in Chapter 3. Like II Thessalonians, this epistle attempts to explain the delay in the second coming of Christ. The objection of the "false teachers" is this: since the world's creation, much time has passed and still nothing has happened; therefore it seems that His promise of returning has failed. In reply, II Peter offers these arguments: *1)* Something *has* happened: the "first creation" of God was destroyed by water; we now await the destruction by fire of the new creation; *2)* God works on an enormous time-table in which "a thousand years (are) as one day" (3:8; cf. Ps. 89:4); *3) There are going to be "new heavens and a new earth" after He comes in judgment* (3:13). This truth was suggested already in Romans 8:19–22, and is in perfect harmony with I Corinthians 15. These and other texts make us bold enough to offer the timetable of eschatological events on the following page.

Resurrection of the Body and Renovation of the Universe

In not a few recent studies the Resurrection of Christ and its implications for His followers have been given new stress. One of the more significant of these is the book by the eminent Protestant theologian, Oscar Cullmann.[7] The title states the issue: "Immortality of the Soul or Resurrection of the Dead?" Showing how the Western mind has been led astray by the Greek (especially Platonic) emphasis on immortality of the soul, Professor Cullmann offers strong evidence from the New Testament for a shift of emphasis to the role of the body in the general resurrection. He points out that the term *flesh* in the Gospels ordinarily is not identical with *body:* the former being a principle of evil, the latter being an integral part of man and therefore good. Nor is *spirit* (Spirit of God, Holy Spirit) identical with *soul* (higher principle in man). In speaking of the Parousia the New Testament regularly gives the body a prominent place in the life to come. Some noteworthy texts are: Romans 8:11; Philippians 3:21; II Corinthians 3:18; and I Corinthians 11:30. In this last text St. Paul is even suggesting that sickness and death among the early Christians resulted from an unworthy reception of the Eucharist! Christ, the "firstborn

---

[7] Oscar Cullmann, *Immortality of the Soul or Resurrection of the Dead?* (London: The Epworth Press, 1958) 60 pp.

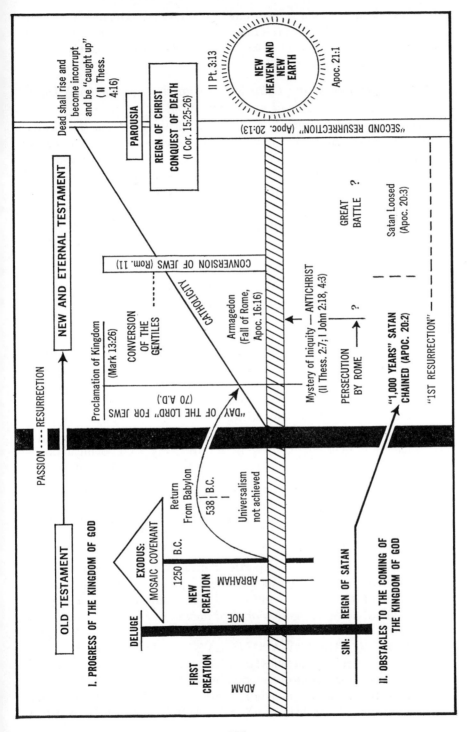

from the dead," did not furnish much inspiration to His followers from the tomb. It was His Resurrection that changed the whole picture; by this medium He wills to restore our *bodies* also—and the whole physical universe (Rom. 8:21).

The Cooperation of the Laity in the Church's Apostolate: A Duty and an Urgent Need

The foregoing paragraph at the very least gives the lie to Dr. Schweitzer's eschatological Jesus, the Savior who saw no hope for the restoration of this world and therefore directed His efforts exclusively toward the Parousia (cf. Chap. II). The Church, as the Body of Christ, has been deputed to carry on His work—the work which He will bring to perfection at His second coming. Inasmuch as this task involves not only the spiritual but also the temporal order, it is thus intimately bound up with the social and political arenas. Here is perhaps the telling and obvious argument for the participation of the laity in the apostolate of the Church: the social and political orders are properly *their* domain. If the market-place is to be rehabilitated, it is the merchants who must address themselves to the task as ambassadors of Christ.

This conclusion is corroborated in many New Testament texts. The sixteenth chapter of the Epistle to the Romans mentions twenty-four "helpers in Christ Jesus" plus two households, with no distinction being made between "clerics" and "laymen." Of the 120 who met in Jerusalem to elect a successor to Judas (Acts 1:15), surely not all had received Orders. A little later in the same book we read:

> Now those who had been dispersed by the persecution that had broken out over Stephen, went all the way to Phoenicia and Cyprus and Antioch, speaking the word to none except to Jews only. But some of them were Cyprians and Cyreneans, who on reaching Antioch began to speak to the Greeks also, preaching the Lord Jesus. And the hand of the Lord was with them, and a great number believed and turned to the Lord. And news concerning them came to the ears of the church in Jerusalem, and they sent Barnabas as far as Antioch (Acts 11:19-22).

From the fact that the Apostle Barnabas was sent to them, it appears that these evangelists were "lay" people; indeed, it was the conviction of the first generations of Christians that *spreading the "Good News" is the obligation of each member of the community.* Recent papal documents have underscored this fact, with the following distinctions: *1)* THE LAY APOSTOLATE IN THE BROAD SENSE is simply a corollary of the lay vocation: the performance of the duties of one's state in life (e.g., housewife, teacher, lawyer) with such zeal that the example influences those with whom the individual comes in contact. *2)* THE LAY APOSTOLATE IN THE STRICT

SENSE is a special calling given to some lay people to exert Christian witness outside of their immediate environment by organized efforts. This can be embraced on either a part or full time basis. The so-called specialized movements belong in this category: Young Christian Workers, Young Christian Students, and the Christian Family Movement. At the same time this does not mean that the clergy can remain unconcerned about these areas. Rather, they must work in harmony with their lay people in developing a modern ethic covering the problems which arise and afford them effective assistance and guidance in carrying it out. Above all the laity should be consulted as true experts in the areas which the Lord has entrusted to them. A system might even be worked out whereby representative laymen and laywomen could be heard on the occasion of the episcopal visitation of a parish.

If one is tempted today to ask why God does not continue to work miracles to hasten the spread of His vineyard, the answer can be gleaned from what we have just said. Although a minority, the Church does have sufficient numbers to make herself effectively representative. *Her greatest efficacy in the modern world lies in the strategic training and organization of the laity.* Here is to be found the sequel to the healings and other prodigies characteristic of the early centuries of Christianity. If the modern world is to be exorcised and rendered worthy to become the spotless bride of Christ, this will come about only through collaboration between the sheep and their shepherds.

Psalm 89: The Divine Timetable

In presenting us with this wisdom poem, the psalmist has borrowed extensively from other Old Testament books: Job 14:1; Isaia 40:6; Genesis 3:19—on which this serves as an excellent commentary. Man must not measure the divine plan by his own petty life-span (vv. 10–11)! The cry in verse 13, "Return, O Lord" reminds us of the early Christian's plea for the Parousia: "Come, Lord Jesus" (Apoc. 22:20).

Suggested Readings

Brown, *The Gospel of St. John and the Johannine Epistles* (New Testament Reading Guide, No. 13), pp. 119–122.

Cullmann, Oscar, *Immortality of the Soul or Resurrection of the Dead?* (London: The Epworth Press, 1958), 60 pp.

Davis, *Theology for Today*, Chap. 20.

Durrwell, *The Resurrection*, pp. 290–300. Page 293, footnote, has a fine statement of the rehabilitation of the universe through charity.

Maly, *The Epistles of Saints James, Jude, Peter* (New Testament Reading Guide, No. 12), pp. 53–69.

Philips, Gerard, *The Role of the Laity in the Church*, 175 pp.

Putz, Louis, *The Modern Apostle* (Fides, 1957), 148 pp.

Theology Digest, VIII:2 (Spring 1960). The whole issue is devoted to the Resurrection.

Thorman, Donald J., *The Emerging Layman* (Garden City, N. Y.: Doubleday and Co., 1962).

Chapter XXVII

Scripture and the Liturgy: The Sanctification of the Laity

READINGS: *One of the readings in the bibliography at the end of the chapter; Psalms 92, 94–99.*

Having completed our journey through Sacred Scripture, we are in a position now to see the relationship between the Bible and the liturgy. The former lies in the area of revelation; the latter pertains to the area of worship. Yet, the two are closely interwoven. Sacred Scripture was never intended to provide purely speculative knowledge of God and His divine plan of salvation. It is eminently practical: it is the kind of Osean knowledge which is sterile unless put into practice. The great interventions of God in history, the continuous series of increasingly intimate divine-human covenants fail in their purpose once they are categorized simply as PAST events. It is precisely in the liturgy that the acts of God are captured and enshrined in all of their timelessness and made contemporary with each succeeding generation. This dimension of Christianity has already been highlighted in Chapter XVI in conjunction with Dom Odo Casel's theory of mystery-presence in the liturgy. Fr. Bouyer underscores the same point in his introduction to *The Paschal Mystery:*

> The Christian religion is not simply a doctrine: it is a fact, an action, and an action, not of the past, but of the present, where the past is recovered and the future draws near. Thus it embodies a mystery of faith, for it declares to us that each day makes our own the action that Another accomplished long ago, the fruits of which we shall see only later in ourselves. . . . For Christ died for us, not in order to dispense us from dying, but rather to make us capable of dying efficaciously, of dying to the life of the old man, in order to live again as the new man who will die no more. . . . The pasch is Christ, who once died and rose from the dead, making us die in His death and raising us to His life. Thus the pasch is not a mere commemoration: it is the empty tomb rendered actual. But it is no longer the Head who must stretch Himself upon the cross in order to rise from the tomb: it is His Body, the Church, and of this Body we are the members.[1]

---

[1] From Louis Bouyer, *Paschal Mystery,* pp. xiii–xiv.

Pope Pius XII had already made this point in his encyclical letter, *Mediator Dei* of 1947, where he states:

> All the elements of the Liturgy, then, would have us reproduce in our hearts through the mystery of the Cross the likeness of the Divine Redeemer according to the words of the Apostle of the Gentiles: 'With Christ I am nailed to the Cross. I live, now not I, but Christ liveth in me' (Gal. 2:19–20). Thus we become a victim, as it were, along with Christ to increase the glory of the Eternal Father.[2]

The Holy Father takes great pains in this encyclical to demonstrate that the liturgy is not merely the *external* worship or rites of the Church; it is above all *internal*. The encyclical vindicates the Church's liturgy as providing not only the official framework of divine worship, but at the same time of satisfying also the internal devotion of the individual Christian. His classic definition of the liturgy expresses it thus:

> The sacred Liturgy is consequently the public worship which our Redeemer as Head of the Church renders to the Father as well as the worship which the community of the faithful renders to its Founder, and through Him to the Heavenly Father. It is, in short, the worship rendered by the Mystical Body of Christ in the entirety of its Head and members.[3]

The Liturgical Year: Normal School of Sanctity for the Laity

In her pedagogical wisdom, the Church spells out each year the principal events of the life of her Founder in what is known as the Liturgical Year. Rather than become monotonous, this liturgical cycle is intended to exert a spiral effect on our lives: each year we are expected to enter the divine mysteries at a deeper level of penetration and hence with a correspondingly profounder effect on our lives. According to the latest calendar reform, the following "seasons" are distinguished: *1)* Advent; *2)* Christmas (until January 13); *3)* Septuagesima (until Mardi Gras); *4)* Lent (Ash Wednesday until the Easter Vigil Mass); *5)* Easter (including the Ascension, Pentecost and its octave). The period following this, as well as the days immediately after January 13 until Septuagesima, is ordinary time. Just how Advent came to be looked upon as the beginning of the liturgical cycle is shrouded in mystery; there are strong reasons for challenging this attitude. In the first place, the early Church knew of only one feast: Easter, the Paschal Mystery, which included Ascension and Pentecost. Only later was Epiphany introduced in the East and Christmas

---

[2] Pope Pius XII, *Mediator Dei*, Par. 102.
[3] *Ibid.*, par. 20.

in the West; in fact, it has been demonstrated that the latter dates only from the fourth century. Its original purpose was to offset the pagan feast, "Sol Invictus" (Unconquered Sun), and at the same time to keep alive the waning expectation of the Parousia by reminding Christians of His first coming at Bethlehem.[4]

In recent times attention has been focused on the greater propriety of seeing Septuagesima as the natural opening of the Church Year. Not only does the Breviary begin its lessons at this time with the Book of Genesis, but according to this plan the year fits into two logical cycles: *a baptismal season* beginning with Septuagesima, and an *eschatological season* beginining with the September Ember Days. The Church Year would work out as follows.[5]

REDEMPTIVE–BAPTISMAL CYCLE	AUTUMN (ESCHATOLOGICAL) CYCLE
Septuagesima—Seventeenth Sunday after Pentecost: •••	Eighteenth Sunday after Pentecost—Candlemas: •••
Three pre-Lenten Sundays	Eighteenth Sunday right through to third Sunday in Advent: the growing spirit of the Parousia (All Saints and Souls; the two Gospels of destruction of Jerusalem)
Lent	
Passiontide and the Sacred Tridua	
The Great Pentecost (7 weeks); Ember Days	
Seventeen weeks to assimilate baptismal rebirth	December Ember Days: the theophanies of Christmas and Epiphany;
Harvest Ember Days (September)	"Hypapante"

The value of this division is that *1)* it would center our lives in the Paschal Mystery; and *2)* it would put a greater seriousness into the celebration of the Christmas cycle by making it a period of moral rearmament each year in preparation for the Parousia (instead of simply a birthday party of the Baby Jesus). As Fr. Parsch observes, "Then it would truly be a 'year of grace,' a year of supernatural life beginning with Easter and its preparatory season and concluding with the final union and marriage to Christ at Epiphany."[6] While awaiting the enlightened insight on the part of some future generation to make the necessary chronological adjustments in the calendar, it is not forbidden us to take advantage of these ideas in bringing our own lives into harmony with the rhythm of the Liturgical Year. Here is the key to lay sanctity as Pius X put it: "The primary and indispensable

---

[4] Cf. *The Bible Today*, I:3 (Dec. 1962), pp. 147–151; and Parsch, *The Church's Year of Grace*, Vol. I, pp. 1–18.

[5] H. A. Reinhold, *The American Parish and the Roman Liturgy* (New York: Macmillan Co., 1958), Chap. 6.

[6] Parsch, *Op. cit.*, p. 11.

source of the true Christian spirit is the active participation of the faithful in the sacred mysteries and in the public and solemn prayer of the Church." Indeed, in primitive times before books were widespread and when Catholic schools were unknown, the only contact of the Church with the faithful was through the repeated drama of the liturgical feasts and the accompanying homilies. What the liturgy accomplished then it can surely accomplish today.

The Divine Office: Praise of the Mystery

What is generally overlooked in connection with the Divine Office is that it originated as a prayer of both faithful and clergy. Fr. Jungmann suggests that the hour of Matins (or Lauds) grew out of the custom of gathering together the clergy in the morning in order to provide instruction for the people (centered around a reading from Scripture) and to offer prayers with them.[7] Vespers seems to have had its beginning in the reading of the psalms and prayers which accompanied the Agape in the early Church. Eventually the Office became the exclusive prerogative of religious and the clergy. Today all religious in solemn vows (including women) and all subdeacons are obliged under pain of serious sin to recite the whole Office each day. Its main purpose is to prolong the fruits of the Mass and consecrate each succeeding segment of time. In fact, before the wave of breviary reforms began, the day's Office included substantial passages from Scripture—sufficient to constitute one's spiritual reading. Today these have been reduced to pericopae. In the following chart showing the composition of the various hours, one can note the pivotal role which the psalms play.

DIVISION	COMPOSITION	TRADITIONAL TIME
1. MATINS	Invitatory Ps. 94, hymn, 9 psalms and 9 (or 3) lessons; the *Te Deum*.	Midnight
2. LAUDS	Five psalms, chapter, hymn, *Benedictus*.	Dawn
3. Prime	Hymn, 3 psalms, chapter, response, Confiteor.	6 A.M.
4. Tierce	Same as Prime, but without Confiteor.	9 A.M.
5. Sext	Same as Prime, but without Confiteor.	Noon
6. None	Same as Prime, but without Confiteor.	3 P.M.
7. VESPERS	Five psalms, chapter, hymn, *Magnificat*.	Before supper
8. Compline	Blessing, lesson, Confiteor, 3 psalms, chapter, hymn, *Nunc Dimittis*, **Salve Regina**.	After supper

[7] Cf. J. A. Jungmann, S. J., *Public Worship* (Collegeville, Minn.: Liturgical Press, 1957), pp. 152–153; 166.

A Final Look at the Psalms: Gelineau Arrangement

In 1951, Fr. Joseph Gelineau, a young Jesuit priest-musician, set out to provide the French people with a version of the psalms which they could both understand and sing. He sought to make them so attractive that they would be sung from the sheer pleasure of the performance. To launch his effort he chose twenty-four of the more representative psalms which he put to a metrical scheme based on the original Hebrew poetry, using the translation in the Jerusalem Bible. He based his compositions on folk-tunes and ancient chant melodies. When he produced a recording of these French psalms together with the antiphons he had composed for them, success was instantaneous. The Ladies of the Grail sponsored an English counterpart, aided by Fr. Clifford Howell, S.J., and Dom Gregory Murray, O.S.B. Subsequently they were introduced into the United States, where they became the favorite of lay apostolic and other groups. Specially adaptable to this effort are the psalms assigned with this chapter. The student is asked to note: *1)* a characteristic common to all; *2)* to which class Psalms 92, 96 and 98 belong (all the same), and Psalms 94, 95, 97, and 99 (likewise the same).

Suggested Readings

Bouyer, *Liturgical Piety;* Chap. 17. This selection deals with the Divine Office.
————, *The Meaning of Sacred Scripture,* Chap. 22 (on the psalms).
Davis, *Liturgy and Doctrine,* Chap. 1.
The Hours of the Divine Office in English and Latin, 3 vols.
Jungmann, *Public Worship,* Chap. 8 (Divine Office); 9 (Church Year).
Parsch, *The Church's Year of Grace,* Vol. 1, pp. 1–18.
Reinhold, *The American Parish and the Roman Liturgy,* Chap. 6.

APPENDIX

Five Catechetical Lectures of St. Cyril of Jerusalem (314-386 A. D.)

MYSTAGOGICAL CATECHESIS I

On the Rites Before Baptism

I Peter 5:8–14

"Be sober, be vigilant; because your adversary the devil, as a roaring lion, walks about, seeking whom he may devour."

1. I have long been wishing, O true-born and dearly beloved children of the Church, to discourse to you concerning these spiritual and heavenly Mysteries; but since I well knew that seeing is far more persuasive than hearing, I waited for the present season; that finding you more open to the influence of my words from your present experience, I might lead you by the hand into the brighter and more fragrant meadow of the Paradise before us; especially as you have been made fit to receive the more sacred Mysteries, after having been found worthy of divine and life-giving Baptism. Since therefore it remains to set before you a table of the more perfect instructions, let us now teach you these things exactly, that you may know the effect wrought upon you on that evening of your baptism.

2. First you entered into the vestibule of the baptistery, and there facing towards the West you listened to the command to stretch forth your hand, and as in the presence of Satan you renounced him. Now you must know that this figure is found in ancient history. For when Pharao, that most bitter and cruel tyrant, was oppressing the free and high-born people of the Hebrews, God sent Moses to bring them out of the evil bondage of the Egyptians. Then the door posts were anointed with the blood of a lamb, that the destroyer might flee from the houses which had the sign of the blood; and the Hebrew people was marvellously delivered. The enemy, however, after their rescue, *pursued after them* (Ex. 14:9, 23), and saw the sea wondrously parted for them; nevertheless he went on, following close in their footsteps, and was all at once overwhelmed and engulfed in the Red Sea.

3. Now turn from the old to the new, from the figure to the reality. There we have Moses sent from God to Egypt; here, Christ, sent forth from His Father into the world: there, that Moses might lead forth an afflicted people out of Egypt; here, that Christ might rescue those who are oppressed in the world under sin: there, the blood of a lamb was the spell against the destroyer; here, the blood of the Lamb without blemish Jesus Christ is made the charm to scare evil spirits: there, the tyrant was pursuing that ancient people even to the sea; and here the daring and shameless spirit, the author of evil, was following you even to the very streams of salvation. The tyrant of old was drowned in the sea; and this present one disappears in the water of salvation.

4. But nevertheless you are bidden to say, with arm outstretched towards him as though he were present, "I renounce thee Satan." I wish also to say why you stand facing to the West; for it is necessary. Since the West is the region of sensible darkness, and he being darkness has his dominion also in darkness, therefore, looking with a symbolic meaning towards the West, you renounce that dark and gloomy potentate. What then did each of you stand up and say, "I renounce thee, Satan,"—you wicked and most cruel tyrant! meaning, "I fear your might no longer; for that Christ has overthrown, having partaken with me of flesh and blood, that through these He *might by death destroy death* (Heb. 2:14–15), that I might not be made *subject to bondage* for ever." "I renounce thee,"—you crafty and most subtle serpent. "I renounce thee"—plotter as you are, who under the guise of friendship did contrive all disobedience, and work apostasy in our first parents. "I renounce thee, Satan,"—the artificer and abettor of all wickedness.

5. Then in a second sentence you are taught to say, "and all thy works." Now the works of Satan are all sin, which also you must renounce; —just as one who has escaped a tyrant has surely escaped his weapons also. All sin therefore, of every kind, is included in the works of the devil. Only know this; that all that you say, especially at that most thrilling hour, is written in God's books; when therefore you do any thing contrary to these promises, you shall be judged as *a transgressor* (Gal. 2:18). You renounce therefore the works of Satan; I mean, all deeds and thoughts which are contrary to reason.

6. Then you say, "And all his pomp." Now the pomp of the devil is the madness of theatres, and horse races, and hunting, and all such vanity: from which that holy man praying to be delivered says unto God, *Turn away mine eyes from beholding vanity* (Ps. 118:37). Be not interested in the madness of the theatre, where you will behold the wanton gestures of the players, carried on with mockeries and all

unseemliness, and the frantic dancing of effeminate men; —not in the madness of them who in hunts expose themselves to wild beasts, that they may pamper their miserable appetite; who, to serve their belly with meats, become themselves in reality meat for the belly of untamed beasts; and to speak justly, for the sake of their own god, their belly, they cast away their life headlong in single combats. Shun also horse-races, that frantic and soul-subverting spectacle. For all these are the pomp of the devil.

7. Moreover, the things which are hung up at idol festivals, either meat or bread, or other such things polluted by the invocation of the unclean spirits, are reckoned in the pomp of the devil. For as the Bread and Wine of the Eucharist before the invocation of the Holy and Adorable Trinity were simple bread and wine, while after the invocation the Bread becomes the Body of Christ, and the Wine the Blood of Christ, so in like manner such meats belonging to the pomp of Satan, though in their own nature simple, become profane by the invocation of the evil spirit.

8. After this you say, "and all thy service." Now the service of the devil is prayer in idol temples; things done in honour of lifeless idols; the lighting of lamps, or burning of incense by fountains or rivers, as some persons cheated by dreams or by evil spirits do thinking to find a cure even for their bodily ailments. Go not after such things. The watching of birds, divination, omens, or amulets, or charms written on leaves, sorceries, or other evil arts, and all such things, are services of the devil; therefore shun them. For if after renouncing Satan and associating yourself with Christ, you fall under their influence, you shall find the tyrant more bitter; perchance, because he treated you of old as his own, and relieved you from his hard bondage, but has now been greatly exasperated by you; so you will be bereaved of Christ, and have experience of the other. Have you not heard the old history which tells us of Lot and his daughters? Was not he himself saved with his daughters, when he had gained the mountain, while his wife became a pillar of salt, set up as a monument for ever, in remembrance of her depraved will and her turning back. Take heed therefore to yourself, and turn not again to *what is behind* (Phil. 3:13), having put your hand to the plough, and then turning back to the salt savor of this life's doings; but escape to the mountain, to Jesus Christ, that *stone hewn without hands* (Dan. 2:35, 45), which has filled the world.

9. When therefore you renounce Satan, utterly breaking all your covenant with him, that ancient league with hell (Isa. 28:15), there is opened to you the paradise of God, which he planted towards the

East, whence for his transgression our first father was banished; and a symbol of this was your turning from West to East, the place of light. Then you were told to say, "I believe in the Father, and in the Son, and in the Holy Spirit, and in one Baptism of repentence." Of which things we spoke to you at length in the former Lectures, as God's grace allowed us.

10. Guarded therefore by these discourses, *be sober. For our adversary the devil,* as was just now read, *as a roaring lion, walks about,* seeking whom he may devour (I Pet. 5:9). But though in former times death was mighty and devoured, at the holy Laver of regeneration God has *wiped away every tear from off all faces* (Isa. 25:8). For you shall no more mourn, now that you have put off the old man; but you shall keep holyday, *clothed in the garment of salvation* (Isa. 41:10), even Jesus Christ.

11. And these things were done in the outer chamber. But if God will, when in the succeeding lectures on the Mysteries we have entered into the Holy of Holies, we shall there know the symbolic meaning of the things which are there performed. Now to God the Father, with the Son and the Holy Spirit, be glory, and power, and majesty, for ever and ever. Amen.

MYSTAGOGICAL CATECHESIS II

On the Rites of Baptism

Romans 6:3–14

"Do you not know that all we who have been baptized into Christ Jesus have been baptized into his death? . . . since you are not under the Law but under grace."

1. These daily introductions into the Mysteries, and new instructions, which are the announcements of new truths, are profitable to us; and most of all to you, who have been renewed from an old state to a new. Therefore, I shall necessarily lay before you the sequel of yesterday's Lecture, that you may learn of what those things, which were done by you in the inner chamber, were symbolical.

2. As soon, then, as you entered, you put off your tunic; and this was an image of *putting off the old man with his deeds* (Col. 3:9). Having stripped yourselves, you were naked; in this also imitating Christ, who was stripped naked on the Cross, and by His nakedness *put off from Himself the principalities and powers, and openly*

triumphed over them on the tree (Col. 2:15). For since the adverse powers made their lair in your members, you may no longer wear that old garment; I do not at all mean this visible one, but the *old man which is being corrupted through its deceptive lusts* (Eph. 4:22). May the soul which has once put him off, never again put him on, but say with the Spouse of Christ in the *Canticle of Canticles, I have put off my garment, how shall I put it on* (Cant. 5:3)? O wondrous thing! you were naked in the sight of all, and were not ashamed; for truly you bore the likeness of the first-formed Adam, who was naked in the garden, and was not ashamed.

3. Then, when you were stripped, you were anointed with exorcised oil, from the very hairs of your head to your feet, and were made partakers of the good olive-tree, Jesus Christ. For you were cut off from the wild olive-tree, and grafted into the good one, and were made to share the fatness of the true olive-tree. The exorcised oil therefore was a symbol of the participation of the fatness of Christ, being a charm to drive away every trace of hostile influence. For as the breathing of the saints, and the invocation of the Name of God, like fiercest flame, scorch and drive out evil spirits, so also this exorcised oil receives such virtue by the invocation of God and by prayer, as not only to burn and cleanse away the traces of sins, but also to chase away all the invisible powers of the evil one.

4. After these things, you were led to the holy pool of Divine Baptism, as Christ was carried from the Cross to the Sepulchre which is before our eyes. And each of you was asked, whether he believed in the name of the Father, and of the Son, and of the Holy Spirit, and you made that saving confession, and descended three times into the water, and ascended again; here also hinting by a symbol at the three days burial of Christ. For as our Savior passed three days and three nights in the heart of the earth, so you also in your first ascent out of the water, represented the first day of Christ in the earth, and by your descent, the night; for as he who is in the night no longer sees, but he who is in the day, remains in the light, so in the descent, as in the night, you saw nothing, but in ascending again you were as in the day. And at the self-same moment you were both dying and being born; and that Water of salvation was at once your grave and your mother. And what Solomon spoke of others will suit you also; for he said, in that case, *There is a time to bear and a time to die* (Eccles. 3:2); but to you, in the reverse order, there was a time to die and a time to be born; and one and the same time effected both of these, and your birth went hand in hand with your death.

5. O strange and inconceivable thing! we did not really die, we were not really buried, we were not really crucified and raised again; but

our imitation was in a figure, and our salvation in reality. Christ was actually crucified, and actually buried, and truly rose again; and all these things He has freely bestowed upon us, that we, sharing His sufferings by imitation, might gain salvation in reality. O surpassing loving-kindness! Christ received nails in His undefiled hands and feet, and suffered anguish; while on me without pain or toil by the fellowship of His suffering He freely bestows salvation.

6. Let no one then suppose that Baptism is merely the grace of remission of sins, or further that of adoption; as John's was a baptism conferring only remission of sins: whereas we know full well, that as it purges our sins, and ministers to us the gift of the Holy Spirit so also it is the counterpart of the sufferings of Christ. For this cause Paul just now cried aloud and said, *Or are you ignorant that all we who were baptized into Christ Jesus, were baptized into His death? We were buried therefore with Him by baptism into His death* (Rom. 6:3). These words he spoke to some who were disposed to think that Baptism ministers to us the remission of sins, and adoption, but has not further the fellowship also, by representation, of Christ's true sufferings.

7. In order therefore that we might learn, that whatsoever things Christ endured, FOR US AND FOR OUR SALVATION He suffered them in reality and not in appearance, and that we also are made partakers of His sufferings, Paul cried with all exactness of truth, *For if we have been planted together with the likeness of His death, we shall be also with the likeness of His resurrection.* Well has he said, *planted together* (Rom. 6:5). For since the true Vine was planted in this place, we also by partaking in the Baptism of death have been *planted together* with Him. And fix your mind with much attention on the words of the Apostle. He said not, "For if we have been planted together with His death," but, *with the likeness of His death.* For in Christ's case there was death in reality, for His soul was really separated from His body, and real burial, for His holy body was wrapt in pure linen; and everything happened really to Him; but in your case there was only a likeness of death and sufferings, whereas of salvation there was not likeness but a reality.

8. Having been sufficiently instructed in these things, keep them, I beseech you, in your remembrance; that I also, unworthy though I be, may say to you, *Now I praise you, because you always remember me, and hold fast the traditions, which I delivered unto you* (I Cor. 11:2). And God, who has presented you *as it were alive from the dead* (Rom. 6:13), is able to grant unto you *to walk in newness of life* (Rom. 6:4): because His is the glory and the power, now and for ever. Amen.

MYSTAGOGICAL CATECHESIS III

On the Chrism
I John 2:20–28

"But you have an anointing from the Holy One . . . so that when he appears we may have confidence, and may not shrink ashamed from him at his coming."

1. Having been *baptized into Christ*, and *put on Christ* (Gal. 3:37), you have been made conformable to the Son of God; for God having *foreordained us unto adoption as sons* (Eph. 1:5), made us *to be conformed to the body of Christ's glory* (Phil. 3:21). Having therefore become *partakers of Christ* (Heb. 3:14), you are properly called Christs, and of you God said, *Touch not My Christs*, or anointed (Ps. 104:15). Now you have been made Christs by receiving the anti-type of the Holy Spirit; and all things have been wrought in you by imitation, because you are images of Christ. He washed in the river Jordan, and having imparted of the fragrance of His Godhead to the waters, He came up from them; and the Holy Spirit in the fulness of His being lighted on Him, like resting upon like. And to you in like manner, after you had come up from the pool of the sacred streams, there was given an Unction, the anti-type of that wherewith Christ was anointed; and this is the Holy Spirit; of whom also the blessed Isaia, in his prophecy respecting Him said in the person of the Lord, *The Spirit of the Lord is upon Me, because He has anointed Me: He has sent Me to preach glad tidings to the poor* (Isa. 61:1).

2. For Christ was not anointed by men with oil or material ointment, but the Father having before appointed Him to be the Savior of the whole world, anointed Him with the Holy Spirit, as Peter says, *Jesus of Nazareth, whom God anointed with the Holy Spirit* (Acts 10:38). David also the prophet cried, saying, *Thy throne, O God, is for ever and ever; a sceptre of righteousness is the sceptre of Thy kingdom; Thou hast loved righteousness and hated iniquity; therefore God even Thy God hath anointed Thee with the oil of gladness above Thy fellows* (Ps. 44:6–7). And as Christ was in reality crucified, and buried, and raised, and you are in Baptism accounted worthy of being crucified, buried, and raised together with Him in a likeness, so is it with the unction also. As He was anointed with an ideal oil of gladness, so you were anointed with ointment, having been made partakers and *fellows of Christ*.

3. But beware of supposing this to be plain ointment. For as the Bread of the Eucharist, after the invocation of the Holy Spirit, is mere bread no longer, but the Body of Christ, so also this holy ointment is no more simple ointment, nor (so to say) common, after

invocation, but it is Christ's gift of grace, and, by the advent of the Holy Spirit, is made fit to impart His Divine Nature. This ointment is symbolically applied to your forehead and your other senses; and while your body is anointed with the visible ointment, your soul is sanctified by the Holy and life-giving Spirit.

4. And you were first anointed on the forehead, that you might be delivered from the shame, which the first man who transgressed bore about with him everywhere; and that *with unveiled face* you might reflect as a mirror the glory of the Lord (II Cor. 3:18). Then on your ears; that you might receive the ears which are quick to hear the Divine Mysteries, of which Isaia said, *The Lord gave me also an ear to hear* (Isa. 50:4); and the Lord Jesus in the Gospel, *He that has ears to hear let him hear* (Matt. 11:15). Then on the nostrils; that receiving the sacred ointment you may say, *We are to God a sweet savor of Christ, in them that are saved* (II Cor. 2:15). Afterwards on your breast; that having put on the *breast-plate of righteousness*, you may *stand against the wiles of the devil* (Eph. 1:14, 11). For as Christ after His Baptism, and the visitation of the Holy Spirit, went forth and vanquished the adversary, so likewise you, after Holy Baptism and the Mystical Chrism, having put on the whole armor of the Holy Spirit, are to stand against the power of the adversary, and vanquish it, saying, *I can do all things through Christ who strengtheneth me* (Phil. 4:13).

5. Having been counted worthy of this Holy Chrism, you are called Christians, verifying the name also by your new birth. For before you were deemed worthy of this grace, you had properly no right to this title, but were advancing on your way towards being Christians.

6. Moreover, you should know that in the old Scripture there lies the symbol of this Chrism. For at the time that Moses imparted to his brother the command of God, and made him High-priest, after bathing in water, he anointed him; and Aaron was called Christ or Anointed, evidently from the typical Chrism. So also the High-priest, in advancing Solomon to the kingdom, anointed him after he had bathed in Gihon (III Kgs. 1:39). To them however these things happened in a figure, but to you not in a figure, but in truth; because you were truly anointed by the Holy Spirit. Christ is the beginning of your salvation; for He is truly the First-fruit, and you the mass (Rom. 11: 16); but if the First-fruit be holy, it is manifest that Its holiness will pass to the mass also.

7. Keep This unspotted: for it shall teach you all things, if it abide in you, as you have just heard declared by the blessed John, discoursing much concerning this Unction (I John 2:20). For this holy thing is a spiritual safeguard of the body, and salvation of the soul. Of this the blessed Isaia prophesying of old said, *And on this mountain,—*

(now he calls the Church a mountain elsewhere also, as when he says, *In the last days the mountain of the Lord's house shall be manifest;)*— *on this mountain shall the Lord make unto all nations a feast; they shall drink wine, they shall drink gladness, they shall anoint themselves with ointment* (Isa. 25:6). And that he may make you sure, hear what he says of this ointment as being mystical; *Deliver all these things to the nations, for the counsel of the Lord is unto all nations* (Isa. 25:7). Having been anointed, therefore, with this holy ointment, keep it unspotted and unblemished in you, pressing forward by good works, and being made well-pleasing to the Captain of your salvation, Christ Jesus, to whom be glory for ever and ever. Amen.

MYSTAGOGICAL CATHECHESIS IV

On the Body and Blood of Christ
I Corinthians 11:23

"For I myself have received from the Lord (what I also delivered to you), that the Lord Jesus, on the night in which he was betrayed, took bread . . ."

1. Even of itself the teaching of the Blessed Paul is sufficient to give you a full assurance concerning those Divine Mysteries, of which having been deemed worthy, you are become of *the same body* (Eph. 3:6) and blood with Christ. *That our Lord Jesus Christ in the night in which He was betrayed, took bread, and when He had given thanks He broke it, and gave to His disciples, saying, Take, eat, this is My Body: and having taken the cup and given thanks, He said, Take, drink, this is My Blood* (I Cor. 11:23). Since then He Himself declared and said of the Bread, *This is My Body,* who shall dare to doubt any longer? And since He has Himself affirmed and said, *This is My Blood,* who shall ever hesitate, saying, that it is not His blood?

2. He once in Cana of Galilee turned the water into wine, akin to blood, and is it incredible that He should have turned wine into blood? When called to a bodily marriage, He miraculously wrought that wonderful work; and *on the children of the bride-chamber* (Matt. 9:15), shall He not much rather be acknowledged to have bestowed the fruition of His Body and Blood?

3. Wherefore with full assurance let us partake as of the Body and Blood of Christ: for in the figure of Bread is given to you His Body, and in the figure of Wine His Blood; that thou by partaking of the Body and Blood of Christ, may be made of the same body and the same blood with Him. For thus we come to bear Christ in us because His Body and Blood are distributed through our members; thus it is

that according to the blessed Peter, *we become partakers of the divine nature* (II Pet. 1:4).

4. Christ on a certain occasion discoursing with the Jews said, *Except you eat My flesh and drink My blood, you have no life in you* (John 6:54). They not having heard His saying in a spiritual sense were offended, and went back, supposing that He was inviting them to eat flesh.

5. In the Old Testament also there was shew-bread; but this, as it belonged to the Old Testament, has come to an end; but in the New Testament there is Bread of heaven, and a Cup of salvation, sanctifying soul and body; for as the Bread corresponds to our body, so is the Word appropriate to our soul.

6. Consider therefore the Bread and the Wine not as bare elements, for they are, according to the Lord's declaration, the Body and Blood of Christ; for even though sense suggests this to you, yet let faith establish you. Judge not the matter from the taste, but from faith be fully assured without misgiving, that the Body and Blood of Christ have been vouchsafed to you.

7. Also the blessed David shall advise you the meaning of this, saying, *Thou hast prepared a table before me in the presence of them that afflict me* (Ps. 22:5). What he says, is to this effect: "Before Your coming the evil spirits prepared a table for men, polluted and defiled and full of devilish influence; but since Your coming. O Lord, *Thou hast prepared before me a table,* what other does he indicate but that mystical and spiritual Table, which God has prepared for us *over against,* that is, contrary and in opposition to the evil spirits? And very truly, for that had communion with devils, but this with God. *Thou hast anointed my head with oil* (Ps. 22:5). With oil He anointed your head upon your forehead, for the seal which you have of God; that you may be made *the engraving of the signet, Holiness unto God* (Ex. 28:36). And *thy cup intoxicateth me, as very strong* (Ps. 22:5). You see that cup here spoken of, which Jesus took in His hands, and gave thanks, and said, *This is My blood, which is shed for many for the remission of sins* (Matt. 26:28).

8. Therefore Solomon also, hinting at this grace, says in Ecclesiastes 9:7–8: *Come hither, eat thy bread with joy* (that is, the spiritual bread; *Come hither,* he calls with the call to salvation and blessing), *and drink thy wine with a merry heart* (that is, the spiritual wine); *and let oil be poured out upon thy head* (you see he alludes even to the mystic Chrism); *and let thy garments be always white, for the Lord is well pleased with thy works;* for before you came to Baptism, your works were *vanity of vanities.* But now having put off your old garments, and put on those which are spiritually white, you must be continually robed in white: of course we mean not this, that you are

always to wear white raiment; but you must be clad in the garments that are truly white and shining and spiritual, that you may say with the blessed Isaia, *My soul shall be joyful in my God; for He hath clothed me with a garment of salvation, and put a robe of gladness around me* (61:10).

9. Having learnt these things, and been fully assured that the apparent bread is not bread, though sensible to taste, but the Body of Christ; and that the apparent wine is not wine, though the taste will have it so, but the Blood of Christ; and that of this David sung of old, saying, *And bread strengtheneth man's heart, to make his face to shine with oil* (Ps. 103:15), "strengthen thou thine heart," by partaking thereof as spiritual, and "make the face of thy soul to shine." And so having it unveiled with a pure conscience, may you *reflect as a mirror the glory* of the Lord (II Cor. 3:18), and proceed from *glory to glory*, in Christ Jesus our Lord: To whom be honour, and might, and glory, for ever and ever. Amen.

MYSTAGOGICAL CATECHESIS V

On the Sacred Liturgy and Communion
I Peter 2:1

"Wherefore putting away all filthiness and all guile, and evil speaking, . . ."

1. By the loving-kindness of God you have heard sufficiently at our former meetings concerning Baptism, and Chrism, and partaking of the Body and Blood of Christ; and now it is necessary to pass on to what is next in order, meaning to-day to set the crown on the spiritual building of your edification.

2. You have seen then the Deacon who gives to the Priest water to wash, and to the Presbyters who stand round God's altar. He gave it not at all because of bodily defilement; it is not that; for we did not enter the Church at first with defiled bodies. But the washing of hands is a symbol that you ought to be pure from all sinful and unlawful deeds; for since the hands are a symbol of action, by washing them, it is evident, we represent the purity and blamelessness of our conduct. Did you not hear the blessed David opening this very mystery, and saying, *I will wash my hands in innocence, and so will I compass Thine Altar, O Lord* (Ps. 25:6)? The washing therefore of hands is a symbol of immunity from sin.

3. Then the Deacon cries aloud, "Receive you one another; and let us kiss one another." Think not that this kiss is of the same character with those given in public by common friends. It is not such: but this kiss blends souls one with another, and courts entire forgiveness

for them. The kiss therefore is the sign that our souls are mingled together, and banish all remembrance of wrongs. For this cause Christ said, *If thou art offering thy gift at the altar, and there remember that thy brother hath aught against thee, leave there thy gift upon the altar, and go thy way; first be reconciled to thy brother, and then come and offer thy gift* (Matt. 5:23). The kiss therefore is reconciliation, and for this reason holy: as the blessed Paul somewhere cried, saying, *Greet you one another with a holy kiss;* and Peter, *with a kiss of charity* (I Pet. 5:14).

4. After this the Priest cries aloud, "Lift up your hearts." For truly ought we in that most awful hour to have our heart on high with God, and not below, thinking of earth and earthly things. In effect therefore the Priest bids all in that hour to dismiss all cares of this life, or household anxieties, and to have their heart in heaven with the merciful God. Then you answer, "We lift them up unto the Lord:" assenting to it, by your avowal. But let no one come here, who could say with his mouth, "We lift up our hearts unto the Lord," but in his thoughts have his mind concerned with the cares of this life. At all times, rather, God should be in our memory; but if this is impossible by reason of human infirmity, in that hour above all this should be our earnest endeavour.

5. Then the Priest says, "Let us give thanks unto the Lord." For verily we are bound to give thanks, that He called us, unworthy as we were, to so great grace; that He reconciled us when we were His foes; that He vouchsafed to us the Spirit of adoption. Then you say, "It is meet and right:" for in giving thanks we do a meet thing and a right; but He did not right, but more than right, in doing us good, and counting us meet for such great benefits.

6. After this, we make mention of heaven, and earth, and sea; of sun and moon; of stars and all the creation, rational and irrational, visible and invisible; of Angels, Archangels, Virtues, Dominions, Principalities, Powers, Thrones; of the Cherubim with many faces: in effect repeating that call of David's, *Magnify the Lord with me* (Ps. 33:3). We make mention also of the Seraphim, whom Isaia in the Holy Spirit saw standing around the throne of God, and with two of their wings veiling their face, and with two their feet, while with two they did fly, crying *Holy, Holy, Holy, is the Lord of Sabaoth* (Isa. 6: 2–3). For the reason of our reciting this confession of God, delivered down to us from the Seraphim, is this, that so we may be partakers with the hosts of the world above in their Hymn of praise.

7. Then having sanctified ourselves by these spiritual Hymns, we beseech the merciful God to send forth His Holy Spirit upon the gifts lying before Him; that He may make the Bread the Body of

Christ, and the Wine the Blood of Christ; for whatsoever the Holy Spirit has touched, is surely sanctified and changed.

8. Then, after the spiritual sacrifice, the bloodless service, is completed, over that sacrifice of propitiation we entreat God for the common peace of the Churches, for the welfare of the world; for kings; for soldiers and allies; for the sick; for the afflicted; and, in a word, for all who stand in need of succour we all pray and offer this sacrifice.

9. Then we commemorate also those who have fallen asleep before us, first Patriarchs, Prophets, Apostles, Martyrs, that at their prayers and intercession God would receive our petition. Then on behalf also of the Holy Fathers and Bishops who have fallen asleep before us, and in a word of all who in past years have fallen asleep among us, believing that it will be a very great benefit to the souls, for whom the supplication is put up, while that holy and most awful sacrifice is set forth.

10. And I wish to persuade you by an illustration. For I know that many say, what is a soul profited, which departs from this world either with sins or without sins, if it be commemorated in the prayer? For if a king were to banish certain ones who had given him offense, and then those who belong to them should weave a crown and offer it to him on behalf of those under punishment, would he not grant a remission of their penalties? In the same way we, when we offer to Him our supplications for those who have fallen asleep, though they be sinners, weave no crown, but offer up Christ sacrificed for our sins, propitiating our merciful God for them as well as for ourselves.

11. Then, after these things, we say that Prayer which the Savior delivered to His own disciples, with a pure conscience entitling God our Father, and saying, *Our Father, who art in heaven.* O most surpassing loving-kindness of God! On them who revolted from Him and were in the very extreme of misery has He bestowed such a complete forgiveness of evil deeds, and so great participation of grace, as that they should even call Him Father. *Our Father, who art in heaven;* and they also are a heaven who *bear the image of the heavenly* (I Cor. 15:49), in whom is God, *dwelling and walking in them* (II Cor. 6:16).

12. *Hallowed be Thy Name.* The Name of God is in its nature holy, whether we say so or not; but since it is sometimes profaned among sinners, according to the words, *Through you My Name is continually blasphemed among the Gentiles* (Isa. 52:5; Rom. 2:24), we pray that in us God's Name may be hallowed; not that it comes to be holy from not being holy, but because it becomes holy in us, when we are made holy, and do things worthy of holiness.

13. *Thy Kingdom come.* A pure soul can say with boldness, *Thy kingdom come;* for he who has heard Paul saying, *Let not therefore sin reign in your mortal body* (Rom. 6:12), and has cleansed himself in deed, and thought, and word, will say to God, *Thy kingdom come.*

14. *Thy will be done as in heaven so on earth.* God's divine and blessed Angels do the will of God, as David said in the Psalm, *Bless the Lord, all ye Angels of His, mighty in strength, that do His pleasure* (Ps. 102:20). So then in effect you mean this by thy prayer, "as in the Angels Thy will is done, so likewise be it done on earth in me, O Lord."

15. *Give us this day our super-substantial bread.* This common bread is not super-substantial bread, but this Holy Bread is super-substantial, that is, appointed for the substance of the soul. For this Bread *goeth* not *into the belly and is cast out into the drain* (Matt. 15:17), but is distributed into your whole system for the benefit of body and soul. But by *this day,* he means, "each day," as also Paul said, *While it is called to-day* (Heb. 3:15).

16. *And forgive us our debts as we also forgive our debtors.* For we have many sins. For we offend both in word and in thought, and very many things we do worthy of condemnation; and *if we say that we have no sin* (I John 1:8), we lie, as John says. And we make a covenant with God, entreating Him to forgive us our sins, as we also forgive our neighbors their debts. Considering then what we receive and in return for what, let us not put off nor delay to forgive one another. The offenses committed against us are slight and trivial, and easily settled; but those which we have committed against God are great, and need such mercy as His only is. Take heed therefore, lest for the slight and trivial sins against you you shut out for yourself forgiveness from God for your very grievous sins.

17. *And lead us not into temptation, O Lord.* Is this then what the Lord teaches us to pray, that we may not be tempted at all? How then is it said elsewhere, "a man untempted, is a man unproved;" and again, *My brethren, count it all joy when you fall into divers temptations* (Jas. 1:2)? But does perchance the entering into temptation mean the being overwhelmed by the temptation? For temptation is, as it were, like a winter torrent difficult to cross. Those therefore who are not overwhelmed in temptations, pass through, showing themselves excellent swimmers, and not being swept away by them at all; while those who are not such, enter into them and are overwhelmed. As for example, Judas having entered into the temptation of the love of money, swam not through it, but was overwhelmed and was strangled both in body and spirit. Peter entered into the temptation of the denial; but having entered, he was not overwhelmed by it, but manfully swam through it, and was delivered from the temptation.

Listen again, in another place, to a company of unscathed saints, giving thanks for deliverance from temptation, *Thou, O God hast proved us; Thou hast tried us by fire into the net; Thou laid affliction upon our loins. Thou hast caused men to ride over our heads; we went through fire and water; and thou brought us out into a place of rest* (Ps. 65:10–12). You see them speaking boldly in regard to their having passed through and not been pierced. *But Thou brought us out into a place of rest;* now their coming into a place of rest is their being delivered from temptation.

18. *But deliver us from the evil.* If *Lead us not into temptation* implied the not being tempted at all, He would not have said, *But deliver us from the evil.* Now evil is our adversary the devil, from whom we pray to be delivered. Then after completing the prayer you say, *Amen;* by this *Amen,* which means "So be it," setting the seal to the petitions of the divinely-taught prayers.

19. After this the Priest says, "Holy things to holy men." Holy are the gifts presented, having received the visitation of the Holy Spirit; holy are you also, having been deemed worthy of the Holy Spirit; the holy things therefore correspond to the holy persons. Then you say, "One is Holy, One is the Lord, Jesus Christ." For One is truly holy, by nature holy; we too are holy, but not by nature, only by participation, and discipline, and prayer.

20. After this you hear the cantor inviting you with a sacred melody to the communion of the Holy Mysteries, and saying, *O taste and see that the Lord is good* (Ps. 33:9). Trust not the judgment to the bodily palate; no, but to faith unfaltering; for they who taste are bidden to taste, not bread and wine, but the anti-typical Body and Blood of Christ.

21. In approaching therefore, come not with the wrists extended, or the fingers spread; but make the left hand a throne for the right, as for that which is to receive a King. And having hollowed the palm, receive the Body of Christ, saying over it, *Amen.* So then after having carefully hallowed your eyes by the touch of the Holy Body, partake of it; giving heed lest you lose any portion thereof; for whatever you lose, it is evidently a loss to you as it were from one of your own members. For tell me, if any one gave you grains of gold, would you not hold them with all carefulness, being on your guard against losing any of them, and suffering loss? Will you not then much more carefully keep watch, that not a crumb fall from you of what is more precious than gold and precious stones?

22. Then after you have partaken of the Body of Christ, draw near also to the Cup of His Blood; not stretching forth your hands, but bending, and saying with an air of worship and reverence, *Amen,* hallow yourself by partaking also of the Blood of Christ. And while

the moisture is still upon your lips, touch it with your hands, and hallow your eyes and brow and the other organs of sense. Then wait for the prayer, and give thanks unto God, who has accounted you worthy of so great mysteries.

23. Hold fast these traditions undefiled and keep yourselves free from offense. Sever not yourselves from the Communion; deprive not yourselves, through the pollution of sins, of these Holy and Spiritual Mysteries. *And the God of peace sanctify you wholly; and may your spirit, and soul, and body be preserved entire without blame at the coming of our Lord Jesus Christ* (I Thess. 5:23). To whom be glory and honor and might, with the Father and the Holy Spirit. now and ever, and world without end. Amen.

Index

Index

James, father(?) of Jude, 106
James of Jerusalem, "brother" of Jesus and probable author of the Epistle, 76, 100, 137, 181
James, son of Alpheus and apostle, 89, 106
James, son of Zebedee, "the Greater," 28–29, 74, 117, 181
James, Epistle of, 9, 28, 83, 100, 101, 163
Jamnes, 142
Jaubert, A., 177
Jechonia, 47
Jeremia (the prophet), 3, 4, 9, 37, 57, 69, 88, 93, 124, 148, 164, 166, 167, 171, 198
Jeremias, J., 108–110, 117
Jerusalem, 4, 33, 39, 57, 74, 82, 118ff., 141
  Council of, 34, 75–76
  destruction of, 4, 32–33, 43, 54, 79, 115, 118, 187ff., 192
  "Heavenly," 192
  last trip to, 49–50, 57, 192, 200
Jerusalem, Bible de, 22, 42, 75, 84, 142, 156, 160, 168, 177, 187, 193, 205, 214
Jesus (name), 44, 46
Jews;
  in Apocalypse, 187ff.
  in Fourth Gospel, 165
  and messianism, 4–8, 31–32
  origin of term, 4
  preaching Gospel to, 82, 105
  religious observances of, 111, 156, 158, 171
  salvation of, 82–86
Joel, Book of, 13, 59
Job, Book of, 51, 61, 92, 117, 209
"Johannine Sacramentary," 169
Johannine Tradition, 119, 121, 161, 163
John the Baptist, St., 7, 15, 25–26, 28, 32, 45, 48–49, 54, 91, 105, 107, 162, 166, 170ff., 192
John Chrysostom, St., 108
John the Evangelist, St., 3, 28–29, 76, 105–106, 117, 161ff., 181
John Mark, 24
John, St., Gospel of, 4, 6, 7, 14, 15, 17, 29, 35, 36, 101, 105, 114, 127, 129, 161ff.

John, Epistles of, 161–163, 203
  I John, 161–165, 203, 221
  II John, 203
  III John, 203–204
John and James, ambition of, 117
John the Presbyter, 203
John XXIII, viii, 204
Jona, father of Peter and Andrew, 106, 113
Jona (prophet), 28, 51, 108
Jones, A., 11, 31, 40, 112
Joseph of Arimathea, 39, 56
Joseph (the Patriarch), 60
Joseph, St., 7, 43–47
Josue, 3, 46, 92
Journet, C., 115, 117, 134
Juda, 6, 166
  Kingdom of, 3–4
  Tribe of, 5, 76
Judaism, 46, 195
Judaizers, 78–79, 126, 135–136
Judas (Iscariot), 13, 36–37, 56, 123, 125–127, 173–174, 177
Jude the Apostle, 106
Jude, "brother" of Jesus and probable author of the Epistle, 106, 151, 181
Jude, Epistle of, 151, 205
Judea, 10, 44
Judges, 3, 140
  Book of, 140
Judgment, General, 33–34, 54
Julicher, A., 109
Jungmann, J., 131–132, 134, 213
Justification, 83, 86, 114
Justin Martyr, St., 146, 184

Kerygma, xi, 15–16, 21, 25, 118, 162, 169
Kerioth, 106
"Key of David," 190
Key, H., 65, 92, 122, 136, 142, 155
King, P., 44
King as title, 22, 31, 38, 101
Kingdom of God, v, 3, 12ff., 37, 39, 49, 51, 59, 82, 101, 116ff., 129ff., 162
  Anawim in, 94, 117
  coming of, 51, 54–55, 57, 59, 70, 101, 117–119, 124, 183
  keys of, 114
  as "Kingdom of Heaven," 90, 94, 108

Index of Psalms

(Page Numbers in Boldface Type Refer to a Formal Treatment of the Psalm)

+ Penitential Psalm

246

Index of Psalms

+ Penitential Psalm
* Gradual or Pilgrim Psalm

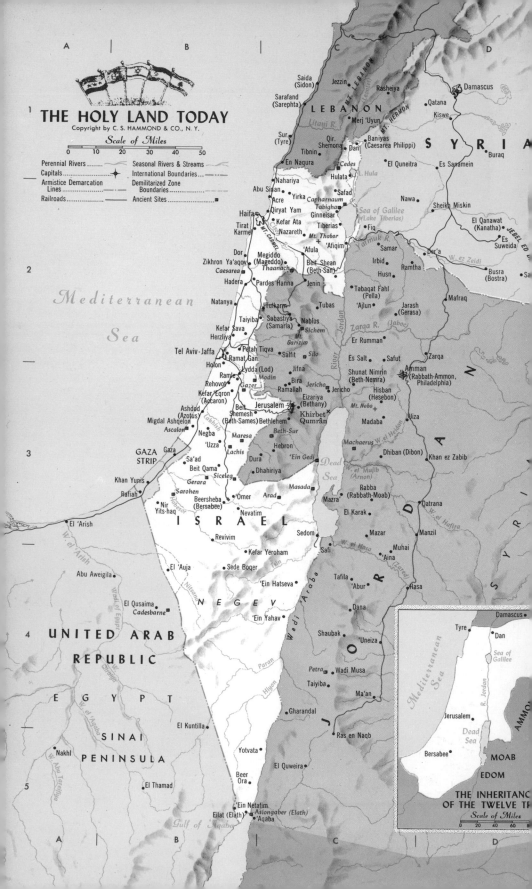

THE HOLY LAND TODAY

Copyright by C. S. HAMMOND & CO., N.Y.

Scale of Miles

0   10   20   30   40   50

Perennial Rivers	Seasonal Rivers & Streams
Capitals	International Boundaries
Armistice Demarcation Lines	Demilitarized Zone Boundaries
Railroads	Ancient Sites

Mediterranean Sea

LEBANON

SYRIA

Saida (Sidon)
Sarafand (Sareptha)
Sur (Tyre)
En Naqura
Nahariya
Abu Sinan
Acre
Qiryat Yam
Kefar Ata
Haifa
Tirat Karmel
Nazareth
Dor
Zikhron Ya'aqov
Caesarea
Hadera
Pardes Hanna
Natanya
Tulkarm
Taiyiba
Kefar Sava
Herzliya
Tel Aviv-Jaffa
Holon
Ramat Gan
Ramle
Rehovot
Kefar Eqron (Accaron)
Ashdod (Azotus)
Migdal Ashqelon
Ascalon
Negba
'Uzza
Lachis
Gaza
GAZA STRIP
Khan Yunis
Rafiah
Sa'ad
Beit Qama
Gerara
Sarohen
Nir Yits-haq
El 'Arish
Abu Aweigila
El Qusaima
Cadesbarne
Beersheba (Bersabee)
'Omer
Nevatim
Revivim
Kefar Yeroham
Sede Boqer
'Ein Hatseva
'Ein Yahav

UNITED ARAB REPUBLIC

EGYPT

SINAI PENINSULA

Nakhl
El Thamad
El Kuntilla
Yotvata
Beer Ora
'Ein Netafim
Eilat (Elath)
Aslongaber (Elath)
'Aqaba

Gulf of Aqaba

NEGEV

ISRAEL

Jezzin
Rasheiya
Damascus
Qatana
Kiswe
Merj 'Uyun
Qir. Shemona
Dan
Baniyas (Caesarea Philippi)
El Quneitra
Es Sanamein
Buraq
Tibnin
Cedes
Hulata
L. Hula
Safad
Nawa
Sheikh Miskin
El Qanawat (Kanatha)
Es Suweida
Yirka
Capharnaum
Tabgha
Ginneisar
Tiberias
Sea of Galilee (Lake Tiberias)
Fiq
Samar
Irbid
Husn
Ramtha
Mafraq
Beit Shean (Beth-San)
Jenin
Tabaqat Fahl (Pella)
'Ajlun
Jarash (Gerasa)
Tubas
Er Rumman
Es Salt
Safut
Amman (Rabbath-Ammon, Philadelphia)
Zarqa
Nablus (Samaria)
Sichem
Salfit
Silo
Jifna
Bira
Ramallah
Jericho
Shunat Nimrin (Beth-Nemra)
Hisban (Hesebon)
Eizariya (Bethany)
Mt. Nebo
Jiza
Khirbet Qumran
Madaba
Bethlehem
Beth-Sur
Hebron
Maresa
Dura
Dhahiriya
'Ein Gedi
Dead Sea
Machaerus (W. el Heidan)
Dhiban (Dibon)
Khan ez Zabib
Rabba (Rabbath-Moab)
Masada
Mazra
Qatrana
Arad
Sedom
El Karak
Mazar
Manzil
Safi
Aina
Muhai
Tafila
'Abur
Hasa
Dana
Shaubak
'Uneiza
Petra
Wadi Musa
Taiyiba
Ma'an
Gharandal
Ras en Naqb
El Quweira

JORDAN

Mt. Thabor
'Afula
'Afiqim
Megiddo (Mageddo)
Thaanach
Yarmuk R.
Der'a
Busra (Bostra)
Zarqa R. (Jaboc)
Tabor
Sabastiya (Samaria)
Mt. Garizim
Patah Tiqva
Lydda (Lod)
Modin
Gazer
Jerusalem
Beit Shemesh (Beth-Sames)
River Jordan
Siceleg
Mt. Carmel
Litani R.
MT. LEBANON
MT. HERMON
JEBEL ED

Inset map

Damascus
Tyre
Dan
Sea of Galilee
Mediterranean Sea
R. Jordan
Jerusalem
AMMON
Dead Sea
Bersabee
MOAB
EDOM

THE INHERITANCE OF THE TWELVE TRIBES

Scale of Miles

0   20   40   60